The Supreme Court

Eighth Edition

Lawrence Baum

Ohio State University

CQ PRESS

A Division of Congressional Quarterly Inc.
Washington, D.C.

CQ Press
1255 22nd St., N.W., Suite 400
Washington, D.C. 20037

(202) 729-1900
Toll-free, 1-866-4CQ-PRESS (1-866-427-7737)

www.cqpress.com

Cover design by Auburn Associates, Inc., Baltimore, Md.

Photo credits: Associated Press: page 10, 16 (Evan Vucci), 64 (Tom Roberts),
74 (Terry Ashe,) 83 (Susan Walsh), 91 (David J. Phillip), 124, 142, 168
(Gregory Bull), 171 (Joe Marquette), 219. Congressional Quarterly:
frontispiece (Ken Heinen). Library of Congress: page 31. Reuters: page 210
(Win McNamee).

Printed and bound in the United States of America

07   06   05   04   03   5   4   3   2   1

Library of Congress Cataloging-in-Publication Data

Baum, Lawrence.
   The Supreme Court / Lawrence Baum.—8th ed.
      p. cm.
   Includes bibliographical references and index.
   ISBN 1-56802-815-6 (alk. paper)
   1. United States. Supreme Court. 2. Constitutional law—United
States. 3. Courts of last resort—United States. 4. Judicial
review—United States. I. Title.

KF8742.B35 2004
347.73'26—dc22   2003016777

To my mother,
Ruth Klein Baum

Contents

Preface

As the Supreme Court's annual term drew to a close in June 2003, anticipation was building about an expected vacancy or two on the Court. The president was Republican, the Senate had a Republican majority, and in 2004 Senate confirmation of a nominee might be more difficult as a presidential election neared. These factors combined to create what seemed to be the ideal time for Chief Justice William Rehnquist (seventy-eight years old) or Justice Sandra Day O'Connor (seventy-three years old), each a conservative Republican, to retire. Journalists wrote articles about the potential nominees, commentators offered their judgments, and senators and interest group leaders made public statements and prepared for the expected political battle.

As it turned out, there was no retirement and thus no vacancy. Barring an unexpected event, the Court would begin its next term in October with the same nine justices who had served since 1994. But the anticipation and preparation for a possible vacancy underscored how much attention people give to the Court and how important they think the Court is. The appointment of a new Supreme Court justice arouses more interest than does the selection of all but a few other public officials in the country.

If the Court's importance is widely recognized, the Court itself is not well understood. Americans know much more about the president and Congress than they do about the Court. One reason is that information about the Court is relatively scarce. The justices do most of their work in private, and their public sessions can be seen only by the small number of people who attend them. Another reason is the Court's role as interpreter of law, a role that adds a degree of complexity to its work. For these reasons, even people who care a good deal about government and politics often know little about how the Court functions or about the forces that shape its decisions and their impact.

This book is an effort to improve understanding of the Supreme Court. It is intended to serve as a short but comprehensive guide to the Court, both for those who already know a good deal about it and for those who have a more limited sense of it. This edition reflects new scholarship on the Court as well as recent developments, such as the Court's decision in *Bush v. Gore* and its repercussions. Both the text and the book's tables and figures have been revised thoroughly to be current.

The first chapter introduces the topic. It discusses the Court's role in general terms, examines the Court's place in the judicial system, analyzes the Court as an institution, and presents a brief summary of its history.

Each of the other chapters deals with an important aspect of the Court. Chapter 2 focuses on the justices: their selection, their backgrounds and careers, and the circumstances under which they leave the Court. Chapter 3 discusses how cases reach the Court and how the Court selects the small portion of those cases that it will hear.

Chapter 4 looks at decision making in the cases that the Court accepts for full decisions. After outlining the Court's decision-making procedures, I turn to the chapter's primary concern: the factors that influence the Court's choices among alternative decisions and policies. Chapter 5 deals with the kinds of issues on which the Court concentrates, the policies it supports, and the extent of its activism in policymaking. I give special attention to changes in the Court's role as a policymaker and the sources of those changes. The final chapter examines the ways in which other government policymakers respond to the Court's decisions as well as the Court's impact on American society as a whole. The chapter concludes with an assessment of the Court's significance as a force in American life.

This new edition reflects the enormous help that many people gave me with earlier editions that now date back more than two decades. In revising the book, I received useful information from Gregory Caldeira, Jon Gould, Richard Pacelle, Christopher Wolfe, and the Office of the Solicitor General, along with helpful suggestions for revision from Wendy Martinek, Binghamton University, SUNY.

The people at CQ Press continue to provide the kind of support that an author hopes for. I appreciate the assistance of Niall O'Donnell and Sally Ryman and the very extensive help that Joan Gossett provided. I am grateful to Charisse Kiino for her planning and encouragement. Brenda Carter has now helped me through five editions of this book, and I have benefited enormously from her professionalism and cheerful handling of any problems that arise. Carolyn Goldinger took on the task of copyediting the new edition, and her work greatly improved the book.

Over the life of this book my mother has given me both her support and a constant flow of clippings on stories that have made their way into the work. I am grateful to her for everything, and the book is dedicated to her.

Chapter 1

The Court

W hen the Supreme Court decided *Bush v. Gore* (2000), which settled the battle over the 2000 presidential election, the Court became a focus of controversy. Meanwhile, a television series called *The West Wing* was achieving great success with its portrayal of the inner workings of the White House. In response to these developments, two television networks prepared series about the Supreme Court. *The Court,* on ABC, and *First Monday,* on CBS, premiered early in 2002. Sally Field starred as a new justice on ABC, and CBS offered James Garner as chief justice. Both shows failed, the ABC show lasting only three weeks.

The failure of a new television series is hardly unusual, and critics found fault with the quality of both shows. But some commentators saw a more fundamental problem: as drama, the Supreme Court is not very compelling. The Court deals with powerful issues such as abortion and the death penalty, but it addresses them in the context of legal arguments that are usually technical and a bit dry. Cases can arouse heated exchanges among the justices, but the exchanges take place mostly on paper. Ultimately, the producers of the television shows were unable to make the Court exciting while maintaining a degree of realism. And so the Court disappeared from prime time, probably to the relief of the nine real justices.

The Supreme Court may be a poor subject for television, but its importance as an institution can hardly be denied. In addition to abortion and the death penalty, the Court shapes policy on questions such as the relationships between government and religion and between the states and the federal government. Before the Court resolved the 2000 presidential election, its decisions were crucial to the impeachment of Bill Clinton and ensured that Richard Nixon's presidency would end early.[1] It is impossible to understand American government and society without understanding the Supreme Court.

This book is an effort to help provide that understanding. Who serves on the Court, and how do they get there? What determines which cases and issues the Court decides? In resolving the cases before it, how does the Court choose between alternative decisions? In what policy areas is it active, and what kinds of policies does it make? Finally, what happens to the Court's decisions after they are handed down, and what impact do they have?

Each of these questions is the subject of a chapter in the book. As I focus on each question, I try to show not only what happens in and around the Court but also why things work as they do. This first chapter is an introduction to the Court, providing background for the chapters that follow.

A Perspective on the Court

The Court in Law and Politics

The Supreme Court is, first of all, a court—the highest court in the federal judicial system. Like other courts, it has a specified jurisdiction, the power to hear and decide particular kinds of cases. Like other courts, it can decide legal issues only in the cases that are brought to it. And, as a court, the Supreme Court makes decisions within a legal framework. While Congress simply writes new law, the policy choices that the Court faces are framed as interpretations of existing law. In this respect, the Court operates within a constraint from which legislators are free.

In another respect, the Supreme Court's identity as a court reduces the constraints on it. The widespread belief that courts should be insulated from the political process gives the Court a certain degree of actual insulation. The justices' lifetime appointments allow them some freedom from concerns about approval by political leaders and voters. Justices usually avoid open involvement in partisan activity, because such involvement is perceived as inappropriate. And because direct contact between lobbyists and justices is generally deemed unacceptable, interest group activity in the Court is basically restricted to the formal channels of legal argument.

The insulation of the Supreme Court from politics should not be exaggerated, however. People sometimes speak of courts as if they are, or at least ought to be, "nonpolitical." In a literal sense, this is impossible: as a part of government, courts are political institutions by definition. What people really mean when they refer to courts as nonpolitical is that courts are separate from the political process and that their decisions are affected only by legal considerations. This too is impossible—for courts in general and certainly for the Supreme Court.

The Court is political chiefly because it makes important decisions on major issues. People care about those decisions and want to influence them. As a result, appointments to the Court frequently involve political battles. Interest groups bring cases and present arguments to the Court in an effort to help shape its policies. Because members of Congress pay attention to the Court's decisions and hold powers over the Court, the justices may take Congress into account when they decide cases. Finally, the justices' political values affect the votes they cast and the opinions they write in the Court's decisions.

Thus, the Supreme Court should be viewed as a legal institution and a political institution. Both the political process and the legal system influence what it does. This ambiguous position makes the Court more complex in some ways than most political institutions; it also makes the Court an interesting case study in political behavior.

The Court as a Policymaker

This book deals with the Supreme Court in general but emphasizes the Court's role in making public policy—the authoritative rules by which government institutions seek to influence the operation of government and to shape society as a whole. Legislation to provide subsidies for wheat farmers, a judge's ruling in an auto accident case, and a Supreme Court decision laying down rules to govern police procedure are all examples of public policy. The Court may be viewed as part of a policymaking system that includes lower courts as well as the other branches of government.

As I have noted, the Supreme Court makes public policy by interpreting provisions of law. Issues of public policy come to the Court in the form of legal questions. In this respect the Court's policymaking differs fundamentally in form from that of Congress.

The Court does not face legal questions in the abstract. Rather, it addresses these questions in the process of settling specific controversies between parties (sometimes called litigants) that bring cases to it. In a sense, then, every decision by the Court has three aspects: it is a judgment about the specific dispute brought to it, an interpretation of the legal issues in that dispute, and a position on the policy questions that are raised by the legal issues.

These three aspects of the Court's rulings are illustrated by its decisions on police powers to search automobiles. In recent years the Court has decided a number of cases involving the circumstances under which car searches are acceptable and the permissible scope of those searches.[2] In each case, it ruled on the specific dispute, determining whether the evidence obtained from a search could be admitted in the trial of a particular defendant. If a state supreme court or federal court of appeals had ruled against the defendant, the Supreme Court could affirm that judgment and allow the defendant's conviction to become final. Alternatively, the Court could reverse the conviction and remand the case, sending it back to the lower court for further action in line with the Court's ruling.

The Court's decision in each case was also a judgment on the law of search and seizure. The Court determines how the Fourth and Fourteenth Amendments should be interpreted in relation to the specific situation in a case. Lower courts then are obliged to apply the Court's interpretation of the Constitution to any other case that involves the same kind of auto search.

Finally, the Court's decisions shape policy on police powers to engage in searches for evidence. In recent years the Court generally has given broad interpretations to those powers, in turn giving law enforcement agencies more freedom to engage in searches. Because the legal limits on police searches are determined primarily by the courts, the Supreme Court's expansions of search powers are an important component of government policy in this field.

The Supreme Court's substantial role in government policy on police searches is not unusual. Through its individual decisions and lines of decisions, the Court contributes a great deal to policy on a variety of important issues. The Court's assumption of this role has been facilitated by several circumstances. For one thing, as the French observer Alexis de Tocqueville noted more than a century ago, "Scarcely any political question arises in the United States that is not resolved, sooner or later, into a judicial question." [3] One reason that policy disputes tend to reach the courts is the existence of a written Constitution whose provisions offer a basis for challenging the legality of government actions.

Because so many policy questions come to the courts, the Supreme Court has the opportunity to shape a wide range of policies. And during much of its history the Court has welcomed that opportunity, frequently ruling on major issues. In doing so the Court has engaged in a good deal of what is often called judicial activism. That term can have many meanings, but it generally refers to court decisions that make significant changes in public policy, particularly in policies established by other institutions.[4]

At the same time, the Court's role in policymaking is limited by three conditions. First, the Court can do only so much with the relatively few decisions it makes in a year. The Court currently issues decisions with full opinions in an average of about eighty cases each year. In deciding such a small number of cases, the Court addresses only a select group of policy issues. Inevitably, there are whole fields of policy that it barely touches. Even in the areas in which the Court does act, it can deal with only a limited number of the issues that exist at a given time.

Second, the justices exercise a degree of judicial restraint, which is the avoidance of activism. They do so in part because they are trained in a legal tradition that emphasizes the value of restraint and in part because they seek to avoid controversy and attacks on the Court. Judicial restraint is reflected in the Court's refusal to hear some important and controversial cases. It is also reflected in the frequent—though not consistent—practice of deciding cases on relatively narrow grounds wherepossible.

Third, the actions of other policymakers limit the impact of even a highly activist Court. The Court is seldom the final government institution to deal with the policy issues it addresses. Its decisions are generally implemented by lower court judges and administrators, who often have considerable discretion in deciding how they will put a ruling into effect. The impact of a decision concerning police searches for evidence depends largely on how police officers react to it. Congress and the president influence how the Court's decisions are carried out, and they can overcome its interpretations of federal statutes simply by amending those statutes. There may be a considerable difference between what the Court rules on an issue and the public policy that ultimately results from government actions on that issue.

For these reasons, those who see the Supreme Court as the dominant force in the U.S. government almost surely are wrong. But if not dominant, the Court is an important policymaker. Certainly, the extent of its power is extraordinary for a court.

The Court in the Judicial System

State and Federal Court Systems

The Supreme Court is part of a court system, and its place in that system structures its role. The United States has a federal court system and a separate court system in each state. Federal courts can hear only those cases that Congress has put under their jurisdiction. Most of the jurisdiction of the federal courts falls into three categories.

First are the criminal and civil cases that arise under federal laws, including the Constitution. A prosecution for bank robbery, which is a violation of federal criminal law, is brought to federal court. So are civil cases based on federal patent and copyright laws.

Second are cases to which the U.S. government is a party. When the federal government sues an individual to recover what it claims to be owed from a student loan, or when an individual sues the federal government over disputed Social Security benefits, the case almost always goes to federal court.

Third are civil cases involving citizens of different states, if the amount in question is at least $75,000; if this condition is met, either party may bring the case to federal court. If a citizen of New Jersey sues a citizen of Texas for $100,000 as compensation for injuries resulting from an auto accident, the plaintiff (the New Jersey resident) might bring the case to federal court, or the defendant (the Texan) might have the case "removed" from state court to federal court. If neither does so, the case will be heard in state court—generally, in the state where the accident occurred.

These categories encompass only a small proportion of all court cases. The most common kinds of cases—criminal prosecutions, personal injury suits, divorces, actions to collect debts—typically are heard in state court. The trial courts of a single populous state such as Illinois or Florida hear far more cases than do the federal trial courts. On the other hand, federal cases are more likely than state cases to raise major issues of public policy.

State court systems vary considerably in their structure, but some general patterns exist (see Figure 1-1). Each state system has courts that are primarily trial courts, which hear cases initially as they enter the court system, and courts that are primarily appellate courts, which review lower court decisions that are appealed to them. Most states have two sets of trial courts, one to handle major cases and the other to deal with minor cases. Major criminal cases usually concern what the law defines as felonies; major civil cases are those involving large sums of money. Most often, appeals from decisions of minor trial courts are heard by major trial courts.

Appellate courts are structured in two ways. In eleven states, generally those with the smallest populations, there is a single appellate court—usually called the state supreme court. All appeals from major trial courts go to this supreme court. The other thirty-nine states have a set of intermediate appellate courts below the supreme court. These intermediate courts initially hear most appeals from major trial courts. State supreme courts are required to hear certain appeals brought directly from the trial courts or from the intermediate courts, but for the most part they have discretionary jurisdiction over challenges to the decisions of intermediate courts. Discretionary jurisdiction means simply that a court can choose to hear some cases and refuse to hear others; cases that a court is required to hear fall under its mandatory jurisdiction.

The structure of federal courts is shown in Figure 1-2. At the base of the federal court system are the federal district courts. The United States has ninety-four district courts; each state has between one and four, and there is one district court in the District of Columbia and in some of the territories such as Guam. The district courts hear all federal cases at the trial level, with the exception of a few types of cases that are heard in specialized courts.

Above the district courts are the twelve courts of appeals, each of which hears appeals in one of the federal judicial circuits. The District of Columbia constitutes one circuit; each of the other eleven circuits has three or more states. The Second Circuit, for example, includes Vermont, New York, and Connecticut. Appeals from the district courts in one circuit generally go to the court of appeals for that circuit, along with appeals from

FIGURE 1-1
Most Common State Court Structures

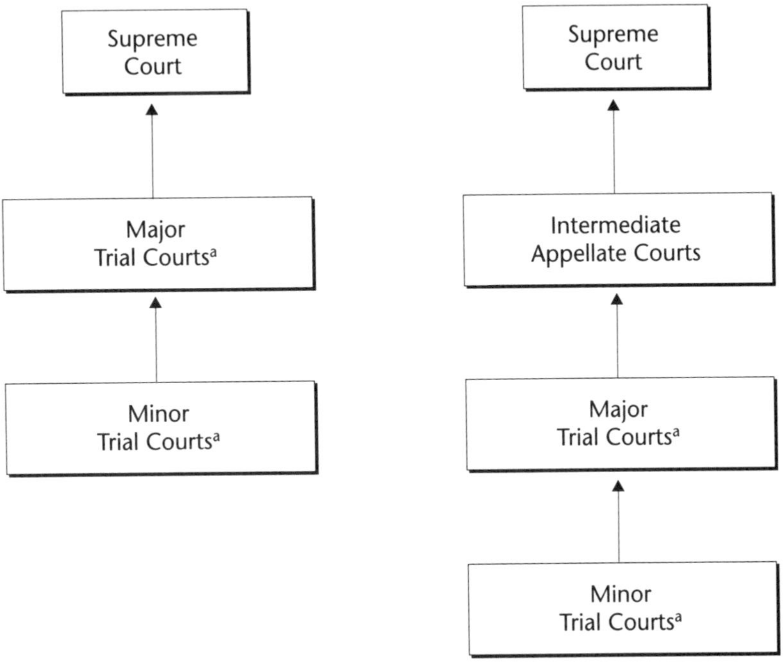

Note: Arrows indicate most common routes of appeals.

a. In many states, major trial courts or minor trial courts (or both) are composed of two or more different sets of courts. For instance, New York has several types of minor trial courts.

the Tax Court and from some administrative agencies. Patent cases and some claims against the federal government go from the district courts to the specialized Court of Appeals for the Federal Circuit, as do appeals from three specialized trial courts. The Court of Appeals for the Armed Forces hears cases from lower courts in the military system.

The Supreme Court's Jurisdiction

The Supreme Court stands at the top of the federal judicial system. Its jurisdiction, summarized in Table 1-1, is of two types. First, the Constitution gives the Court jurisdiction over certain specified classes of cases as a trial court—what is called original jurisdiction. Those cases may be brought directly to the Court. The Court's original jurisdiction includes some cases to

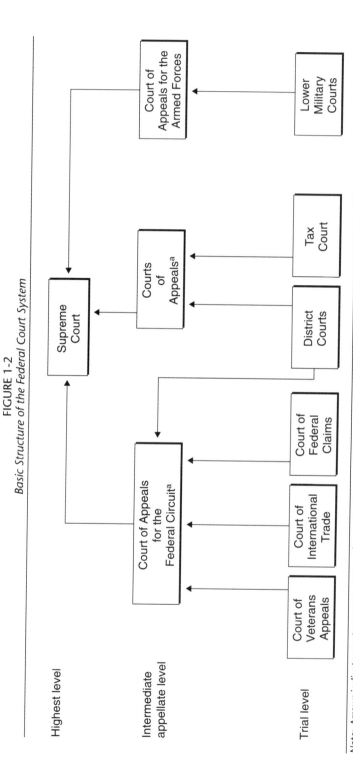

FIGURE 1-2
Basic Structure of the Federal Court System

Highest level

Intermediate
appellate level

Trial level

Supreme Court

Court of Appeals for the Armed Forces

Lower Military Courts

Courts of Appeals[a]

Tax Court

District Courts

Court of Appeals for the Federal Circuit[a]

Court of Federal Claims

Court of International Trade

Court of Veterans Appeals

Note: Arrows indicate most common routes of appeals. Some specialized courts of minor importance are excluded.

a. These courts also hear appeals from administrative agencies.

TABLE 1-1
Summary of Supreme Court Jurisdiction

A. Original jurisdiction
  1. Disputes between states[a]
  2. Some types of cases brought by a state
  3. Disputes between a state and the federal government
  4. Cases involving foreign diplomatic personnel

B. Appellate jurisdiction[b]
  1. All decisions of federal courts of appeals and specialized federal appellate courts
  2. All decisions of the highest state court with jurisdiction over a case, concerning issues of federal law
  3. Decisions of special three-judge federal district courts (mandatory)

a. It is unclear whether these cases are mandatory, and the Court treats them as discretionary.
b. Some minor categories are not listed.

which a state is a party and cases involving ambassadors. Most cases within the Court's original jurisdiction can be heard alternatively by a district court. Lawsuits between two states can be heard only by the Supreme Court, and these lawsuits—often involving disputed state borders—account for most of the decisions based on the Court's original jurisdiction. The Court frequently refuses to hear cases under its original jurisdiction, even some lawsuits by one state against another. In part for this reason, full decisions in these cases are not plentiful—only about 175 such decisions in the Court's history.[5] When the Court does accept a case under its original jurisdiction, it usually appoints a "special master" to gather facts and propose a decision, which the Court tends to ratify.[6]

Second, the Court has appellate jurisdiction to hear cases brought by parties dissatisfied with certain lower court decisions. In the federal system, such cases can come from the federal courts of appeals and from the two specialized appellate courts. Cases may also come directly from special three-judge district courts that hear a few classes of cases. Most cases that reach the Court from the three-judge district courts concern voting and election issues.

Cases can come to the Supreme Court after decisions by the state supreme courts if they involve claims arising under federal law, including the Constitution. If a state supreme court chooses not to hear a case, the losing party can then go to the Supreme Court. For example, in 2003 the Court decided a case that had been heard only by a West Virginia trial

Ellis Island, the first stopping point for millions of immigrants to the United States. In a 1998 decision based on the Supreme Court's original jurisdiction, the Court ruled that most of the island belongs to New Jersey rather than New York.

court.[7] Table 1-2 shows that a substantial majority of the cases that come to the Court, and an even larger majority of the cases that it hears, originated in federal court rather than in state court.

The rule by which state cases come to the Supreme Court may be confusing, because cases arising under federal law ordinarily start in federal court. But cases brought to state courts on the basis of state law sometimes contain issues of federal law as well. This situation is common in criminal cases. A person accused of burglary under state law will be tried in a state court. During the state court proceedings, the defendant may argue that the police violated his rights under the U.S. Constitution during a search. The case eventually can be brought to the Supreme Court on that issue. If it is, the Court will have the power to rule only on the federal issue, not on the issues of state law involved in the case. For example, the Court cannot rule on whether the defendant actually committed the burglary.

Nearly all cases brought to the Court are under its discretionary jurisdiction, so it can choose whether to hear them. They come to the Court primarily in the form of petitions for a writ of certiorari, a legal device by which the Court calls up a case for decision from a lower court. The Court must hear certain cases, called appeals. In a series of steps culminating in 1988, Congress converted the Court's jurisdiction from mostly mandatory

TABLE 1-2
Sources of Supreme Court Cases in Recent Periods (in percentages)

	Federal courts			
	Courts of appeals	*District courts*	*Specialized courts*	State courts
Cases brought to the Court[a]	78.5	0.1	1.3	20.1
Cases heard by the Court[b]	81.8	1.3	6.5	10.4

Source: Data on cases heard by the Court are from U. S. Supreme Court Database, compiled by Harold Spaeth, Michigan State University.

Note: Original jurisdiction cases are not included.

a. Cases in which the Court granted or denied hearings, October 7, 2002 (1,898 cases).
b. Cases in which the Court heard oral argument, 2001 term (78 cases).

to almost entirely discretionary. Today, appeals can be brought in only the few small classes of cases that come directly from three-judge district courts. The McCain–Feingold campaign funding law of 2002 provided this procedure for constitutional challenges to the law, so the appeals from the three-judge district court decision that upheld some parts of the law and struck down others went directly to the Supreme Court in 2003.[8] Because of a sense of urgency about resolving the issues in this case, the Court took the rare step of holding oral arguments during its summer recess.

The Supreme Court hears only a fraction of 1 percent of the cases brought to federal and state courts. As this figure suggests, courts other than the Supreme Court have ample opportunity to make policy on their own. Moreover, their decisions help to determine the ultimate impact of the Court's policies. Important though it is, the Supreme Court is hardly the only court that matters.

An Overview of the Court

The Court's Structure

The Supreme Court did not move into its own building until 1935. In its first decade, the Court met first in New York and then in Philadelphia. The Court moved to Washington, D.C., with the rest of the federal government at the beginning of the nineteenth century. For the next 130 years, it sat in the Capitol, a "tenant" of Congress.

The Court's accommodations in the Capitol were not entirely adequate. Among other things, the lack of office space meant that justices did most of their work at home. After an intensive lobbying effort by Chief Justice

William Howard Taft, Congress appropriated money for the Supreme Court building in 1929. The five-story structure, completed in 1935, occupies a full square block across the street from the Capitol. Because the primary material in the impressive building is marble, it has been called a "marble palace."

The building houses all the facilities necessary for the Court's operation. Formal sessions are held in the courtroom on the first floor. The justices sit behind a bench at the front of the courtroom. The attorneys' tables face the bench, and other participants and spectators fill the rest of the room. Behind the courtroom is the conference room, where the justices meet to decide cases. Also near the courtroom are the chambers that contain offices for the associate justices and their staffs. (Reflecting the chief justice's special status, the chief's chambers are attached to the conference room.) Since 1935 the justices have conducted all official business in the Supreme Court building, except for one week in 2001 when oral arguments were held at a nearby federal court building because of the possibility that the Court's own building had been contaminated with anthrax bacteria.

Personnel: The Justices

Under the Constitution, members of the Supreme Court must be nominated by the president and confirmed by a majority vote in the Senate. The Constitution establishes that they will hold office "during good behavior"—that is, for life unless they relinquish their posts voluntarily or are removed through impeachment proceedings. Beyond these basic rules, questions such as the number of justices, their qualifications, and their duties have been settled by federal statutes and by tradition.

People today are accustomed to a Court of nine members, but the number of justices was changed several times during the Court's first century. The Judiciary Act of 1789 provided for six justices. Subsequent statutes changed the number successively to five, six, seven, nine, ten, seven, and nine. The changes were made in part to accommodate the justices' duties in the lower federal courts, in part to serve partisan and policy goals of the president and Congress. The most recent change to nine members was made in 1869, and any further changes in size appear quite unlikely.

In 2003 each associate justice received a salary of $190,000, and the chief justice received $198,600. Substantial as these salaries are, they are not much higher than what some large law firms pay new attorneys. Some justices also have considerable personal wealth: Sandra Day O'Connor, John Paul Stevens, Ruth Bader Ginsburg, David Souter, and Stephen Breyer apparently are millionaires.[9]

The primary duty of the justices is to participate in the collective decisions of the Court: determining which cases to hear, deciding cases, and writing and contributing to opinions. Ordinarily, the Court's decisions are made by all nine members, but exceptions occur. At times the Court has only eight members because a justice has resigned, retired, or died, and a replacement has not been appointed. A justice's illness may leave the Court temporarily shorthanded. Or a justice may decide not to participate in a case because of a perceived conflict of interest. Under federal law, judges should withdraw from cases—"recuse" themselves—when a decision would affect their self-interest substantially or their impartiality "might reasonably be questioned." [10]

Justices do not explain the reasons for their recusals, but the most common reason is a financial interest in a case. Justices Breyer and O'Connor occasionally recuse themselves because of their stock holdings. Justices Stevens and O'Connor stayed out of a 2001 case that would affect taxation of their salaries.[11]

Other recusals result from personal ties between justices and the litigants or lawyers in a case. Three justices did not vote on a 2001 stay of execution because of their friendship with the murder victim's son, a federal judge.[12] Several current justices have spouses or children in law or politics. In George W. Bush's administration, for example, Antonin Scalia's son served for a time as the top legal official in the Labor Department, and William Rehnquist's daughter served as the inspector general of Health and Human Services. This reality creates some difficult choices for justices. In a 2000 case, Rehnquist took the unusual step of writing an opinion to explain why he had participated in a case in which his son was working as an attorney.[13]

When only eight justices participate in a decision, the Court may divide 4–4. This was the result in a 2002 environmental case from which Justice Anthony Kennedy withdrew because he was acquainted with one of the litigants.[14] In the 2001 case involving a stay of execution, the three recusals resulted in a 3–3 vote. A tie vote affirms the lower court decision, the votes of individual justices are not announced, and no opinions are written. In rare instances, the Court fails to achieve a quorum of six members. This situation, like a tie vote, results in affirmance of the lower-court decision.

In addition to their participation in collective decisions, the justices make some decisions individually, as circuit justices. The United States has always been divided into federal judicial circuits. Originally, most appeals within a circuit were heard by ad hoc courts composed of a federal trial judge and two members of the Supreme Court assigned to that area as circuit justices. The circuit duties were arduous, particularly when long-distance travel was difficult. Some justices even suffered ill health from "circuit riding." [15] The justices' circuit-riding responsibilities were reduced in several steps and eliminated altogether when Congress created the courts of appeals in 1891.

The twelve judicial circuits continue to have circuit justices assigned to them, with three justices doing double duty. The circuit justices deal with applications for special action, such as a request to stay a lower court decision (prevent it from taking effect) until the Court decides whether to hear the case. Ordinarily, such an application must go first to the circuit justice. That justice may rule on the application as an individual or refer the case to the whole Court. If the circuit justice rejects an application, it can then be made to a second justice. That justice ordinarily refers it to the whole Court.

The most common subject of stay requests is the death penalty. The Court is confronted with numerous requests to grant or vacate (remove) stays of execution, many of which come almost at the scheduled execution time. These requests put considerable pressure on the justices, and they sometimes divide the Court along ideological lines. In one 2002 case, three liberal justices dissented from the Court's denial of a stay of execution in a case involving the use of the death penalty for murders committed by juveniles. A few months earlier, three conservatives joined a long opinion that dissented from the granting of stays in two cases involving the death penalty for mentally retarded defendants.[16] The current Court grants stays of execution only in circumstances that seem especially compelling to most justices. One example was a 2003 case in which a former federal prosecutor and three former federal judges, one of whom had been head of the FBI, supported the prisoner.[17]

For the most part, the nine justices are equal in formal power. The exception is the chief justice, who is the formal leader of the Court and of the federal judicial system. The official title, "Chief Justice of the United States," symbolizes the chief's responsibilities for the federal judicial system as a whole. In this role, the chief chairs the Judicial Conference and conveys to Congress the views of the conference on legislative issues. The chief also delivers an annual "state of the judiciary" message, directed primarily at Congress.[18]

The Constitution requires that the chief justice preside over Senate trials in impeachment proceedings against presidents, a duty that attracted attention to Chief Justice Rehnquist during President Clinton's trial in 1999. It also attracted attention to Rehnquist's distinctive robe with four gold stripes on each sleeve, modeled on the costume of the British lord chancellor in a theater production that he attended in 1995.[19]

Within the Court, the chief justice presides over the Court's public sessions and conferences. The chief also supervises administration of the Court, with the assistance of committees of justices such as the Committee for the Budget and the Cafeteria Committee. One justice serves as "social secretary."[20]

Personnel: Law Clerks and Other Support Staff

A staff of more than four hundred people supports the justices. A large majority of the staff members carries out custodial and police functions under the supervision of the marshal of the Court. Several other offices help carry out the Court's work. The clerk of the Court is responsible for the clerical processing of all the cases that come to the Court. The reporter of decisions supervises preparation of the official record of the Court's decisions, *United States Reports.* The librarian is in charge of the libraries in the Supreme Court building.

Of all the members of the support staff, the law clerks have the most direct impact on the Court's decisions. Justices may employ four clerks each, but Chief Justice Rehnquist chooses to use only three. (Rehnquist likes to play tennis with his clerks, and one reporter pointed out that three are "just enough to fill a doubles team." [21]) The typical clerk is a recent, high-ranked graduate of a prestigious law school. In the 1998–2002 terms, 41 percent came from Harvard and Yale. The great majority clerked in a federal court of appeals before coming to the Supreme Court, and some spent a short time in legal practice between their stints in a court of appeals and the Supreme Court.[22] There has been a growing tendency for the justices, especially the most conservative, to draw clerks from court of appeals judges who share their ideological positions.[23]

Clerkships are prized positions, and more than a thousand people apply for them each year.[24] Most apply to several justices. Clerks usually work with a justice for only one year. After leaving the Court, clerks have little difficulty obtaining good positions at high salaries. Many go on to distinguished careers. Indeed, William Rehnquist, John Paul Stevens, and Stephen Breyer were once law clerks in the Court.

Clerks typically spend much of their time on the petitions for hearings by the Court, digesting information in the petitions and the lower court records and summarizing it for the justices. Clerks also work on cases that have been accepted for decision. This work includes analysis of case materials and issues, discussions of issues with their justices, and drafting opinions.

The extent of law clerks' influence over the Court's decisions is a matter of considerable interest and wide disagreement.[25] Observers who depict the clerks as quite powerful probably underestimate the justices' ability to maintain control over their decisions. Still, the jobs that justices give to their clerks ensure significant influence. One former clerk estimated that "well over half of the text the Court now produces was generated by law clerks," and he concluded that "delegation of the initial drafting task inevitably entails a substantial transfer of responsibility over the final

Justice Stephen Breyer, wearing a "Cat in the Hat" hat and tie,
at an elementary school where he read from a Dr. Seuss book.

content of an opinion." [26] The same is true of the other work that clerks
do.

The Court and the Outside World

Busy as Supreme Court justices may be with their judicial work, they engage in a good deal of activity outside the Court. Most common are
speeches and lectures at law schools and legal conferences, but justices
speak at other forums as well. Some justices are quite active speakers; Justice O'Connor, for example, reports that she has spoken in every state.[27]

Some of the justices engage in off-the-Court writing. Chief Justice
Rehnquist has written three books about law and courts, with a fourth
scheduled for publication in 2004. Rehnquist has a remarkable ability to
anticipate what topics will become relevant: in 1992 he published a book

on impeachments, and his 1998 book was on civil liberties during wartime.[28] Justice O'Connor has published a book about her childhood on a ranch and one with essays on the Court's history and other topics. Justice Thomas has arranged to write a book about his life, for what was reported to be a $1 million advance payment.[29]

The justices' outside activities can have implications for policy or politics. Their speeches and lectures often convey a sense of their views on public issues. At a 2002 judicial conference, for example, Justice Stevens argued that state legislatures should consider limiting the death penalty to people who commit crimes after reaching the age of eighteen.[30] Justice Scalia has expressed his views on a number of issues, including the role of religion in public life.[31]

Some justices have become involved in the political process more directly, primarily by consulting with presidents. This was true of President Lyndon Johnson's appointees Abe Fortas and Thurgood Marshall. Fortas, a long-time adviser to Johnson, continued to serve in that role after his appointment. He dealt with some issues that could have come before the Court, and he disclosed to an FBI official information on the Court's deliberations in two cases.[32] Warren Burger, appointed chief justice by President Nixon, later discussed pending cases with Nixon.[33] Since Burger and Nixon, however, it appears that no justice has engaged in that kind of presidential consultation.

Some of the justices receive a good deal of attention in the mass media. Justice Scalia has even been the occasional subject of a comic strip that appears in weekly newspapers. The cartoonist depicts Scalia as a motorcycle-riding avenger who attacks enemies such as Saddam Hussein and the Florida Supreme Court.[34] Yet few justices are well known. In a 2002 survey, only 11 percent of the respondents could name three justices, and 64 percent could recall none of their names. (Sandra Day O'Connor received the most mentions, 24 percent, Stephen Breyer and John Paul Stevens the fewest.)[35]

Most justices seem to like their anonymity, which allows them a freedom that more visible public figures lack. During a parade of anti-abortion marchers in front of the Court, Harry Blackmun, author of the 1973 opinion legalizing abortion, was able to stand nearby and watch unnoticed.[36] As one biographer said of William Brennan, who exerted great influence on civil liberties law, "He enjoyed all the benefits of power with none of the annoyances."[37]

This anonymity results in part from the justices' own choices. Most important, they have refused to allow televising of oral arguments and announcements of decisions. As Justice Souter put it, "The day you see a camera coming into our courtroom, it's going to roll over my dead body."[38]

The release of audiotapes of arguments is delayed, so excerpts cannot be played on same-day newscasts, although the justices allowed immediate release of the arguments in *Bush v. Gore* and the 2003 cases involving affirmative action in admissions to the University of Michigan. And the justices grant few on-the-record interviews to journalists. Justice Scalia makes many public speeches, but he refuses to allow radio and television coverage of them. Some reporters found it ironic that Scalia applied that policy to an appearance in which he was given an award for his support of free speech.[39]

The Court reveals little about its decision-making processes, which its public information officer once said "are cloaked in a security . . . possibly rivaled only by the National Security Agency or the CIA." [40] This degree of secrecy suggests that the justices' efforts to keep out of the public eye have another purpose as well. By limiting the flow of information about themselves and the Court, the justices may be trying to maintain an impression that the Court is above ordinary politics. Indeed, Barbara Perry has argued that the justices and the Court's staff engage in a careful strategy to give the Court an exalted image among the general public.[41]

If there is such a strategy, it has achieved considerable success. Although the Court receives some criticism in the mass media, on the whole it is treated far more deferentially than Congress or the president. One scholar has said that the reporters who cover the Court "are in essence tools of the Court." [42] And the Court's public approval ratings are usually more positive than those of the other branches, especially Congress. Such a high level of approval may provide the Court with some protection from criticism and from more concrete attacks by other policymakers.

The Court's Schedule

The Court keeps to a constant annual schedule. It holds one term each year, lasting from the first Monday in October until the beginning of the succeeding term a year later.[43] The term is designated by the year in which it begins: the 2003 term began in October 2003. Ordinarily, the Court does its collective work from late September to late June. This work begins when the justices meet to dispose of the petitions for hearings that have accumulated during the summer and ends when the Court has issued decisions in all the cases it heard during the term.

Most of the term is divided into sittings of about two weeks, when the Court holds sessions to hear oral arguments in cases and to announce decisions, and recesses of two weeks or longer. The justices meet in conference during the sittings and less frequently during recesses. After the Court begins its last sitting in mid-May, it hears no more cases and holds one or more sessions each week to announce decisions.

The Court issues few decisions early in the term because of the time required after oral arguments to write opinions and reach final positions. Typically, about one-third of the decisions are announced in June, as the justices scramble to finish their work by the end of the term. This deadline creates considerable pressure. At the end of the term, reported one former law clerk, "marriages got put on hold. Friendships disappeared." [44] Another said, "I still have nightmares" about the end of the term. [45]

When the Court has reached and announced decisions in all the cases it heard during the term, the summer recess begins. Cases that the Court accepted for hearing but that were not argued during the term are carried over to the next term. In summer the justices generally spend some time away from Washington but continue their work on the petitions for hearings that arrive at the Court. During that time the Court and individual circuit justices respond to applications for special action. When the justices meet at the end of summer to dispose of the accumulated petitions, the cycle begins again.

The schedule of weekly activities, like the annual schedule, is fairly regular. During sittings, the Court generally holds sessions on Monday through Wednesday of two weeks and Monday of the third week. The sessions begin at ten o'clock in the morning. Oral arguments usually are held during each session except on the last Monday of the sitting. They may be preceded by several types of business. On Mondays the Court announces the filing of its order list, which is a report of the Court's decisions on petitions for hearing and other actions taken at its conference on the preceding Friday. On Tuesdays and Wednesdays, as well as the last Monday of the sitting, justices announce their opinions in cases the Court has resolved. During the last sitting of the term, however, opinions may be announced on any day of the week.

The oral arguments consume most of the time during sessions. The usual practice is to allot one hour, equally divided between the two sides, for argument in a case. With the reduced numbers of cases accepted by the Court in recent years, sessions have become shorter, and on most argument days, the Court hears two cases.

During sittings, the Court holds two conferences each week. The Wednesday afternoon conference is devoted to discussion of the cases that were argued on Monday. In a longer conference on Friday, the justices discuss the cases argued on Tuesday and Wednesday, as well as all the other matters the Court must decide. The most numerous of these matters are the petitions for hearing.

The Court also holds a conference on the last Friday of each recess to deal with the continuing flow of business. The remainder of the justices' time during recess periods is devoted to their individual work: study of petitions for hearing and of cases scheduled for argument, writing of opinions, and reaction to other justices' opinions. That work continues during the sittings.

The Court's History

This book is concerned primarily with the Supreme Court at present and in the recent past, but I frequently refer to the Court's history to provide perspective on the current Court. It is useful at this point to take an overview of that history.

The Court from 1790 to 1865

The Framers of the Constitution explicitly created the Supreme Court, but the Constitution says much less about the Court than about Congress and the president. In the Judiciary Act of 1789, which set up the federal court system, the Court's jurisdiction under the Constitution was used as the basis for granting the Court broad powers. Still, what it would do with its powers was uncertain, in part because their scope was ambiguous.

The Court started slowly, deciding only about fifty cases and making few significant decisions between 1790 and 1799.[46] Several nominees rejected offers to serve on the Court, and two justices—including Chief Justice John Jay—resigned to take more attractive positions in state government. The Court's fortunes improved considerably under John Marshall, chief justice from 1801 to 1835. Marshall, appointed by President John Adams, dominated the Court to a degree that no other justice has matched. He used his dominance to strengthen the Court's position and advance the policies he favored.

The Court's most important assertion of power under Marshall was probably its decision in *Marbury v. Madison* (1803), in which the Court struck down a federal statute for the first time. In his opinion for the Court, Marshall argued that when a federal law is inconsistent with the Constitution, the Court must declare the law unconstitutional and refuse to enforce it. A few years later, the Court also claimed the right of judicial review over state acts.

The Court's aggressiveness brought denunciations and threats, including an effort by President Thomas Jefferson to have Congress remove at least one justice through impeachment. But Marshall's skill in minimizing confrontations helped to protect the Court from a successful attack. The other branches of government and the general public gradually accepted the powers that he claimed for the Court and the Court's role in policy-making.

This acceptance was tested by the Court's decision in *Scott v. Sandford* (1857), generally known as the *Dred Scott* case. Prior to that decision, the Court had overturned only one federal statute, the minor law involved in *Marbury v. Madison*. In *Dred Scott,* however, Marshall's successor, Roger Taney (1836–1864), wrote the Court's opinion holding that Congress had exceeded its constitutional powers when it prohibited slavery in some territories. That decision was intended to resolve the legal controversy over slavery. Instead, the level of controversy increased, and the Court was vilified in the North. The Court's prestige suffered greatly, but its basic powers survived without serious challenge.[47]

During this period, the Court was concerned with more than its own position; it was addressing major issues of public policy. The primary area of its concern was federalism, the legal relationship between the national government and the states. Under Marshall, the Court gave strong support to national powers. Marshall wanted to restrict state policy where that policy interfered with activities of the national government, especially its power to regulate commerce. Under Taney, the Court was not as favorable to the national government, but Taney and his colleagues did not reverse the Marshall Court's general expansion of federal power. As a result, the constitutional power of the federal government remained strong; the Court had permanently altered the lines between the national government and the state governments.

The Court from 1865 to 1937

After the Civil War, the Court began to focus its attention on government regulation of the economy. By the late nineteenth century, all levels of government were adopting new laws to regulate business activities. Among them were the federal antitrust laws, state regulations of railroad practices, and federal and state laws concerning employment conditions. Inevitably, much of this legislation was challenged in the courts on constitutional grounds.

Although the Supreme Court upheld a great many government policies regulating business in this period, it gradually became less friendly toward those policies. That position was reflected in the development of constitutional doctrines limiting government power to control business activities. Those doctrines were used with increasing frequency to attack regulatory legislation; in the 1920s, the Supreme Court held unconstitutional more than 130 regulatory laws.[48]

In the 1930s, the Supreme Court's attacks on economic regulation brought it into serious conflict with the other branches. President Franklin Roosevelt's New Deal program to combat the Great Depression included sweeping statutes to control the economy, measures that enjoyed widespread support. In a series of decisions in 1935 and 1936, the Court struck down several of these statutes, including laws broadly regulating industry and agriculture, generally by 6–3 and 5–4 margins.[49]

Roosevelt responded in 1937 by proposing legislation under which an extra justice could be added to the Court for every sitting justice over the age of seventy who had served at least ten years, up to a maximum of six. If the legislation were enacted, Roosevelt could appoint six new justices, thereby "packing" the Court with justices favorable to his programs. While this plan was being debated in Congress, however, the Court weakened the impetus behind it. In several decisions in 1937, the Court reversed direction and upheld New Deal legislation and similar state laws by narrow margins.[50] Although some disagree, most observers have concluded that this shift was a deliberate effort to mend the contentious relationship with the other branches.[51] In any event, the Court-packing plan died.

During the congressional debate, one of the conservative justices retired. Several other justices left the Court in the next few years, giving Roosevelt the ideological control of the Court that he had sought through the Court-packing legislation. The new Court created by his appointments fully accepted the economic regulation that had been viewed unfavorably by its predecessor, giving very broad interpretations to the constitutional powers to tax and to regulate interstate commerce.

The Court from 1937 to the Present

Since its retreat in the late 1930s, the Court has continued to uphold major economic policies of the federal government. The Court hears many cases concerning economic regulation, but this field has become less central to its role. Instead, the Court's primary emphasis in the current era is civil liberties. More precisely, the Court gives the most attention to the interpretation of legal protections for freedom of expression and freedom of religion, for the procedural rights of criminal defendants and others, and for equal treatment of disadvantaged groups.

The Court's general position on civil liberties issues has varied considerably during this period, mostly as a result of changes in its membership. The one constant has been the Court's collective interest in addressing civil liberties issues.

The Court gave the most support to civil liberties during the 1960s, the latter part of the period when Earl Warren was chief justice (1953–1969). The Court's policies during that period are often identified with Warren, but other liberal justices played roles of equal or greater importance: Hugo Black and William Douglas, Roosevelt appointees who served through the Warren Court, and Eisenhower appointee William Brennan.

The most prominent decision of the Warren era was *Brown v. Board of Education* (1954), in which the Court ordered the desegregation of school systems that assigned students to schools by race. The Court supported the rights of African Americans in several other policy areas as well. During the 1960s, the Court expanded the rights of criminal defendants in state cases. It issued landmark decisions on the right to counsel (*Gideon v. Wainwright*, 1963), police search and seizure practices (*Mapp v. Ohio*, 1961), and the questioning of suspects (*Miranda v. Arizona*, 1966). The Court supported freedom of expression by expanding First Amendment rights, especially on obscenity and libel. In a line of cases beginning with *Baker v. Carr* (1962), the Court required that legislative districts be equal in population.

When Earl Warren retired in 1969, he was succeeded as chief justice by Warren Burger, President Nixon's first Court appointee. Nixon made three more appointments in 1970 and 1971. The Court's membership changed much more slowly after that. But each new member until 1993 was appointed by a conservative Republican president—one by Gerald Ford, three by Ronald Reagan, and two by George Bush. In 1986 Reagan named Nixon appointee William Rehnquist, the most conservative justice on the Court, to succeed Warren Burger as chief justice. The string of Republican appointments was broken with Bill Clinton's two appointments in 1993 and 1994. No justice left the Court between 1994 and 2003, the longest period of membership stability since the 1820s.

The Republican appointments from 1969 through 1991 gradually moved the Court's civil liberties policies in a conservative direction. But the movement was not uniform. For example, the Court continued to give considerable support to freedom of expression. Perhaps the most decisive shift came on issues of criminal procedure, although the Court did not directly overturn any of the Warren Court's landmark expansions of defendants' rights. The Rehnquist Court's interpretations of federal antidiscrimination statutes tended to narrow their impact, with exceptions on some issues such as sexual harassment.

The Court's policies in other areas changed as well. Its interpretations of environmental and labor laws became more conservative. Beginning in 1995, it narrowed congressional power to regulate the private sector and especially state governments.[52]

The Supreme Court's policies continue to evolve in complex ways, providing a reminder of how difficult it is to predict where the Court is going. The Court's history also demonstrates that its direction is largely a reflection of its membership, so the selection of justices is a crucial process. I examine that process in the next chapter.

NOTES

1. The decisions affecting Clinton were *Morrison v. Olson* (1988) and *Clinton v. Jones* (1997); the decision on Nixon was *United States v. Nixon* (1974).
2. Examples include *Maryland v. Dyson* (1999); *City of Indianapolis v. Edmond* (2000); and *Florida v. Thomas* (2001).
3. Alexis de Tocqueville, *Democracy in America*, trans. Henry Reeve, rev. Francis Bowen (New York: Knopf, 1945), vol. 1, 280.
4. Bradley C. Canon, "A Framework for the Analysis of Judicial Activism," in *Supreme Court Activism and Restraint,* ed. Stephen C. Halpern and Charles M. Lamb (Lexington, Mass.: Lexington Books, 1982), 385–419; Richard L. Pacelle Jr., *The Role of the Supreme Court in American Politics: The Least Dangerous Branch?* (Boulder, Colo.: Westview Press, 2002).
5. See Vincent L. McKusick, "Discretionary Gatekeeping: The Supreme Court's Management of Its Original Jurisdiction Docket Since 1961," *Maine Law Review* 45 (1993): 185–242.
6. Anne-Marie Carstens, "Lurking in the Shadows of Judicial Process: Special Masters in the Supreme Court's Original Jurisdiction Cases," *Minnesota Law Review* 86 (February 2002): 625–715.
7. *Norfolk & Western Railway Co. v. Ayers* (2003).
8. The district court decision was *McConnell v. Federal Election Commission* (D.D.C. 2003).
9. "At Least 5 Millionaires on the Supreme Court," *Washington Post,* June 1, 2002, A5.
10. 28 U.S.C., sec. 455.
11. *United States v. Hatter* (2001).
12. David G. Savage, "In Rare 3–3 Vote, High Court Refuses to Delay Execution," *Los Angeles Times,* August 14, 2001. The case was *Beazley v. Johnson* (2001).
13. *Microsoft Corporation v. United States* (2000).
14. Linda Greenhouse, "Tie Affirms Clean Water Act's Reach," *New York Times,* December 17, 2002. The case was *Borden Ranch Partnership v. U.S. Army Corps of Engineers* (2002).
15. David N. Atkinson, *Leaving the Bench: Supreme Court Justices at the End* (Lawrence: University Press of Kansas, 1999), chap. 2.
16. The cases were, respectively, *Patterson v. Texas* (2002) and *Moore v. Texas* (2002). See Ira Mickenberg, "Hostility Grows over Death Penalty," *National Law Journal,* August 5, 2002, C9.
17. Peter T. Kilborn, "Texas Death Row Inmate Gets a Last-Minute Stay," *New York Times,* March 13, 2003, A16. The case was *Banks v. Cockrell* (2003).
18. See, for example, Charles Lane, "Rehnquist Calls on Lawmakers to Address 'Crisis' in Courts," *Washington Post,* January 1, 2003, A2.
19. See Joan Biskupic, "Emerging from Margins, Rehnquist Adapts to Role," *Washington Post,* January 23, 1999, A13.
20. See Bernard Schwartz, *Decision: How the Supreme Court Decides Cases* (New York: Oxford University Press, 1996), 73–74.
21. David Savage, *Turning Right: The Making of the Rehnquist Supreme Court* (New York: Wiley, 1992), 306.
22. Tony Mauro, "Clerks Follow New Path to High Court," *Legal Times,* October 21, 2002, 1.

23. Corey Ditslear and Lawrence Baum, "Selection of Law Clerks and Polarization in the U.S. Supreme Court," *Journal of Politics* 63 (August 2001): 869–885.

24. Joan Biskupic, "Clerks Gain Status, Clout in the Temple of Justice," *Washington Post,* January 2, 1994, A23.

25. See Richard A. Posner, *The Federal Courts: Challenge and Reform* (Cambridge: Harvard University Press, 1996), 139–159; Mark Tushnet, "Thurgood Marshall and the Brethren," *Georgetown Law Journal* 80 (August 1992): 2110–9; and Edward Lazarus, *Closed Chambers: The First Eyewitness Account of the Epic Struggles Inside the Supreme Court* (New York: Times Books, 1998).

26. Sean Donahue, "Behind the Pillars of Justice: Remarks on Law Clerks," *The Long Term View* 3 (spring 1995): 81–82.

27. Sandra Day O'Connor, *The Majesty of the Law: Reflections of a Supreme Court Justice* (New York: Random House, 2003), xvi.

28. William H. Rehnquist, *Grand Inquests: The Historic Impeachments of Justice Samuel Chase and President Andrew Johnson* (New York: Morrow, 1992); Rehnquist, *All the Laws but One: Civil Liberties in Wartime* (New York: Alfred A. Knopf, 1998).

29. Charles Lane, "Clarence Thomas Sells Memoirs," *Washington Post,* January 9, 2003, C1, C4.

30. Bob Egelko, "Death Penalty for Juveniles Hit," *San Francisco Chronicle,* July 19, 2002, A4.

31. "Scalia Attacks Church-State Court Rulings," *New York Times,* January 13, 2003, A19.

32. James Rowen, "FBI Files Show Justice Violated Court Secrecy," *Milwaukee Journal,* January 21, 1990, 1A, 20A. See also Juan Williams, *Thurgood Marshall: American Revolutionary* (New York: Times Books, 1998), 340–344.

33. Seymour M. Hersh, "Nixon's Last Cover-Up: The Tapes He Wants the Archives to Suppress," *New Yorker,* December 14, 1992, 81.

34. The comic strip is "Tom the Dancing Bug," by Ruben Bolling.

35. Charles M. Madigan, "Name Supremes? Not Diana Ross," *Chicago Tribune,* April 28, 2002, sec. 2, 5; The Polling Company, "Shocking Poll: More Americans Can Name Rice Krispies Characters than Supreme Court Justices!" at *www.pollingcompany.com,* accessed March 12, 2003. For a more positive assessment of public knowledge about the Court, see James L. Gibson, Gregory A. Caldeira, and Lester Kenyatta Spence, "Public Knowledge of the United States Supreme Court, 2001," (working paper, 2001).

36. Savage, *Turning Right,* 236.

37. Kim Isaac Eisler, *A Justice for All: William J. Brennan, Jr., and the Decisions that Transformed America* (New York: Simon & Schuster, 1993), 247.

38. Ronald Goldfarb, "The Invisible Supreme Court," *New York Times,* May 4, 1996, A15.

39. Charles Lane, "Recordings Banned as Scalia Accepts Free Speech Award," *Washington Post,* March 20, 2003, A27.

40. Annie Groer and Joan Biskupic, "Toni House, Washington's Supreme Spokeswoman," *Washington Post,* September 30, 1998, D10.

41. Barbara A. Perry, *The Priestly Tribe: The Supreme Court's Image in the American Mind* (Westport, Conn.: Praeger, 1999).

42. Robert Schmidt, "May It Please the Court," *Brill's Content,* October 1999, 73. On coverage of the Court, see Elliot E. Slotnick and Jennifer A. Segal,

Television News and the Supreme Court: All the News That's Fit to Air? (New York: Cambridge University Press, 1998).

43. The Court's schedule is described in Robert L. Stern, Eugene Gressman, Stephen M. Shapiro, and Kenneth S. Geller, *Supreme Court Practice,* 8th ed. (Washington, D.C.: Bureau of National Affairs, 2002), 9–16.

44. Joan Biskupic, "In June, Rulings Move with Supreme Speed," *Washington Post,* May 26, 1998, A15.

45. Joan Biskupic, "The Art of 'Holding Five' in Peak Season," *Washington Post,* June 7, 1999, A17.

46. See William R. Casto, *The Supreme Court in the Early Republic: The Chief Justiceships of John Jay and Oliver Ellsworth* (Columbia: University of South Carolina Press, 1995). For another perspective, see Scott Douglas Gerber, ed., *Seriatim: The Supreme Court Before John Marshall* (New York: New York University Press, 1998).

47. Robert G. McCloskey, *The American Supreme Court,* 3d ed., rev. Sanford Levinson (Chicago: University of Chicago Press, 2000), 64–66.

48. This figure was calculated from data in Congressional Research Service, *The Constitution of the United States of America: Analysis and Interpretation* (Washington, D.C.: Government Printing Office, 1987), 1885–2113.

49. The cases included *Carter v. Carter Coal Co.* (1936); *United States v. Butler* (1936); and *Schechter Poultry Corp. v. United States* (1935).

50. The cases included *National Labor Relations Board v. Jones & Laughlin Steel Corp.* (1937); *Steward Machine Co. v. Davis* (1937); and *West Coast Hotel Co. v. Parrish* (1937).

51. See Barry Cushman, *Rethinking the New Deal Court: The Structure of a Constitutional Revolution* (New York: Oxford University Press, 1998).

52. Among these decisions were *United States v. Lopez* (1995) and *Board of Trustees v. Garrett* (2001).

Chapter 2

The Justices

The social and political environment of the Supreme Court exerts considerable effect on the Court's decisions. But the most direct influence on those decisions, and probably the most powerful, is the Court's membership. When the Court decides a case by a 5–4 vote, as it frequently does, that one-vote margin emphasizes how much difference it makes that some people sit on the Court rather than others. With one change in the set of justices who served from 2000 to 2003, the Court might have taken some very different steps. It might have prohibited tuition vouchers for students at religious schools rather than allowing them.[1] It might have prohibited affirmative action in university admissions rather than upholding it in some forms.[2] And the presidential election of 2000 might have been resolved even later than it was—and perhaps with a different result. The identities of the people who become justices are a matter of fundamental importance.

As of mid-2003, presidents had made 148 nominations to the Supreme Court, and 108 justices have served. Four candidates were nominated and confirmed twice, eight declined appointments or died before beginning service on the Court, and twenty-eight did not secure Senate confirmation.[3] Table 2-1 lists the forty-five nominations to the Court since 1930 and the thirty-six justices chosen since that time.

This chapter focuses on the past several decades. The chapter's three sections discuss the selection of justices, the characteristics of the people who are selected, and how and why they leave the Court.

The Selection of Justices

The selection of a Supreme Court justice begins with the creation of a vacancy, when a member of the Court resigns, retires, or dies. Inevitably, vacancies occur at an irregular rate. President Bill Clinton was able to select

TABLE 2-1
Nominations to the Supreme Court since 1930

Name	Nominated by	Replaced	Years served
Charles Evans Hughes (CJ)	Hoover	Taft	1930–41
John Parker	Hoover	(Sanford)	Defeated for confirmation, 1930
Owen Roberts	Hoover	Sanford	1930–45
Benjamin Cardozo	Hoover	Holmes	1932–38
Hugo Black	F. Roosevelt	Van Devanter	1937–71
Stanley Reed	F. Roosevelt	Sutherland	1938–57
Felix Frankfurter	F. Roosevelt	Cardozo	1939–62
William Douglas	F. Roosevelt	Brandeis	1939–75
Frank Murphy	F. Roosevelt	Butler	1940–49
James Byrnes	F. Roosevelt	McReynolds	1941–42
Harlan Fiske Stone (CJ)[a]	F. Roosevelt	Hughes	1941–46
Robert Jackson	F. Roosevelt	Stone	1941–54
Wiley Rutledge	F. Roosevelt	Byrnes	1943–49
Harold Burton	Truman	Roberts	1945–58
Fred Vinson (CJ)	Truman	Stone	1946–53
Tom Clark	Truman	Murphy	1949–67
Sherman Minton	Truman	Rutledge	1949–56
Earl Warren (CJ)	Eisenhower	Vinson	1953–69
John Harlan	Eisenhower	Jackson	1955–71
William Brennan	Eisenhower	Minton	1956–90
Charles Whittaker	Eisenhower	Reed	1957–62
Potter Stewart	Eisenhower	Burton	1958–81

Name	Seat	President	Years/Notes
Byron White	Whittaker	Kennedy	1962–93
Arthur Goldberg	Frankfurter	Kennedy	1962–65
Abe Fortas	Goldberg	Johnson	1965–69
Thurgood Marshall	Clark	Johnson	1967–91
Abe Fortas (CJ)[a]	(Warren)	Johnson	Nomination withdrawn, 1968
Homer Thornberry	(Fortas)	Johnson	Nomination became moot, 1968[b]
Warren Burger (CJ)	Warren	Nixon	1969–86
Clement Haynsworth	(Fortas)	Nixon	Defeated for confirmation, 1969
G. Harrold Carswell	(Fortas)	Nixon	Defeated for confirmation, 1970
Harry Blackmun	Fortas	Nixon	1970–94
Lewis Powell	Black	Nixon	1971–87
William Rehnquist	Harlan	Nixon	1971–
John Paul Stevens	Douglas	Ford	1975–
Sandra Day O'Connor	Stewart	Reagan	1981–
William Rehnquist (CJ)[a]	Burger	Reagan	1986–
Antonin Scalia	Rehnquist	Reagan	1986–
Robert Bork	(Powell)	Reagan	Defeated for confirmation, 1987
Douglas Ginsburg	(Powell)	Reagan	Withdrew before formal nomination, 1987
Anthony Kennedy	Powell	Reagan	1988–
David Souter	Brennan	G. Bush	1990–
Clarence Thomas	Marshall	G. Bush	1991–
Ruth Bader Ginsburg	White	Clinton	1993–
Stephen Breyer	Blackmun	Clinton	1994–

a. Nominated as chief justice while serving as associate justice.

b. When Fortas's nomination for chief justice was withdrawn, no vacancy for his seat as associate justice existed.

two new justices in his first eighteen months in office, but none during the rest of his eight-year tenure. Indeed, by the spring of 2003, no vacancies had occurred in nine years, an extraordinary length of time, and the absence of retirements that summer ensured an even longer gap between appointments.

The formal process for selection of justices is simple. When a vacancy occurs, the president makes a nomination, which must be confirmed by a majority of those voting in the Senate. When the chief justice's position is vacant, the president has two options: to nominate a sitting justice to that position and also nominate a new associate justice, or to nominate a person as chief justice from outside the Court. Presidents usually take the latter course, primarily to have a wider field from which to select the chief, but President Reagan elevated Justice William Rehnquist to the position of chief justice after Warren Burger retired in 1986.

The actual process of selection is more complicated than the simple formal process suggests. The president and the Senate make their decisions surrounded by individuals and groups with a deep interest in these decisions, and the process of nomination and confirmation can be quite complex. It will be useful to first discuss the roles of unofficial participants and then consider how the president and Senate reach their decisions.

Unofficial Participants

Because Supreme Court appointments are so important, a variety of individuals and groups seek to influence the president and Senate. When a vacancy occurs, presidents and their staffs may hear from a wide array of groups, government officials, other prominent people, and ordinary individuals.[4] Apart from members of the president's administration, the most important of these participants fall into three categories: the legal community, other interest groups, and potential justices. The president and Senate also seek to influence each other. The need for Senate confirmation gives the president an incentive to listen to members of Congress, especially when opposition control of the Senate or other conditions weaken the president's position.[5]

The Legal Community. Lawyers have a particular interest in the Court's membership, and their views about potential justices may carry particular weight. As the largest and most prominent organization of lawyers, the American Bar Association (ABA) has occupied a special position. An ABA committee investigates presidential nominees who await confirmation and evaluates them as "well qualified," "qualified," or "not qualified." The

The justices in 1994. These nine justices remained on the Court in 2003; that nine-year period was the longest without a Court appointment since the 1820s.

committee has never rated a nominee as "not qualified," but its level of enthusiasm for a nominee can affect the confirmation process. A unanimous rating of "well qualified," which both Ruth Bader Ginsburg and Stephen Breyer received, helps to smooth the path to Senate approval. By the same token, when four committee members rated Robert Bork as "not qualified" in 1987 and two gave that rating to Clarence Thomas in 1991, their prospects for confirmation were weakened.

Those negative ratings of two conservative Republicans, one of them (Bork) a prestigious legal scholar, helped convince many conservatives that the ABA had become unduly liberal. For that reason some Republican senators give little weight to its judgment, and President George W. Bush discontinued the practice of allowing the ABA committee to rate prospective nominees to lower courts before their selection.

Other legal groups and individual lawyers also participate in the selection process. Law professors and other prominent attorneys often announce their evaluations of nominees the Senate is considering. Such evaluations may have considerable impact. The criticism of President Nixon's nominees Clement Haynsworth and G. Harrold Carswell by prominent attorneys countered the ABA's official judgment that the two nominees were qualified and contributed to their rejection by the Senate.

The lawyers involved in the selection of justices sometimes include sitting members of the Supreme Court. But justices usually stay out of the selection process, despite their interest in who their colleagues will be. When justices do participate, most often it is by recommending a potential nominee.

The most active Supreme Court lobbyist in the past half century was Chief Justice Warren Burger. Appointed by Richard Nixon in 1969, he was active in suggesting names to fill other vacancies during the Nixon administration. He played an important role in Carswell's nomination and a critical role in the nomination of his longtime friend Harry Blackmun. But Burger's advocacy sometimes annoyed Nixon, especially when he told Nixon's attorney general in 1971 that he would resign if the president appointed undistinguished lawyers to the Court. When this threat was relayed to the president, he responded, "Let him resign." [6]

Other Interest Groups. Many interest groups have a stake in Supreme Court decisions, so groups often seek to influence the selection of justices. At the nomination stage, groups that are politically important to the president are in a good position to exert influence. A Democratic president, for example, generally gives some weight to the views of labor and civil rights groups. Such groups usually can communicate directly with the president or with top presidential advisers, the best way to affect the president's views. They can also make their wishes known publicly. Some conservative groups have campaigned publicly and privately in support of their view that George W. Bush should nominate strong conservatives rather than moderate conservatives to fill any vacancies on the Court during his presidency.

Once a nomination has been announced, groups often work for or against Senate confirmation. Group opposition to a nominee is more common than support, because groups that favor a nominee may perceive confirmation as assured even if they do nothing.

Significant interest group activity at the confirmation stage can be traced back as far as 1881, but it was fairly limited and sporadic until the late 1960s.[7] Conservative groups helped to bring about the defeat of Abe Fortas, nominated for elevation to chief justice by President Lyndon Johnson in 1968, while labor and civil rights groups helped to secure the defeats of Nixon nominees Haynsworth and Carswell. Several liberal groups worked against the elevation of William Rehnquist to chief justice in 1986, helping to build significant opposition, but ultimately Rehnquist was confirmed with about a two-thirds majority.

President Reagan's nomination of Robert Bork in 1987 gave rise to an unprecedented level of group activity.[8] Liberal groups feared that the strongly conservative Bork would move an ideologically divided Court to the right. Accordingly, they devoted considerable effort, and an estimated $12 million to $15 million, to achieving his defeat.[9] Their activities ranged from newspaper advertisements to direct lobbying of senators. Groups favorable to Bork's nomination took action as well. The pro-Bork groups did not mobilize as quickly or as fully as the opposition groups, and the higher level of activity against Bork helped to bring about his defeat.[10]

The nomination of Clarence Thomas in 1991 also provoked considerable group activity. Among Thomas's supporters were the United States Chamber of Commerce and Young Americans for Freedom. Opponents included the Leadership Conference on Civil Rights, a coalition of 185 groups concerned with civil rights and civil liberties, and a smaller coalition called the Alliance for Justice; both had played central roles in the opposition to Bork as well. Individual groups such as the AFL-CIO and the National Abortion Rights Action League were also involved. The opposition groups were unable to achieve the same kind of massive campaign against Thomas that they had launched against Bork. But their opposition helped to create concern about Thomas among liberal senators and thereby contributed to the decisions by most Democratic senators to vote against Thomas's confirmation.

Interest groups played a more limited role in the confirmations of Ruth Bader Ginsburg in 1993 and Stephen Breyer in 1994. In the current era as a whole, however, the level of group involvement in the confirmation process is higher than ever. That change reflects the increased number of interest groups and the increased intensity of group activity, greater awareness that nominations to the Court are important, and group leaders' learning from past episodes how to participate effectively in the confirmation process.[11] Ideological groups have also found that opposition to controversial nominees is a good way to generate interest in their causes and monetary contributions from their supporters.

Candidates for the Court. One difference between the Supreme Court and the lower federal courts is that people often become members of the Court without taking any actions to obtain their appointments. Because presidents consider Court appointments so important, they look for candidates who best serve presidential goals rather than restricting their choices to candidates who seek the job openly. For this reason most potential justices believe it is counterproductive to conduct campaigns in their own behalf.

Some people do work to obtain appointments, and some of them are successful. While serving on a federal court of appeals, Warren Burger exerted considerable effort to make himself a candidate for the Supreme Court. When his effort succeeded, President Nixon's attorney general said that "Burger's the first guy to run for the job of Chief Justice—and get it." [12] Actually, at least one predecessor campaigned even harder. William Howard Taft became chief justice in 1921 after years of efforts that began even when he was president. An ex-president often has considerable influence, and one commentator described Taft as "virtually appointing himself" chief justice. [13]

In the case of Ruth Bader Ginsburg, it was her husband who did the campaigning. Apparently without his wife's knowledge, Martin Ginsburg mobilized support for her candidacy among legal scholars and members of the women's movement. [14] His activity on her behalf may have been decisive in making Ginsburg a leading candidate and ultimately the successful nominee.

One possible approach for a judge who wants a Supreme Court nomination is to take public positions that would appeal to an appointing president. Some observers thought that Judge Michael Luttig of the federal court of appeals in Virginia engaged in a complicated version of this strategy in June 2000. Luttig wrote two opinions strongly criticizing his colleague J. Harvie Wilkinson for taking more liberal positions in those cases. Because both Luttig and Wilkinson were widely mentioned as potential nominees if George W. Bush became president in 2001, Luttig might have been trying to advance his candidacy. [15]

Although some people actively seek appointments to the Court, others are reluctant to accept them. A number of candidates have declined nominations or taken themselves out of the running when they appeared likely to be nominated. In 1993 and 1994 at least four candidates for nominations to the Court withdrew from consideration. One, Senate Majority Leader George Mitchell, was even offered a nomination. [16]

Among those who accept nominations, some are ambivalent about doing so. Byron White in 1962, Abe Fortas in 1965, and Lewis Powell in 1971 were all reluctant to take the nominations that they ultimately accepted. According to Justice Sandra Day O'Connor, when President Reagan telephoned her to ask whether it would be "all right with you" if he announced her nomination to the Court the next day, "I didn't know if it was or not." [17]

Such cases are exceptions, however. Whether or not they actively sought a position on the Supreme Court, most of those who are offered a nomination have little difficulty in accepting it. Speaking of William Brennan's appointment in 1956, President Dwight Eisenhower's press secretary reported, "I never saw a man say 'yes' so fast when the President asked him to take the job." [18]

In past eras, nominees typically played little part in the confirmation process. Today, they participate actively in that process. Nominees visit with senators (Clarence Thomas, setting a record, paid "courtesy calls" on more than half of the senators) and testify before the Senate Judiciary Committee.

That testimony presents challenges to nominees. When there is already substantial opposition to confirmation, nominees try to use their testimony to win the support of wavering senators. When confirmation seems assured, nominees seek to avoid saying something that raises doubts about them.

For most nominees, the greatest challenge arises from questions about their views on legal issues. Senators try to determine where a nominee stands on issues such as abortion and the death penalty. For their part, nominees prefer not to make their positions clear, so that they do not "prejudge" issues that might come before the Court or arouse opposition from senators who disagree with their positions. Yet nominees also know that refusal to respond to questions about their views may anger senators.

Nominees' typical response to this dilemma is to offer some information about their views but to speak only vaguely about matters that might create trouble for them. Clarence Thomas was asked repeatedly and in various ways where he stood on abortion as a constitutional issue, and he adamantly refused to indicate his views. In response to questions from Senator Patrick Leahy of Vermont, Thomas said that he had never "debated the contents" of *Roe v. Wade*. He also said, "I have not made, Senator, a decision one way or the other" about whether the case was properly decided.[19]

Not only the specifics of nominees' testimony but also the general impression they create can make a difference when confirmation is not assured. Robert Bork's appearance before the committee in 1987 left no doubt about his impressive legal skills, but many liberal and moderate senators remained convinced that he was too conservative, and some felt that he had not been candid about his views. Thomas's answers to questions about abortion and other issues also raised doubts in some senators' minds about his candor. Their testimony thereby contributed to Bork's Senate defeat and to the narrowness of Thomas's victory. In contrast, David Souter's testimony avoided raising concerns about his views and reassured many senators that he was not strongly conservative; as a result, his confirmation was assured.

The President's Decision

For the president, a Supreme Court vacancy provides a valuable opportunity to influence the Court's direction, and presidents seek to make the most of these opportunities. But the individuals and groups for whom nominations are important can subject the president to heavy and conflicting pressures, and the pressures have grown stronger in recent years. As a result, according to Mark Silverstein, for the Clinton White House the nominations of two justices "emerged as an unexpected burden rather than a cause for celebration." [20]

Presidents differ in their decision-making styles, and these differences are reflected in the nomination process. In his examination of presidents since Harry Truman, David Yalof has described two kinds of differences.[21] One concerns what Yalof calls the "decisional framework." In some instances, major decisions about priorities and criteria for a nomination are made only after a vacancy arises. This approach, predominant in the Truman administration, has been rare since then. At the other extreme, some nominees effectively are chosen even before a vacancy arises. This was true for each of Johnson's nominees. But most common, especially among recent presidents, is an intermediate approach: general criteria for selection of nominees are developed prior to a vacancy, but those criteria are not used to select a nominee until the vacancy arises.

The second kind of difference is the extent to which presidents delegate work on nominations to other officials in the executive branch. Reagan and George H.W. Bush gave considerable responsibility to officials in the White House and Justice Department, while Clinton exerted far more direct control over the selection process even in its early stages. Delegation can save presidents time and increase the options and information available to them, but if advisers have narrow perspectives or get into conflicts with each other, the decision-making process may suffer. Some of Reagan's nominations encountered this difficulty. On the other hand, when presidents play an active part throughout the selection process, they can introduce a degree of chaos to the process if they change their minds in midstream. This was true of Clinton, and Nixon's nomination of William Rehnquist was the unexpected outcome of a haphazard selection process that reflected Nixon's frequently changing views about potential nominees.[22]

The criteria used to select nominees fall into several categories: the "objective" qualifications of potential nominees, their policy preferences, rewards to political and personal associates, and the building of political support. Cutting across these criteria and helping to determine their use is the inescapable reality that the Senate must confirm a nominee.

"Objective" Qualifications.   Presidents have strong incentives to select Supreme Court nominees who have demonstrated high levels of legal competence and adherence to ethical standards. A candidate who falls

short on either of these criteria is vulnerable to opposition and potential defeat in the Senate. Further, most presidents have considerable respect for the Supreme Court and want to uphold high standards in selection.

In general, presidents' choices reflect a concern for competence. This does not mean that all nominees are highly skilled in the law, but only in a few cases has a nominee's capacity to serve on the Court been questionable. One of those nominees was Nixon's choice, G. Harrold Carswell, in 1970; Carswell was denied confirmation.

The ethical behavior of several nominees has been questioned. Abe Fortas (when nominated to be chief justice), Clement Haynsworth, and Stephen Breyer were attacked for alleged financial conflicts of interest; Fortas was also criticized for continuing to consult with President Johnson while serving as an associate justice. The charges against Fortas and Haynsworth helped bring about their defeats in the Senate. After Douglas Ginsburg was announced as a Reagan nominee, disclosures were made about a possible financial conflict of interest when he was in the Justice Department and about his past use of marijuana. The latter disclosure was especially damaging, and Ginsburg withdrew his name from consideration. An allegation that Clarence Thomas had sexually harassed an assistant while he was a federal administrator resulted in a special set of Senate hearings on the charge and put his confirmation in jeopardy.

To minimize the possibility of such embarrassments, administrations today give close scrutiny to potential nominees. After its difficulty with Douglas Ginsburg, the Reagan administration wanted to ensure that Anthony Kennedy, its choice as the next nominee, had no problems in his personal life. White House counsel A. B. Culvahouse came to Kennedy with a twenty-one-page list of questions. The FBI, itself embarrassed by its failure to discover Ginsburg's drug use, undertook a massive investigation of its own. Culvahouse stopped Kennedy during a visit to the White House to tell him that the investigation had uncovered a problem: Kennedy's daughter had an unpaid parking ticket. When nothing else turned up, Kennedy was nominated.[23]

Competence and ethics can be considered screening criteria for potential nominees. These criteria may eliminate some people from consideration, but enough candidates survive the screening process to give presidents a wide range of choices for a nomination.

Policy Preferences. By policy preferences, I mean an individual's attitudes toward policy issues. These criteria have always been a major consideration in the selection of Supreme Court justices, because presidents recognize that the ability of their appointees to influence the Court's policies is among the presidents' major legacies.

Presidents differ in their levels of concern with the policy preferences of potential nominees. Presidents who seek to usher in a new political era are especially concerned with bringing the Supreme Court more in line with their own positions.[24] This was true of Richard Nixon and Ronald Reagan, who sought to move the country and the Court in a more conservative direction. Speaking of potential nominees, Nixon told his chief of staff that he did not care "if the guy can read or write, just so he votes right." [25] In periods when the Court plays an especially prominent role in policymaking, as it does today, presidents give more weight to the policy positions of potential nominees. In any period, some specific issues are especially important to presidents and their political allies, as abortion has been in recent years.

It is in relation to this criterion that the Senate's role creates the greatest complications. Most Democratic presidents are distinctly liberal, most Republicans distinctly conservative. If a strongly liberal president chose a nominee whose preferences were also strongly liberal, that nominee's views would be somewhat distant from the views of Senate moderates and quite distant from the views of many Republican senators. A strongly conservative president is in a similar situation with Democratic senators. Thus, most presidents face a dilemma: choose a nominee whose views mirror their own and risk difficulty with confirmation, or choose a more moderate nominee and reduce their ability to reshape the Court.

Presidents react to this dilemma in different ways, giving varying weights to the collective views of the Senate. When President Reagan nominated Robert Bork and President George Bush chose Clarence Thomas, even though the Senate had a Democratic majority, they risked a Senate battle and defeat of their nominee in the interest of putting a strong conservative on the Court. Bill Clinton was more cautious, declining to nominate people whose reputations for strong liberalism might arouse opposition in the Senate. Indeed, Clinton gave greater weight than most presidents to the goal of avoiding confirmation battles.[26]

It is not always easy for presidents to ascertain the policy preferences of a potential nominee and to determine how those preferences would be reflected in votes and opinions on the Supreme Court. This is the primary reason that every nominee since 1986 has come from a federal court of appeals. As Reagan's attorney general Edwin Meese said, "You know the judicial philosophy of those judges because they've had experience and they've written opinions you can look at." [27] On the whole, sitting judges appointed to the Court have been less likely to disappoint their nominators with their votes and opinions than have other justices.[28]

Whether or not candidates are judges, their views about legal issues can be gauged from their public expressions or from their interactions with people whom the president trusts. Sometimes presidents or their representatives question prospective nominees directly about their views. Sandra Day O'Connor was questioned by two sets of administration officials and then by President Reagan himself, with whom she discussed abortion and other issues.

On the other hand, presidents sometimes choose nominees whose views on major issues are not very clear to give potential opponents less of a target. In doing so, however, they run the risk of guessing wrong themselves about a nominee's views. President George Bush chose David Souter in 1990 partly because Souter had a very short record of statements and positions on controversial judicial issues, but people who knew Souter assured Bush that he was suitably conservative. Souter indeed was confirmed without great difficulty, but his record as a justice suggests that he was not nearly as conservative as Bush thought. Some members of George W. Bush's administration reportedly "invoke a 'no more David Souters' mantra." [29]

Souter is not the only justice whose positions on the Court have surprised the appointing president. Dwight Eisenhower was unhappy about the liberalism of two of his appointees, Earl Warren and William Brennan. Indeed, according to a story that is widely circulated but of uncertain accuracy, when Eisenhower was asked if he had made any mistakes as president, he replied, "Yes, two, and they are both sitting on the Supreme Court." [30]

Such disappointments are not rare, but most justices turn out to be ideologically compatible with the presidents who appoint them. And presidents who were especially careful to select compatible justices have suffered relatively few disappointments. Both Franklin Roosevelt and Richard Nixon did well in getting what they wanted from the justices they selected. Presidents who emphasized other criteria or chose with less care, such as Truman and Eisenhower, often did less well.

When careful presidents suffer disappointments, it is often because a justice shifts position after reaching the Court. Indeed, one study found that justices tend to move away from the views of their appointing president over time.[31] Nixon's one "failure" was Harry Blackmun, who had a distinctly conservative record in his early years on the Court but gradually adopted more liberal positions. To a lesser degree, Anthony Kennedy also may have shifted in a liberal direction after reaching the Court—most notably, on abortion. In 1996 a conservative publication referred to Kennedy as "surely Reagan's biggest disappointment." [32]

Presidents cannot be assured of their appointees' support even on cases that affect the president directly. President Clinton's two appointees, Ruth Bader Ginsburg and Stephen Breyer, joined in the unanimous decision in *Clinton v. Jones* (1997) that allowed a lawsuit against him for sexual harassment to go forward. Three of President Nixon's appointees joined in the unanimous decision in *United States v. Nixon* (1974) that required him to yield tape recordings of his conversations as president. (The fourth, William Rehnquist, did not participate because he had worked in the Justice Department during the Nixon administration.) After learning of the Court's decision, Nixon reportedly "exploded, cursing the man he had named chief justice, reserving a few choice expletives for Blackmun and Powell, his other appointees." [33]

Political and Personal Reward. Abe Fortas was one of Lyndon Johnson's closest associates. In 1948 Fortas's legal skills had helped preserve Johnson's victory in a disputed Senate election. As his professional reputation grew, Fortas continued to advise Johnson, who came to rely heavily on his counsel. When Johnson had his first opportunity to choose a Supreme Court justice, he selected Fortas. The nomination rewarded someone who had done much for Johnson, even if Fortas was quite reluctant to accept the reward. It also put on the Court someone whose ability and policy views Johnson knew well from personal experience. Three years later, Johnson nominated Fortas for elevation to chief justice. To replace Fortas as associate justice, Johnson selected Homer Thornberry, a federal judge from Texas who was also a close friend.

In choosing Fortas and Thornberry, Johnson was taking a common approach. About 60 percent of the nominees to the Court had known the nominating president personally.[34] Most of Johnson's recent predecessors—Franklin Roosevelt, Harry Truman, and John F. Kennedy—had selected primarily personal acquaintances. For Truman, reward for political associates seemed to be the main criterion for selection.

Some appointments to the Court were direct rewards for political help. Eisenhower selected Earl Warren to serve as chief justice in part because of Warren's crucial support of Eisenhower at the 1952 Republican convention. As governor of California and leader of that state's delegation, Warren had provided needed votes on a preliminary issue, and Eisenhower's success on that issue helped to secure his nomination.

Since the 1968 nominations of Fortas and Thornberry (both of which failed when Fortas's confirmation was blocked), no president has chosen a close associate or political ally to serve on the Supreme Court. Only William Rehnquist, an official in the Nixon Justice Department, might qualify as an associate. And Nixon, three months before nominating Rehnquist, recalled his name as "Renchburg." (Two weeks before the nomination Nixon was unable to recall *any* version of Rehnquist's name; when a visitor offered "Bill Rensler," Nixon responded, "Oh, I know Rensler well.")[35]

Perhaps the main reason for the decline in the selection of personal acquaintances is that such nominees are vulnerable, as Fortas was, to charges of "cronyism." In any case, one element of political reward continues to be important: about 90 percent of all nominees to the Court—and all those chosen since 1975—have been members of the president's party. One reason is that lawyers who share the president's policy views are more likely to come from the same party, but there is also a widespread feeling that such an attractive prize should go to one of the party faithful.

Building Political Support. If nominations can reward those who helped the president politically in the past, they can also be used to seek political benefits in the future. Most often, presidents select justices with certain characteristics in order to appeal to leaders and voters who share those characteristics.

For most of the Court's history, the most important characteristic was geography. Presidents sought to provide each region with representation on the Court. In part, this reflected a high level of regional consciousness among voters. And until 1891 the justices "rode circuit," helping to staff lower federal courts in designated regions of the country, and it made sense to choose justices from the circuits they would represent. But with the end of circuit-riding and a perceived decline in sectional consciousness, geography has become less important to presidents. Religious affiliations were of some importance during much of the twentieth century, as presidents sought to maintain Catholic and Jewish representation on the Court. But the relevance of religion has also declined.

In contrast, representation by race, gender, and ethnicity has become quite important. President George Bush's nomination of Clarence Thomas to succeed Thurgood Marshall reflected the pressure he felt to maintain black representation on the Court. George W. Bush has shown an interest in selecting the first Hispanic justice.[36] According to one scholar, "gender was the primary and decisive factor" in President Reagan's nomination of Sandra Day O'Connor at a time when there was a widespread feeling that a woman should be appointed.[37]

A large proportion of voters say that prospective Supreme Court appointments are important to their choice of a presidential candidate,[38] but it is uncertain whether actual nominations have much direct impact on people's votes in presidential elections. It is more certain that nominations help presidents gain support from political leaders and activists that can improve their electoral prospects indirectly. And in nominating a woman (to take one example), a president may act not just for political advantage but in the belief that the country benefits from female representation on the Court.

Summary. Nominations to the Supreme Court depend on a variety of criteria, and most appointments serve multiple goals. All the considerations discussed here have been important to some nominations, but their importance has changed over time and varies from one nomination to another.

The Court's importance has at least two effects on the criteria for selection of justices. First, it makes presidents and their representatives weigh all the criteria more carefully than they generally do in making lower court nominations. Second, it leads to an emphasis on the criteria of competence and policy preferences rather than on the "political" considerations of reward and support building. If Supreme Court justices are better jurists than lower court judges, and if their policy preferences are more accurate reflections of their nominators' views, it is largely because presidents have a strong incentive to achieve those results.

Senate Confirmation

A president's nomination to the Court goes to the Senate for confirmation. The nomination is referred to the Judiciary Committee, which gathers extensive information on the nominee, holds hearings at which the nominee and other witnesses testify, and then votes its recommendation for Senate action. After this vote, the nomination is referred to the floor, where it is debated and a confirmation vote taken. The length of this process depends primarily on the degree of controversy concerning the nomination, although the general trend in recent years has been toward lengthier consideration of nominees.

The Senate's Role. When the president nominates someone to any position in the executive branch or the judiciary, the presumption typically is in favor of confirming that nominee. That presumption applies to the Supreme Court. But the Senate gives Supreme Court nominations a collective scrutiny that district court nominations seldom receive, and the occasional defeats of nominees are reminders that confirmation is not automatic. Thus, the president has good reason to take the Senate's likely reaction into account in making a nomination.

The Senate's Record. Through mid-2003 the Senate had failed to confirm twenty-six nominations to the Supreme Court, either through an adverse vote or a refusal to act. These twenty-six cases constituted about one-sixth of the nominations that the Senate considered. This proportion of defeats is higher than for any other position to which the president makes appointments. For example, presidents have made far more nominations of cabinet members, but only nine have been defeated.

Presidents in the twentieth century were more successful with Supreme Court nominations than were presidents in the nineteenth. Since 1900 only five of the sixty nominations considered by the Senate have failed: Herbert Hoover's nomination of John Parker in 1930, Johnson's elevation of Abe Fortas to chief justice in 1968 (withdrawn after Fortas's supporters failed to end an anticonfirmation filibuster), Nixon's nominations of Clement Haynsworth in 1969 and G. Harrold Carswell in 1970 (both for the same vacancy), and Reagan's nomination of Robert Bork in 1987. Only two successful nominees were confirmed by less than a two-thirds margin in the Senate.

To a degree, however, this record of success is misleading. The Senate has continued to scrutinize nominations carefully. This has been especially true since the late 1940s. Of the twenty-eight nominees the Senate considered from 1949 through mid-2003, four were defeated, seven received more than ten negative votes, and others faced serious opposition. The Senate votes in this period are shown in Table 2-2. As the table suggests, nominees have faced especially close scrutiny since 1968.

Nominees vary a great deal in the number of confirmation votes they win, from those who receive unanimous approval to those who fail to win the needed majority. This variation reflects the characteristics of nominees and of the situations in which the Senate considers them.[39]

Nominees and Situations. As noted, the most important characteristics of nominees in the confirmation process are their perceived ideological positions and qualifications. Nominees who are thought to be highly liberal or highly conservative have greater difficulty than those who seem to be moderate, simply because extremists are more distant ideologically from the average senator. Nominees who seem less qualified also may arouse opposition. A perceived weakness in legal skills or ethical standards might cause senators who are otherwise favorable to oppose a nominee. More important, senators who are ideologically distant from a nominee often use questions about a nominee's qualifications as an "objective" justification for opposing the nominee.

Whatever may be a nominee's personal characteristics, the outcome of the confirmation process is also influenced by several aspects of the situation that exist at the time. One is the president's political strength in the Senate. According to one count, presidents whose party holds a Senate majority have had 90 percent of their nominees confirmed, as against 61 percent for presidents who faced an opposition majority.[40] One reason for this difference is that senators of the majority party chair the Judiciary Committee and schedule votes on the floor. Another reason is that a Senate controlled by the opposition has more senators who are

TABLE 2-2
Senate Votes on Supreme Court Nominations Since 1949

Nominee	Year	Vote
Tom Clark	1949	73–8
Sherman Minton	1949	48–16
Earl Warren	1954	NRV[a]
John Harlan	1955	71–11
William Brennan	1957	NRV
Charles Whittaker	1957	NRV
Potter Stewart	1959	70–17
Byron White	1962	NRV
Arthur Goldberg	1962	NRV
Abe Fortas	1965	NRV
Thurgood Marshall	1967	69–11
Abe Fortas[b]	1968	withdrawn[c]
Homer Thornberry	(1968)	no action
Warren Burger	1969	74–3
Clement Haynsworth	1969	45–55
G. Harrold Carswell	1970	45–51
Harry Blackmun	1970	94–0
Lewis Powell	1971	89–1
William Rehnquist	1971	68–26
John Paul Stevens	1975	98–0
Sandra Day O'Connor	1981	99–0
William Rehnquist[b]	1986	65–33
Antonin Scalia	1986	98–0
Robert Bork	1987	42–58
Douglas Ginsburg	(1987)	no action
Anthony Kennedy	1988	97–0
David Souter	1990	90–9
Clarence Thomas	1991	52–48
Ruth Bader Ginsburg	1993	96–3
Stephen Breyer	1994	87–9

Source: Joan Biskupic and Elder Witt, *Guide to the U.S. Supreme Court,* 3d ed. (Washington, D.C.: Congressional Quarterly, 1997), 1099.

a. No recorded vote.

b. Elevation to chief justice.

c. Nomination withdrawn after Senate vote failed to end filibuster against nomination; vote was 45–43 to end filibuster, and two-thirds majority was required.

politically opposed to the president and who are ideologically distant from a nominee.

Other factors affect the president's strength. Presidents with high public approval have an advantage, because strong public support deters opposition to their nominees. And nominations made late in a president's term are more vulnerable because the president's popularity tends to decline, some presidents are "lame ducks" who will leave office shortly, and partisanship often increases. Nearly half of the nominees selected in the last year of a presidential term were defeated in the Senate.[41]

A second aspect of the situation is the mobilization of activity for and against the nominee. Substantial interest group activity against a nomination can overcome the assumption that a nominee will be confirmed and thus cause senators to consider voting against confirmation. It is also important whether some senators decide to play an active role in mustering votes against a nominee and whether the administration mounts a strong effort to secure confirmation.[42]

Finally, the perceived impact of a nomination helps to determine whether senators feel that efforts to defeat the nominee are worthwhile. Probably the central explanation for the intense scrutiny given to recent nominations is the increased prominence of the Supreme Court in the resolution of controversial policy issues. If a nominee has the potential to change the Court's policies substantially, senators will attach particular importance to that nomination.

Among recent nominees, David Souter and Clarence Thomas illustrate the importance of personal characteristics. The two were chosen by President George Bush a year apart, with the Democrats holding majorities in the Senate. Each would replace a strongly liberal justice and therefore change the Court's ideological balance considerably. Souter won confirmation with only moderate difficulty, but Thomas's margin was only four votes. The difference can be explained primarily by two widespread perceptions: that Souter was a moderate conservative and Thomas a strong conservative, and that Souter was well qualified while Thomas's qualifications might be questioned.

Another pair of nominees illustrates the importance of the situation. President Reagan selected Antonin Scalia in 1986 and Robert Bork in 1987. Both were viewed as highly conservative, and both were former legal scholars who were thought to be well qualified for service on the Court. Scalia was confirmed unanimously, and Bork was defeated. One difference was that the Senate in 1986 had a Republican majority, but Bork the next year faced a Democratic majority. Another was that Scalia would replace another strong conservative, while Bork would replace a moderate conservative on a Court with a close ideological balance.

Finally, in 1986 liberal senators and interest groups focused their efforts on defeating William Rehnquist, nominated for elevation to chief justice, and largely ignored Scalia. In 1987, in contrast, Senator Edward Kennedy took the lead in opposing Bork and liberal interest groups mounted a massive campaign against him, while the Reagan administration did relatively little to mobilize support for him.

These generalizations can be applied to the Senate's treatment of nominations since 1968. The Senate's actions in this period fall into three categories: confirmations that involved little difficulty, confirmations that were achieved with more difficulty, and defeats of nominees.

The Easy Confirmations. Of the seventeen nominees who were considered by the Senate between 1968 and 1994, nine achieved relatively easy confirmation: Warren Burger, Harry Blackmun, Lewis Powell, John Paul Stevens, Sandra Day O'Connor, Antonin Scalia, Anthony Kennedy, Ruth Bader Ginsburg, and Stephen Breyer. Five of these nominees received no negative votes, Powell received one negative vote, and Burger and Ginsburg each received three. Breyer also fits in this category, even though nine senators voted against his confirmation.

Their easy confirmations do not mean that these nominees aroused universal enthusiasm. Liberal Democrats certainly would have preferred nominees less conservative than Burger and Scalia. Anti-abortion groups opposed O'Connor and Ginsburg. But these nominees escaped strong challenges because their objective qualifications seemed strong and because concern about their ideological positions was limited.

Circumstances favored other nominees besides Scalia. Blackmun probably would have won confirmation easily in any case, but that result was ensured by the Senate's collective desire to avoid a third consecutive battle over a Nixon nomination. Observers disagreed about how liberal Ginsburg was, but her presence on the Court could do no more than moderate its conservative tendencies.

Breyer received negative votes from nine Republican senators. Some argued that his investment in Lloyd's of London, an insurance syndicate, showed a lack of prudence in making a risky investment and that it had created conflicts of interest in some cases in which he had participated. Other opponents said that the justice was too liberal. But most senators saw Breyer as only moderately liberal, so that his replacement of the moderate liberal Harry Blackmun would have little impact on the Court. His abilities as lawyer and judge were clear, and he had won the respect of both Democrats and Republicans while serving on the staff of the Senate Judiciary Committee. His confirmation was never in real jeopardy.

The Difficult Confirmations. Some of the successful nominees have been confirmed with difficulty. They include William Rehnquist, when nominated as associate justice in 1971 and as chief justice in 1986; Clarence Thomas in 1991; and—with somewhat less difficulty—David Souter in 1990. In each instance, the nominee's apparent conservatism aroused opposition from liberal senators and interest groups.

When Rehnquist was first nominated in 1971, the Leadership Conference on Civil Rights led the opposition. Rehnquist's opponents argued that his conservatism on civil liberties was so extreme as to be unacceptable in a Supreme Court justice. The case against him was weakened, however, by the general perception that he was a highly competent lawyer. The opposition thus had to be based almost entirely on ideological grounds, and even for some liberals those grounds were insufficient to justify a negative vote. Rehnquist was confirmed by a 68–26 vote.

Rehnquist's record as an associate justice was as conservative as expected, so his prospective elevation to chief justice in 1986 also aroused strong opposition from liberal interest groups and senators. These opponents sought to gain support by raising questions about Rehnquist's ethical standards. They made several charges, the most important of which was that Rehnquist had sought to intimidate black and Hispanic voters in Arizona during the 1960s. These charges attracted attention but ultimately had little impact. Rehnquist was confirmed by a 65–33 vote; with few exceptions, northern Democrats voted against him, and other senators voted for him.

When David Souter was nominated in 1990, the prospective replacement of liberal William Brennan by a conservative on a closely divided Court helped to spur opposition from some liberal senators and interest groups. But Souter's objective qualifications were generally considered quite good. His record offered few clues about his views on policy issues, but his testimony gave the impression that he was moderate in his views and personal style. That impression assured his confirmation; the Senate vote was 90–9.

A year later, Clarence Thomas won confirmation by the smallest margin in the twentieth century. His very conservative record aroused opposition from several liberal interest groups, but initially they had little impact. Thomas benefited from effective support by the Bush administration, and many Democrats favored the continuation of black representation on the Court.

Opposition grew after Thomas testified before the Judiciary Committee. His testimony raised doubts about his candor and abilities, and the committee split 7–7 on whether to recommend his confirmation. Still, as senators announced their positions, Thomas seemed assured of success.

The disclosure of Anita Hill's sexual harassment charge against Thomas threatened his confirmation. After committee hearings on that charge, however, few senators changed their positions, and Thomas was confirmed by a 52–48 vote. The vote was primarily along party lines. But Thomas won crucial support from eleven southern Democrats, responding in part to their perception of support for Thomas by black constituents.[43] This response underlines the public visibility of controversial confirmation decisions in the current era.

The Defeats. Of the four confirmation defeats since 1968, three came in a two-year period, 1968–1970. The first was that of Abe Fortas, a sitting justice nominated to be chief justice by President Johnson in 1968. Fortas's strong liberalism on the liberal Warren Court caused early opposition from conservative senators. Moreover, some Republicans wanted to prevent Fortas's confirmation in order to reserve the vacancy for a new president—expected to be Republican—in 1969. These opponents pointed to two activities that raised doubts about Fortas's ethical fitness: his continued consultation with the president about policy matters while a member of the Court and an arrangement by which he gave nine lectures at American University, in Washington, D.C., for a fee of $15,000 raised from businesses. The Judiciary Committee approved the nomination by a divided vote, but it ran into a filibuster on the Senate floor. A vote to end the filibuster fell fourteen votes short of the two-thirds majority then required; the opposition came almost entirely from Republicans and southern Democrats. President Johnson withdrew the nomination at Fortas's request.

In 1969 Fortas resigned from the Court. President Nixon selected Clement Haynsworth, chief judge of a federal court of appeals, to replace him. Haynsworth was opposed by labor groups and the National Association for the Advancement of Colored People (NAACP), both of which disliked his judicial record. Liberal senators, concerned about this record, sought revenge for Fortas's defeat as well. Haynsworth was also charged with unethical conduct: he had sat in two cases involving subsidiaries of companies in which he owned stock, and in another case he had bought the stock of a corporation in the interval between his court's decision in its favor and the announcement of the decision. These charges aroused additional opposition by Senate moderates. Haynsworth ultimately was defeated by a 55–45 vote, with a large minority of Republicans voting against confirmation.

President Nixon then nominated another court of appeals judge, G. Harrold Carswell. After the fight over Haynsworth, most senators were inclined to support the next nominee. One senator predicted that any new Nixon nominee "will have no trouble getting confirmed unless he has committed murder—recently." [44] But Carswell drew almost immediate opposition from civil rights groups for what they perceived as his hostility to their interests, and their cause gained strength from a series of revelations about the nominee that suggested an active opposition to black civil rights. Carswell was also criticized for an alleged lack of judicial competence. After escorting Carswell to talk with senators, one of Nixon's staffers reported to the president that "they think Carswell's a boob, a dummy. And what counter is there to that? He is." [45] The nomination was defeated by a 51–45 vote; the lineup was similar to that in the vote on Haynsworth.

Robert Bork's 1987 defeat differed from the three that preceded it in that no serious charges were made about his competence or his ethical standards. But liberals were concerned about his strong conservatism on civil liberties issues and his potential to shift the Court's ideological balance. As noted earlier, Senator Kennedy and liberal interest groups worked hard to secure votes against Bork. Concern about Bork's views was intensified by his testimony before the Senate Judiciary Committee, in which he discussed in detail his positions on issues such as the right to privacy.

This growing concern, combined with the unprecedented level of interest group activity against Bork, made his defeat possible. Also important was President Reagan's political weakness: not only did the Democrats control the Senate, but Reagan's popularity both inside and outside Congress had declined. Even so, a more effective campaign for Bork by the administration might have secured his confirmation. In any event, confirmation was denied by a 42–58 vote. All but eight senators voted along party lines; the overwhelming and unexpected opposition of southern Democrats made the difference in the outcome.

Summary. Since 1968 the Senate has taken a more active role in scrutinizing nominees to the Supreme Court. One reason for this change is the growth in efforts by interest groups to defeat nominees whose views run counter to group positions. Another spur has been the growing awareness that a single Court appointment can have considerable impact on national policy. In both respects one issue—abortion—has been especially important. As a result of these developments, the confirmation battles over Robert Bork and Clarence Thomas became national spectacles. And even relatively uncontroversial nominations received a good deal of scrutiny.

Even so, the great majority of nominees since 1968 were confirmed— most with little difficulty. One reason for this success is that presidents often sought nominees whom they expected the Senate to accept. More fundamentally, the Senate as a whole still typically began with a presumption in favor of confirming nominees. Because of this presumption, presidents continued to hold most of the power to determine who would sit on the Supreme Court.

This situation is not necessarily permanent. After they gained majority status in 1995, Senate Republicans took an assertive stance in slowing the confirmation of President Clinton's lower court nominees and blocked some nominees on ideological grounds. When Democrats regained a Senate majority during the first year of George W. Bush's presidency, they returned the favor, and even as a minority in 2003 they used Senate procedures to try to prevent some confirmations. This confrontational style may create greater constraints on presidents, especially when the Senate is controlled by the opposite party. The roles of the president and Senate in selecting Supreme Court justices should be viewed as dynamic, especially in a period of strong partisan contention.

The Impact of the Selection Process

The process of selecting people to hold a particular office is likely to affect the office itself. Certainly this is true of the Supreme Court. Most important, the process helps to determine what kinds of people become justices. In the current era, for example, the eagerness of many senators to oppose nominees whose views they dislike gives presidents an incentive to choose people who seem ideologically moderate and who have avoided controversial positions on policy issues.

Further, the intense scrutiny that nominees now undergo may affect people's willingness to be considered as candidates for nomination. David Souter told his friend and Senate sponsor Warren Rudman, "If I had known how vicious this process is, I wouldn't have let you propose my nomination." [46] Prospective nominees may take themselves out of the running because they want to spare themselves and their families what has become a considerable ordeal. [47]

Among those who win confirmation, the experience may shape their behavior as justices. Hugo Black's 1937 confirmation was difficult, largely because of charges that he had been a member of the Ku Klux Klan — charges that he admitted to be true after his confirmation. One commentator concluded that Black "came on the Court determined to prove that he was not a racist member of the Klan," [48] and he did establish himself as one of the strongest civil libertarians in the Court's history. Years after the hard-fought battle over his confirmation, Clarence Thomas remained bitter about what he called "a plain whipping." [49] Observers have suggested that this experience strengthened his resolve to take strongly conservative positions on the Court. [50] Whatever may be true of Black and

Thomas, undoubtedly some justices are changed by what they go through to achieve their positions.

Who Is Selected

A children's book about Justice O'Connor concludes with a set of suggestions "if you want to be a Supreme Court justice." [51] While other observers might add or delete specific suggestions, the list underlines an important reality: because of the workings of the selection process, certain kinds of people are more likely to reach the Supreme Court than others.

Career Paths

The kinds of people who become justices can be understood in terms of the paths that they take to the Court. These paths have changed over time. In this section I give particular attention to the period extending from the presidency of Franklin Roosevelt to the present. In that period thirty-three justices were selected. Some characteristics of these justices are listed in Table 2-3. The box on pages 54–55 summarizes the careers of the justices who sat on the Court in 2003.

The Legal Profession. The Constitution does not require that Supreme Court justices be attorneys. In practice, however, this restriction has been absolute. Nearly everyone involved in the selection process assumes that only a person with legal training can serve effectively on the Court. If a president nominated a nonlawyer to the Court, this assumption—and the large number of lawyers in the Senate—probably would prevent confirmation.

Thus, holding a law degree constitutes the first and least flexible requirement for recruitment to the Court. Most of the justices who served during the first century of the Court's history had followed what was then the standard practice, apprenticing under a practicing attorney. In several instances, the practicing attorney was a leading member of the bar.[52] James Byrnes (chosen in 1941) was the last justice to study law through apprenticeship; all his successors have taken what is now the conventional route of law school training. A high proportion of justices have graduated from the more prestigious schools. Of the nine justices sitting in 2003, seven received their law degrees from Harvard, Yale, or Stanford.

High Positions. If legal education is a necessary first step in the paths to the Court, almost equally important as a last step is attaining a high position in government or the legal profession. Obscure private practitioners or state

TABLE 2-3
Selected Characteristics of Justices Appointed since 1937

Justice	Age[a]	State of residence[b]	Law school	Position at appointment[c]	Years as judge	Elective office[d]	Administrative position[e]
Black	51	Ala.	Alabama	Senator	1	Senate	—
Reed	53	Ky.	Columbia	Solicitor general	0	State leg.	Solicitor general
Frankfurter	56	Mass.	Harvard	Law professor	0	—	Subcabinet
Douglas	40	Wash.	Columbia	Chair, Sec. & Exchange Comm.	0	—	Sec. & Exchange Comm.
Murphy	49	Mich.	Michigan	Attorney general	7	Governor	Attorney general
Byrnes	62	S.C.	None	Senator	0	Senate	—
Jackson	49	N.Y.	Albany	Attorney general	0	—	Attorney general
Rutledge	48	Iowa	Colorado	U.S. Ct. App.	4	—	—
Burton	57	Ohio	Harvard	Senator	0	Senate	—
Vinson	56	Ky.	Centre (Ky.)	Sec. of Treasury	5	House of Rep.	Sec. of Treasury
Clark	49	Texas	Texas	Attorney general	0	—	Attorney general
Minton	58	Ind.	Indiana	U.S. Ct. App.	8	Senate	Asst. to president
Warren	62	Calif.	Calif.	Governor	0	Governor	—
Harlan	55	N.Y.	New York	U.S. Ct. App.	1	—	Asst. U.S. attorney
Brennan	50	N.J.	Harvard	State Sup. Ct.	7	—	—
Whittaker	56	Mo.	Kansas City	U.S. Ct. App.	3	—	—
Stewart	43	Ohio	Yale	U.S. Ct. App.	4	City council	—
White	44	Colo.	Yale	Dep. atty general	0	—	Dep. atty general
Goldberg	54	Ill.	Northwestern	Sec. of labor	0	—	Sec. of labor

Justice	Age[a]	State[b]	Law school	Position[c]	Years	Elective office[d]	Appointive office[e]
Fortas	55	D.C.	Yale	Private practice	0	—	Subcabinet
Marshall	59	N.Y.	Howard	Solicitor general	4	—	Solicitor general
Burger	61	Minn.	St. Paul	U.S. Ct. App.	13	—	Asst. atty general
Blackmun	61	Minn.	Harvard	U.S. Ct. App.	11	—	—
Powell	64	Va.	Wash. & Lee	Private practice	0	—	State Bd. of Education
Rehnquist	47	Ariz.	Stanford	Asst. atty general	0	—	Asst. atty general
Stevens	55	Ill.	Northwestern	U.S. Ct. App.	5	—	—
O'Connor	51	Ariz.	Stanford	State Ct. App.	6	State leg.	State asst. atty general
Scalia	50	D.C.	Harvard	U.S. Ct. App.	4	—	Asst. atty general
Kennedy	51	Calif.	Harvard	U.S. Ct. App.	11	—	—
Souter	51	N.H.	Harvard	U.S. Ct. App.	12	—	State atty general
Thomas	43	D.C.	Yale	U.S. Ct. App.	1	—	Equal Empl. Opp. Comm.
Ginsburg	60	D.C.	Harvard, Columbia	U.S. Ct. App.	13	—	—
Breyer	56	Mass.	Harvard	U.S. Ct. App.	13	—	—

Sources: Leon Friedman and Fred L. Israel, *The Justices of the United States Supreme Court, 1789–1969: Their Lives and Major Opinions* (New York: R. R. Bowker Co., 1969; 1978 supplement); Harold W. Chase and Craig R. Ducat, *Constitutional Interpretation,* 2d ed. (St. Paul: West, 1979), 1361–1376; Joan Biskupic and Elder Witt, *Guide to the U.S. Supreme Court,* 3d ed. (Washington, D.C.: Congressional Quarterly, 1997), 930–962.

a. Age at time of appointment.

b. Primary state of residence before selection.

c. In this and following columns, positions are federal except where noted otherwise.

d. Highest office.

e. Highest appointive administrative position. Minor position omitted.

Careers of the Supreme Court . . .

William H. Rehnquist (born 1924)

Law degree, Stanford University, 1952
Supreme Court law clerk, 1952–1953
Private law practice, 1953–1969
U.S. Justice Department, 1969–1971
Appointed to Supreme Court, 1971
Appointed chief justice, 1986

John Paul Stevens (born 1920)

Law degree, Northwestern University, 1947
Supreme Court law clerk, 1947–1948
Private law practice, 1949–1970
Judge, U.S. Court of Appeals, 1970–1975
Appointed to Supreme Court, 1975

Sandra Day O'Connor (born 1930)

Law degree, Stanford University, 1952
Deputy county attorney, 1952–1953
Civilian attorney, U.S. Army, 1954–1957
Private law practice, volunteer work, family
  responsibilities, 1957–1965
Assistant state attorney general, 1965–1969
Arizona legislator, 1969–1975
Arizona trial judge, 1975–1979
Judge, Arizona Court of Appeals, 1979–1981
Appointed to Supreme Court, 1981

Antonin Scalia (born 1936)

Law degree, Harvard University, 1960
Private law practice, 1960–1967
Law school teaching, 1967–1971
Legal positions in federal government, 1971–1977
Law school teaching, 1977–1982
Judge, U.S. Court of Appeals, 1982–1986
Appointed to Supreme Court, 1986

Anthony M. Kennedy (born 1936)

Law degree, Harvard University, 1961
Private law practice, 1961–1975
Judge, U.S. Court of Appeals, 1975–1988
Appointed to Supreme Court, 1988

David H. Souter (born 1939)

Law degree, Harvard University, 1966
Private law practice, 1966–1968

. . . Justices (2003)

David H. Souter (continued)

New Hampshire attorney general's office,
1968–1978

Attorney general, New Hampshire, 1976–1978

Judge, New Hampshire trial court, 1978–1983

Justice, New Hampshire Supreme Court,
1983–1990

Judge, U.S. Court of Appeals, 1990

Appointed to Supreme Court, 1990

Clarence Thomas (born 1948)

Law degree, Yale University, 1974

Missouri attorney general's office, 1974–1977

Attorney for Monsanto Company, 1977–1979

Legislative assistant to a U.S. senator, 1979–1981

Assistant U.S. secretary of education, 1981–1982

Chair, U.S. Equal Employment Opportunity Commission,
1982–1990

Judge, U.S. Court of Appeals, 1990–1991

Appointed to Supreme Court, 1991

Ruth Bader Ginsburg (born 1933)

Law degree, Columbia University, 1959

Federal district court law clerk, 1959–1961

Law school research position, 1961–1963

Law school teaching, 1963–1980

Judge, U.S. Court of Appeals, 1980–1993

Appointed to Supreme Court, 1993

Stephen G. Breyer (born 1938)

Law degree, Harvard University, 1964

Supreme Court law clerk, 1964–1965

U.S. Justice Department, 1965–1967

Law school teaching, 1967–1980

Staff, U.S. Senate Judiciary Committee,
1974–1975, 1979–1980

Judge, U.S. Court of Appeals, 1980–1994

Appointed to Supreme Court, 1994

Source: Based chiefly on information in Kenneth Jost, *The Supreme Court Yearbook, 1998–1999* (Washington, D.C.: CQ Press, 2000), 321–339.

Note: With the exception of Justice Breyer's Senate staff service, only the primary position held by a future justice during each career stage is listed.

trial judges might be superbly qualified for the Court, but their qualifications would be questioned because of their lowly positions. A high position in government or the legal profession also makes a person more visible to the president and to others involved in the nomination process.

At the time they were selected, the thirty-three justices appointed since 1937 held positions of four types. They were executive branch officials, judges, elected officials, or well-respected leaders in the legal profession.

Ten justices served in the federal executive branch, seven in the Justice Department. The other three justices served as chair of the Securities and Exchange Commission (Douglas), secretary of the Treasury (Vinson), and secretary of labor (Goldberg).

Sixteen of the justices appointed in this period were appellate judges at the time of selection. Fourteen of them sat on the federal courts of appeals; the other two (Brennan and O'Connor) served on state courts. Five of the fourteen federal judges came from the District of Columbia circuit, which is especially visible to the president and other federal officials.

Of the other seven justices appointed since 1937, four held high elective office; three were senators (Black, Byrnes, and Burton) and the fourth was governor of California (Warren). The other three held positions outside government. Each had attained extraordinary success and respect—as a legal scholar (Frankfurter), a Washington lawyer (Fortas), and a leader of the legal profession (Powell). Frankfurter and Fortas had also been informal presidential advisers.

The Steps Between.   The people who have become Supreme Court justices took a variety of routes from legal education to the high positions that made them credible candidates for the Court. Frankfurter, Fortas, and Powell illustrate one simple route: entry into legal practice or academia, followed by a gradual rise to high standing in the legal profession. Some justices took a similar route through public office. Earl Warren held a series of appointive and elective offices, leading to his California governorship. Clarence Thomas served in several nonelected government positions, culminating in appointments as chair of the federal Equal Employment Opportunity Commission and then as judge on a federal court of appeals.

Since 1975 the most common route to the Court has been through private practice or law teaching, often combined with some time in government, before appointment to a federal court of appeals. Antonin Scalia, Stephen Breyer, and Ruth Bader Ginsburg were law professors. John Paul Stevens and Anthony Kennedy went directly from private practice to a court of appeals. During their careers, all five had held government positions or participated informally in the governmental process.

The path that Justice O'Connor took was unusual. She spent time in private practice and government legal positions, with some career interruptions for family reasons, before becoming an Arizona state senator and majority leader of the senate. O'Connor left the legislature for a trial judgeship. Her promotion to the state court of appeals through a gubernatorial appointment put her in a position to be considered for the Supreme Court.

O'Connor's career underlines the multiplicity of paths to the Court. Justices have brought to the Court a broad range of career experiences. What they have shared is their credential as lawyers and their success in reaching the higher levels of the legal profession or government that make them candidates for nomination to the Court.

Implications of the Career Paths

The paths to the Supreme Court help to explain some significant characteristics of the justices. They also underline the role of chance in determining who becomes a justice.

Age. Young people are not appointed to the Supreme Court. Most of the justices selected in the twentieth century were in their fifties when they joined the Court; of the remainder, most were over the age of sixty. William Douglas was the youngest appointee, at age forty; only three other appointees—Potter Stewart, Byron White, and Clarence Thomas—were under forty-five.

In one sense, this pattern is surprising. We might expect presidents to select relatively young candidates to maximize the length of time "their" justices would serve. The main reason they do not is the time required to achieve the high positions that most justices hold when they are selected and to attain the eminence that makes one a serious candidate for selection.

Within this constraint, most recent presidents have sought to select justices who are relatively young. Thomas was forty-three when selected; the other four Reagan and George Bush appointees were all aged fifty or fifty-one. This pattern reflects strong presidential interest in the Court's future direction. In this respect, Clinton's selection of sixty-year-old Ruth Bader Ginsburg—the oldest appointee in more than twenty years—stands out.

Class, Race, and Sex. The Supreme Court's membership has been quite unrepresentative of the general population in terms of social class; most justices grew up in families that were relatively well off. One study found that one-third of the justices were from the upper class and one-quarter were from the upper middle class. Only one-quarter were from the lower middle class or below.[53]

Since the 1930s, an unusually high percentage of appointees to the Court, especially Democrats, have had lower-status backgrounds. Still, the recent justices as a group grew up in better than average circumstances. The 2003 Court included one justice from the upper class (Stevens), four from the upper middle class, three from the middle class, and one (Thomas) whose family was impoverished.

The predominance of higher-status backgrounds can be explained by the career paths that most justices take. First and most important, a justice must obtain a legal education. To do so is easiest for individuals of high status, because of the cost of law school and the college education that necessarily precedes it. Second, individuals of high status have a variety of advantages in their careers. Those who can afford to attend elite law schools, for instance, have the easiest time obtaining positions in successful law firms.

The partial deviation from this pattern since the 1930s reflects the increasing availability of legal education. In addition, the larger size of the legal profession, the judiciary, and the federal government has made high positions in these sectors more accessible to individuals with lower-status backgrounds who previously might have been excluded. If these explanations have some validity, the proportion of justices with lower-status backgrounds will remain relatively large and may increase in the future.

Until 1967 all the justices were white men. This pattern is not difficult to understand. Women and members of racial minority groups had extreme difficulty pursuing an education in the law because of legal and other restrictions. As a result, the number of potential justices from these groups who passed the first barrier to selection was quite small. Moreover, prejudice against women and members of racial minorities limited their ability to advance in the legal profession and in politics. As a result, very few individuals who were not white men could achieve the high positions that people generally must obtain to be considered for nomination to the Court.

Since 1967 two women (O'Connor and Ginsburg) and two African Americans (Marshall and Thomas) have won appointments to the Court. These appointments reflect changes in society that made it at least somewhat less difficult for people other than white men to achieve high positions. They also reflect the growing willingness of presidents to consider women and members of racial minority groups as prospective nominees. Still, because of the various advantages they enjoy, white men are likely to enjoy disproportionate representation on the Court for some time.

If the Court has been composed primarily of white men with higher-status backgrounds, what has been the effect on its policies? One possible effect concerns the legal claims of racial minority groups and of women. It seems likely that those claims would have been taken seriously at an earlier time if members of these groups had sat on the Court, because these justices would have influenced their colleagues' perceptions of discrimination. As Justice O'Connor pointed out, Thurgood Marshall had that kind of influence once he joined the Court.[54]

Political and social attitudes differ somewhat between people of higher and lower socioeconomic status, so justices' class origins might affect the Court's decisions. But the justices typically are people who have achieved high status themselves even if their origins were humble. The sympathies of people who have "climbed" upward from a low socioeconomic level may differ little from those of people who started out with social and economic advantages. Notably, the justices with humble backgrounds have included solid conservatives such as Warren Burger and Clarence Thomas as well as liberals such as Earl Warren and Thurgood Marshall. Some commentators argue that the Court's decisions generally reflect the values and interests of people who are well off.[55] If so, this may result from the status that the justices achieve in their own lives more than from their origins.

Prior Judicial Service.   Recent presidents have preferred to nominate lower court judges to the Supreme Court because these candidates' judicial records provide information about their policy views. As a result, the current Supreme Court has eight justices (all but Rehnquist) who served on lower courts. Historically, a majority of the justices had judicial experience before reaching the Court. Many commentators think that such service is desirable, even a prerequisite to superior work on the Supreme Court. On a different level, some conservatives have argued that a lack of lower court service encourages judicial activism.

Yet a comparison of justices with and without lower court experience indicates that the two groups do not behave very differently. To take one example, the leaders of the activist Warren Court were Earl Warren, with no lower court experience, and former state supreme court justice William Brennan. Their strongest opponents were John Marshall Harlan, who came to the Court from a federal court of appeals, and Felix Frankfurter, who came from Harvard Law School. And all four of these justices have been widely viewed as outstanding.

This apparent lack of difference is easy to explain. Of the twenty justices appointed since 1937 who had lower court experience, the justice with the most experience had served for thirteen years; ten justices had been lower court judges for five years or less. Undoubtedly, any service on a lower court shapes a justice's perspective, but a stint of three or five years—or even of thirteen years—is not likely to have as much impact on a person's thinking and approach to judicial policy issues as the much longer period of education and professional development that preceded it.

Partisan Political Activity. One characteristic shared by most current justices, like their predecessors, is a degree of involvement in partisan politics. Antonin Scalia, for example, held several positions in the Nixon and Ford administrations. Anthony Kennedy drafted a state ballot proposition for California governor Ronald Reagan. William Rehnquist was active in the Arizona Republican Party. Clarence Thomas worked with John Danforth when Danforth was the Missouri attorney general and a U.S. senator, and Thomas later served in the Reagan and George Bush administrations.

This pattern reflects the ways that justices are chosen. Even if nominations to the Court are not used as political rewards, presidents look more favorably on those who have contributed to their party's success. Partisan activity also brings people to the attention of presidents, their staff members, and others who influence nomination decisions. Perhaps more important, it enables people to win the high offices and appointive positions that make them credible candidates for the Court. To take the most important current example, lawyers who avoid any involvement in politics are unlikely to win federal judgeships. Historically, many justices were career politicians who achieved high elective office. Of the current justices, only O'Connor comes close to fitting that pattern. She became majority leader of the Arizona Senate but left the legislature after only six years to run for (and win) a trial court judgeship. In filling two Court vacancies, Bill Clinton seriously considered three people who had won high elective office but ultimately followed the example of Ford, Reagan, and George Bush in choosing lower court judges who had never run for office.

Changes in Career Paths. Even in the period since 1937, the paths to the Supreme Court and the characteristics of people who become justices have changed. The numerical dominance of people from privileged backgrounds and of white men has declined, a decline reflecting social and political changes in the United States. That trend is unlikely to be reversed.

Justices' career patterns have also changed. Among the twelve justices appointed since 1969, only one (O'Connor) ever held elective office, only one (Rehnquist) came to the Court directly from the executive branch, and all but two (Rehnquist and Powell) were appellate judges when they received their Court appointments. In a sense, there is less politics and more law in the backgrounds of justices than there used to be. This change may be temporary, the result of a series of specific appointment decisions. But it might represent a long-term shift. If the backgrounds of justices *are* becoming more legal and less political, this represents a note-worthy change in the ways that people reach the Supreme Court.

The change may also be consequential. In the view of one commentator, the Court has been transformed

from an institution that once drew on the collective experience of people who had lived both sides of the vital intersection of law and politics . . . to one staffed by a smart, highly professional cadre of academic judges who often appear disconnected from the practical implications of the court's work.[56]

That specific judgment aside, people whose backgrounds are primarily in politics probably tend to have different perspectives from those who have worked chiefly in the legal system.

The Role of Chance. No one becomes a Supreme Court justice through an inevitable process. Rather, advancement from membership in the bar to a seat on the Court results from luck as much as anything else. This luck comes in two stages. First, good fortune is often necessary to achieve the high positions in government or law that make individuals possible candidates for the Court; it is not necessarily the "fittest" who become cabinet members or federal appellate judges. Second, even after they achieve such positions, whether candidates are seriously considered for the Court and actually win an appointment depends largely on the existence of several favorable circumstances.

For one thing, a potential justice gains enormously by belonging to a particular political party at the appropriate time. Every appointment to the Court between 1969 and 1992 was made by a Republican president. As a result, potential justices who were liberal Democrats had to watch their chances slip away. Further, someone whose friend or associate achieves a powerful position becomes a far stronger candidate for a seat on the Court. David Souter was fortunate that someone who described Souter as "my closest friend" (Warren Rudman) became a U.S. senator and that a person who knew and admired him (John Sununu) became the president's chief of staff.[57]

More generally, everyone appointed to the Court has benefited from a favorable series of circumstances. Eisenhower's attorney general became aware of William Brennan because Brennan gave a conference address in place of a colleague on the New Jersey Supreme Court who was ill. John Paul Stevens has reported that his *pro bono* volunteer services for a client led to favorable publicity that later helped him win a judicial appointment.[58]

This does not mean that the effects of presidential appointments on the Court are random. No matter which individuals they choose, Demo-

TABLE 2-4
Reasons for Leaving the Court Since 1965

Year	Justice	Age	Primary reasons for leaving	Length of time from leaving until death
1965	Goldberg	56	Appointment as ambassador to U.N.	24 years
1967	Clark	67	Son's appointment as attorney general	10 years
1969	Fortas	58	Pressures based on possible ethical violations	13 years
1969[a]	Warren	78[a]	Age	5 years
1971	Black	85	Age and ill health	1 month
1971	Harlan	72	Age and ill health	3 months
1975	Douglas	77	Age and ill health	4 years
1981	Stewart	66	Age	4 years
1986	Burger	78	Responsibilities for Commission on the Bicentennial of the Constitution, possibly age	9 years
1987	Powell	79	Age and health concerns	11 years
1990	Brennan	84	Age and ill health	7 years
1991	Marshall	83[b]	Age and ill health	2 years
1993	White	76[b]	Desire to allow another person to serve, possibly age	9 years
1994	Blackmun	85	Age	5 years

Sources: Joan Biskupic and Elder Witt, *Guide to the U.S. Supreme Court,* 3d ed. (Washington, D.C.: Congressional Quarterly, 1997), 931–954; other biographical sources, newspaper stories.

a. Warren originally announced intent to leave the Court in 1968 at age 77.

b. Marshall announced intent to leave the Court at 82, White at 75.

cratic presidents generally nominate people with liberal views and Republicans tend to select conservatives. But it does mean that specific individuals achieve membership on the Court in large part through good fortune. "You have to be lucky," said Sandra Day O'Connor about her appointment,[59] a statement that reflects realism as well as modesty.

Leaving the Court

In the Supreme Court's first century, Congress sometimes increased the Court's size to allow new appointments of justices. Such legislation has become very unlikely, almost unthinkable. Today new members come to the Court only when a sitting justice leaves.

Justices can leave the Court in three ways: through death, voluntary decisions, or external pressure.[60] In contrast with the nineteenth century, justices today seldom stay on the Court until they die. Indeed, the last justice to die in office was Robert Jackson in 1954. Thus, departures from the Court result primarily from voluntary choices and external pressure. Table 2-4 summarizes the reasons for departures since 1965.

Voluntary Departures

After its somewhat rocky start, the Supreme Court became a prestigious body with considerable influence on American life. As a result, justices typically are reluctant to leave the Court.

This reluctance is reflected in the infrequency with which justices leave to take other positions or opportunities. In the past century, only a handful of justices have done so. The most recent was Arthur Goldberg, who resigned in 1965 to become U.S. ambassador to the United Nations.

The primary choice that justices face, then, is when to retire from the Court. Financial considerations once played an important part in those choices: several justices stayed on the Court, sometimes with serious infirmities, to keep receiving their salaries. Congress established a judicial pension in 1869, and it is now quite generous. Justices who are at least seventy years old and who have served as federal judges for ten years or more, or who are at least sixty-five and have served for fifteen years, can retire and continue to receive the salaries they earned at the time of their retirements. Justices who meet those criteria can retire and receive any salary increases granted sitting justices if they are disabled or if they perform a certain amount of service for the federal courts—generally equal to one-quarter of full-time work.

In this situation, older justices weigh the satisfactions of remaining on the Court against the somewhat different satisfactions of retirement and against concern about their capacity to handle their work. The satisfactions are so great that most justices stay well past the usual retirement age. But age and health problems eventually tip the balance in favor of retirement. When justices do retire, they usually cite one or both of those factors. When Harry Blackmun retired from the Court in 1994, he explained that "it's not easy to step aside, but I know what the numbers are, and it's time."[61] The "numbers" referred to his age. Later, Blackmun said,

Justice John Paul Stevens in 2002. In 2003, at the age of 83, Stevens gave no indication that he had considered retiring that year.

"Eighty-five is pretty old. I don't want to reach a point where my senility level reaches unacceptable proportions." [62]

Some justices do stay on the Court past the time at which they can function effectively as justices. One clear case is William Douglas, whose health problems had become so great by 1975 that his colleagues took the extraordinary step of agreeing to set aside for later rehearing any case in which Douglas was part of a 5–4 majority. (Such action was never taken because Douglas retired a few weeks later, before there were any decisions that met this criterion.) [63] Other cases are more ambiguous. One scholar has argued that since World War II, seven justices remained on the Court "years or months" too long after their mental capacities should have led to their departures. The most recent justices on his list were Lewis Powell and Thurgood Marshall. [64]

The justices are well aware that their departures may change the ideological balance on the Court, and that awareness sometimes affects the timing of retirements. Yet the satisfactions of serving on the Court may outweigh this consideration. Justice O'Connor, a Republican, reportedly made a remark at an election-night party in 2000 that seemed to indicate she would be willing to retire only if Republican George W. Bush became president.[65] Whether or not this report was accurate, O'Connor did not retire at the end of the Court's term despite Bush's victory. When the Republicans regained control of the Senate in 2002, it was widely expected that either O'Connor or fellow Republican William Rehnquist would retire in the summer of 2003, thereby allowing Bush to appoint a successor in a situation that favored confirmation of his nominee. But neither justice retired, and the long period since the last Court retirement in 1994 became even longer.

One current justice has given very early notice of his retirement. In 1993, two years after he joined the Court, Clarence Thomas told two of his clerks that he would remain on the Court until 2034. He explained, "The liberals made my life miserable for 43 years, and I'm going to make their lives miserable for 43 years." [66]

External Pressure

Although justices make their own decisions whether to resign or retire, Congress and the president can try to influence those decisions. For example, the legislation creating attractive pension rights has had considerable impact. The other branches can also try to persuade specific justices to leave the Court. Presidents have good reason to do so—to create vacancies they can fill. Occasionally, they try to induce retirements. John Kennedy reportedly persuaded Felix Frankfurter to retire after ill health had decreased his effectiveness, but Thurgood Marshall bitterly resisted efforts by the Carter administration to convince him to retire.[67]

Presidents can also try to lure justices away from the Court by offering them other positions. Lyndon Johnson offered Arthur Goldberg the position of ambassador to the United Nations and then exerted intense personal pressure to induce him to accept that position. Byron White, however, rejected the idea of becoming FBI director when the Reagan administration sounded him out about it.

As the examples of Marshall and White indicate, justices can resist pressure to give up their positions on the Court, but impeachment is beyond their control. Under the Constitution, justices, like other federal officials, can be removed through impeachment proceedings for "treason, bribery, or other high crimes and misdemeanors." [68] President Thomas Jefferson actually sought to gain control of the largely Federalist (and anti-Jefferson) judiciary through the use of impeachment, and Congress did impeach and convict a federal district judge in 1803. Justice Samuel Chase made himself vulnerable to impeachment by participating in President John Adams's campaign for reelection in 1800 and by making some injudicious and partisan remarks to a Maryland grand jury in 1803. Chase was impeached, an action justified chiefly by his handling of political trials, but the Senate acquitted him in 1805. His acquittal effectively ended Jefferson's plans to seek the impeachment of other justices.

No justice has been impeached since then, but the possible impeachment of two justices has been the subject of serious discussion. Several efforts were made to remove William Douglas (most seriously in 1969 and 1970), motivated by opposition to his strong liberalism. The reasons stated publicly by opponents were his financial connections with a foundation and his outside writings.[69] A special House committee failed to approve a resolution to impeach Douglas, however, and the resolution died in 1970.

Had Abe Fortas not resigned from the Court in 1969, he actually might have been removed through impeachment proceedings.[70] Fortas had been criticized for his financial dealings at the time he was nominated unsuccessfully to be chief justice in 1968. A year later, it was disclosed that he had a lifetime contract as a consultant to the Wolfson Foundation and had received money from that foundation at a time when the person who directed it was being prosecuted by the federal government. Under considerable pressure, Fortas resigned. The resignation came too quickly to determine how successful an impeachment effort would have been, but it almost certainly would have been serious.

The campaigns against Douglas and Fortas came primarily from the Nixon administration, which sought to replace the two liberals with more conservative justices. John Dean, a lawyer on Nixon's staff, later reported that Fortas's resignation led to "a small celebration in the attorney general's office" that "was capped with a call from the president, congratulating" Justice Department officials "on a job well done." [71] In contrast, according to Dean, the unsuccessful campaign against Douglas "created an intractable resolve by Douglas never to resign while Nixon was president." [72]

The Fortas episode seems unlikely to be repeated, in part because it reminded justices of the need to avoid questionable financial conduct. The removals of three federal judges through impeachment proceedings between 1987 and 1989 make it clear that impeachment is a real option. But it is used only in cases with strong evidence of serious misdeeds, often involving allegations of corrupt behavior.

Thus, the timing of a justice's leaving the Court reflects primarily the justice's own inclinations, health, and longevity. Those who want to affect the Court's membership may have their say when a vacancy occurs, but they have little control over the creation of vacancies.

Conclusion

The recruitment of Supreme Court justices is a complex process. People do not "rise" to the Court in an orderly fashion. Rather, whether they become credible candidates for the Court and whether they actually win appointments depend on a wide range of circumstances. Indeed, something close to pure luck plays a powerful role in determining who becomes a justice.

The recruitment process has evolved over the Court's history. To take one example, the balance of power between president and Senate in selecting justices has shifted back and forth. Further, justices today are drawn from a larger portion of American society than they were during most of the Court's history, and their backgrounds are more "legal" and less "political" than they once were.

The Court's power and prestige have fundamental effects on its membership. For one thing, presidents take nominations to the Court very seriously, and they have a wide range of prospective nominees to choose from. For another, justices are usually reluctant to give up their positions.

Also consequential is the perception of a strong link between the Court's membership and its decisions. Because of this perception, presidents accord heavy weight to the policy preferences of candidates when they choose a nominee. For the same reason, the Senate gives Court nominees greater scrutiny than it does nominees to any other positions. Interest groups regularly seek to influence president and Senate, and they sometimes engage in massive campaigns over nominees.

This perception is well founded. In later chapters I will discuss how the identities of the justices shape the Court's positions on legal and policy issues.

NOTES

1. The decision was *Zelman v. Simmons-Harris* (2002).
2. The decisions were *Gratz v. Bollinger* (2003) and *Grutter v. Bollinger* (2003).
3. The four who were nominated and confirmed twice include three individuals elevated from associate justice to chief justice (Edward White, Harlan Stone, and William Rehnquist) and one (Charles Evans Hughes) who resigned from the Court and was later appointed chief justice. Douglas Ginsburg is counted as a nominee even though he withdrew from consideration in 1987, before he was officially nominated.

4. Christine Nemacheck, "Strategic Selection: Presidential Selection of Supreme Court Justices from Hoover Through Reagan" (Ph.D. diss., George Washington University, 2001), 48–50.

5. Ibid., chap. 2.

6. Richard Reeves, *President Nixon: Alone in the White House* (New York: Simon & Schuster, 2001), 383. Burger's role in the Nixon nominations is discussed in John W. Dean, *The Rehnquist Choice* (New York: Free Press, 2001), 19, 52, 179–185.

7. This discussion is based in part on John Anthony Maltese, *The Selling of Supreme Court Nominees* (Baltimore: Johns Hopkins University Press, 1995); and Gregory A. Caldeira and John R. Wright, "Lobbying for Justice: The Rise of Organized Conflict in the Politics of Federal Judgeships," in *Contemplating Courts,* ed. Lee Epstein (Washington, D.C.: CQ Press, 1995), 44–71.

8. Michael Pertschuk and Wendy Schaetzel, *The People Rising: The Campaign Against the Bork Nomination* (New York: Thunder's Mouth Press, 1989); Patrick B. McGuigan and Dawn M. Weyrich, *Ninth Justice: The Fight for Bork* (Washington, D.C.: Free Congress Research and Education Foundation, 1990); Mark Gitenstein, *Matters of Principle: An Insider's Account of America's Rejection of Robert Bork's Nomination to the Supreme Court* (New York: Simon & Schuster, 1992).

9. Richard Hodder-Williams, "The Strange Story of Judge Robert Bork and a Vacancy on the United States Supreme Court," *Political Studies* 36 (December 1988): 628.

10. Gregory A. Caldeira and John R. Wright, "Lobbying for Justice: Organized Interests and the Bork Nomination in the United States Senate" (Paper presented at the annual meeting of the American Political Science Association, Chicago, September 1992).

11. Caldeira and Wright, "Lobbying for Justice: The Rise of Organized Conflict," 59–69.

12. Dean, *The Rehnquist Choice,* 14.

13. Henry J. Abraham, *Justices, Presidents, and Senators: A History of the U.S. Supreme Court Appointments from Washington to Clinton,* rev. ed. (Lanham, Md.: Rowman & Littlefield, 1999), 140.

14. Eleanor Randolph, "Husband Triggered Letters Supporting Ginsburg for Court," *Washington Post,* June 17, 1993, A25.

15. Alan Cooper, "Rivalry on 4th Circuit?" *Richmond Times-Dispatch,* August 7, 2000. The decisions were *Urofsky v. Gilmore* (4th Cir. 2000) and *Gibbs v. Babbitt* (4th Cir. 2000).

16. Naftali Bendavid, "Just Saying No to Chance for Supreme Court," *Legal Times,* April 18, 1994, 1, 22, 23.

17. From an interview of Justice O'Connor by Katie Couric on *Dateline NBC,* January 25, 2002 (NBC News Transcript).

18. Abraham, *Justices, Presidents, and Senators,* 200.

19. U.S. Congress, *Nomination of Judge Clarence Thomas to Be Associate Justice of the Supreme Court of the United States,* Committee on the Judiciary, U.S. Senate, 102d Cong., 1st sess. (Washington, D.C.: Government Printing Office, 1993), 222–223.

20. Mark Silverstein, "Bill Clinton's Excellent Adventure: Political Development and the Modern Confirmation Process," in *The Supreme Court in*

American Politics: New Institutionalist Interpretations, ed. Howard Gillman and Cornell Clayton (Lawrence: University Press of Kansas, 1999), 136.

21. David Alistair Yalof, *Pursuit of Justices: Presidential Politics and the Selection of Supreme Court Justices* (Chicago: University of Chicago Press, 1999), esp. 6–7.

22. Dean, *The Rehnquist Choice.*

23. David Savage, *Turning Right: The Making of the Rehnquist Supreme Court* (New York: Wiley, 1992), 180–181.

24. This formulation is adapted from one presented in Sheldon Goldman, "Judicial Appointments and the Presidential Agenda," in *The Presidency in American Politics,* ed. Paul Brace, Christine B. Harrington, and Gary King (New York: New York University Press, 1989), 19–47.

25. Dean, *The Rehnquist Choice,* 96.

26. See George Stephanopoulos, *All Too Human: A Political Education* (Boston: Little, Brown, 1999), 168.

27. Fred Barnes, "Reagan's Full Court Press," *New Republic,* June 10, 1985, 18.

28. Data supporting this conclusion are presented in David W. Rohde and Harold J. Spaeth, *Supreme Court Decision Making* (San Francisco: W. H. Freeman, 1976), 107–109.

29. Joan Biskupic, "Election Still Splits Court," *USA Today,* January 22, 2001, 2A; see also Neil A. Lewis, "Presidential Candidates Differ Sharply on Judges They Would Appoint," *New York Times,* October 8, 2000, A28.

30. Alyssa Sepinwall, "The Making of a Presidential Myth" (letter), *Wall Street Journal,* September 4, 1990, A11; Tony Mauro, "Leak of Souter Keeps McGuigan in Plan," *Legal Times,* September 10, 1990, 11.

31. Jeffrey A. Segal, Richard J. Timpone, and Robert M. Howard, "Buyer Beware? Presidential Success Through Supreme Court Appointments," *Political Research Quarterly* 53 (September 2000): 557–595.

32. "Justice Anthony Kennedy: Surely Reagan's Biggest Disappointment," *Human Events,* May 31–June 7, 1996, 3.

33. J. Anthony Lukas, *Nightmare: The Underside of the Nixon Years* (New York: Viking Press, 1976), 569.

34. Robert Scigliano, *The Supreme Court and the Presidency* (New York: Free Press, 1971), 95, updated by the author.

35. Dean, *The Rehnquist Choice,* 86, 132. The quotation is from page 132.

36. Charles Lane and Amy Goldstein, "At High Court, a Retirement Watch," *Washington Post,* June 17, 2001, A4.

37. Barbara A. Perry, *A "Representative" Supreme Court? The Impact of Race, Religion, and Gender on Appointments* (New York: Greenwood Press, 1991), 122.

38. Stuart Taylor Jr., "The Supreme Question," *Newsweek,* July 10, 2000, 21.

39. See George L. Watson and John A. Stookey, *Shaping America: The Politics of Supreme Court Appointments* (New York: HarperCollins, 1995), chaps. 2 and 3; and Jeffrey A. Segal, Charles M. Cameron, and Albert D. Cover, "A Spatial Model of Roll Call Voting: Senators, Constituents, Presidents, and Interest Groups in Supreme Court Confirmations," *American Journal of Political Science* 36 (February 1992): 96–121.

40. These percentages are based on figures in Jeffrey Segal, "Senate Confirmation of Supreme Court Justices: Partisan and Institutional Politics," *Journal of Politics* 49 (November 1987): 1008, updated by the author. Percentages differ among sources, chiefly because of differences in assignment of partisan affiliation to some presidents.

41. Based on ibid., updated by the author. Nominations made during a president's fourth year but after the president's reelection are not included.

42. See Maltese, *Selling of Supreme Court Nominees.*

43. L. Marvin Overby, Beth M. Henschen, Michael H. Walsh, and Julie Strauss, "Courting Constituents? An Analysis of the Senate Confirmation Vote on Justice Clarence Thomas," *American Political Science Review* 86 (December 1992): 997–1003.

44. "Here Comes the Judge," *Newsweek,* February 2, 1970, 19. Quoted in John Massaro, *Supremely Political: The Role of Ideology and Presidential Management in Unsuccessful Supreme Court Nominations* (Albany: State University of New York Press, 1990), 105.

45. Reeves, *President Nixon,* 161.

46. Warren B. Rudman, *Combat: Twelve Years in the U.S. Senate* (New York: Random House, 1996), 181.

47. Bendavid, "Just Saying No," 23.

48. Kim Isaac Eisler, "Black Bio Lacks Shades of Gray," *Legal Times,* November 25, 1996, 78. See Roger K. Newman, *Hugo Black: A Biography* (New York: Pantheon, 1994), 233–268.

49. Jeff Franks, "Justice Thomas Still Healing From 'Whipping' on Hill," *Washington Post,* February 13, 1998, A9.

50. On Thomas's reaction to the confirmation battle, see John C. Danforth, *Resurrection: The Confirmation of Clarence Thomas* (New York: Viking Press, 1994); and Jeffrey Toobin, "The Burden of Clarence Thomas," *The New Yorker,* September 27, 1993, 38–51.

51. Lisa Tucker McElroy, *Meet My Grandmother: She's a Supreme Court Justice* (Brookfield, Conn.: Millbrook Press, 1999), 32.

52. For this observation and for much of the information on which the analysis in this section is based, I am indebted to John R. Schmidhauser, *Judges and Justices: The Federal Appellate Judiciary* (Boston: Little, Brown, 1979), 41–100.

53. Lee Epstein, Jeffrey A. Segal, Harold J. Spaeth, and Thomas G. Walker, *The Supreme Court Compendium,* 2d ed. (Washington, D.C.: Congressional Quarterly, 1996), 227–238. This source was also used to classify the justices sitting in 2000.

54. Sandra Day O'Connor, *The Majesty of the Law: Reflections of a Supreme Court Justice* (New York: Random House, 2003), 132–138.

55. See William J. Daniels, "Justice Thurgood Marshall: The Race for Equal Justice," in *The Burger Court: Political and Judicial Profiles,* ed. Charles M. Lamb and Stephen C. Halpern (Urbana: University of Illinois Press, 1991), 235.

56. Linda Greenhouse, "Impolitic: The Separation of Justice and State," *New York Times,* July 1, 2001, sec. 4, p. 1.

57. See Rudman, *Combat,* 152–194. The quotation is on p. 153.

58. Richard C. Reuben, "Justice Stevens: I Benefited from Pro Bono Work," *Los Angeles Daily Journal,* August 11, 1992, 11. See Kenneth A. Manaster, *Illinois Justice: The Scandal of 1969 and the Rise of John Paul Stevens* (Chicago: University of Chicago Press, 2001).

59. Laurence Bodine, "Sandra Day O'Connor," *American Bar Association Journal* 69 (October 1983): 1394.

60. This discussion of resignation and retirement draws on David N. Atkinson, *Leaving the Bench: Supreme Court Justices at the End* (Lawrence: University Press of Kansas, 1999).

61. "Departing Justice Blackmun Garners Clinton's Praise," *Congressional Quarterly Weekly Report,* April 9, 1994, 859.

62. Douglas Jehl, "Mitchell Viewed as Top Candidate for High Court," *New York Times,* April 7, 1994, A1.

63. Dennis J. Hutchinson, *The Man Who Once Was Whizzer White: A Portrait of Justice Byron R. White* (New York: Free Press, 1998), 434–436, 463–465. See Bruce Allen Murphy, *Wild Bill: The Legend and Life of William O. Douglas* (New York: Random House, 2003), 481–495.

64. David J. Garrow, "Mental Decrepitude on the U.S. Supreme Court: The Historical Case for a 28th Amendment," *University of Chicago Law Review* 67 (fall 2000): 1085. See also Artemus Ward, *Deciding to Leave: The Politics of Retirement from the United States Supreme Court* (Albany: State University of New York Press, 2003).

65. Evan Thomas and Michael Isikoff, "The Truth Behind the Pillars," *Newsweek,* December 25, 2000/January 1, 2001, 46.

66. Neil A. Lewis, "2 Years After His Bruising Hearing, Justice Thomas Still Shows the Hurt," *New York Times,* November 27, 1993, 6.

67. Juan Williams, "Marshall's Law," *Washington Post Magazine,* January 7, 1990, 29; from an interview with Marshall conducted by Carl Rowan, quoted in "The Justice and the President," *Washington Post,* September 11, 1987, A23.

68. U.S. Constitution, Art. 2, Sec. 4.

69. John Ehrlichman, *Witness to Power: The Nixon Years* (New York: Simon & Schuster, 1982), 122.

70. Laura Kalman, *Abe Fortas: A Biography* (New Haven: Yale University Press, 1990), 359–376; Bruce Allen Murphy, *Fortas: The Rise and Ruin of a Supreme Court Justice* (New York: Morrow, 1988).

71. Dean, *The Rehnquist Choice,* 11.

72. Ibid., 26.

Chapter 3

The Cases

In the current era, the Supreme Court reaches full decisions in about eighty cases a year. The justices choose those cases from more than seven thousand petitions for hearings. But even those seven thousand petitions are a very small portion of all the actions and events that could become Supreme Court cases. From that perspective, a Supreme Court decision is a very rare event.

This chapter examines the process of agenda setting that produces those rare events. In the first stage of that process, people make the series of decisions that bring their cases to the Supreme Court. In the second stage, the Court selects from those cases the ones that it fully considers and decides.

Several kinds of people and institutions play a part in setting the Court's agenda. In the first stage, litigants play a necessary part by filing cases and bringing them through the legal system to the Court. Most of those litigants are represented by lawyers for at least part of this process, and some receive direct or indirect assistance from interest groups. Although the Court plays no direct part in this stage, expectations about what it *might* do affect decisions whether to bring cases to the Court.

In the second stage, the justices choose cases to hear. These choices may be influenced by the litigants, lawyers, and interest groups that participate in cases. Finally, the other branches of government structure both stages of the process by setting the Court's jurisdiction and writing the statutes on which most cases are based.

The first two sections of this chapter examine the two stages of agenda-setting in the Court. In the first section, I consider how and why cases are brought to the Court. The second section discusses how and why the justices choose some of those cases to decide. The final section takes a different perspective on agenda-setting by examining the impact of growth in the Court's caseload.

Reaching the Court: Litigants, Attorneys, and Interest Groups

As noted, cases reach the Supreme Court through the efforts of litigants, their attorneys, and interest groups. I will examine the role of each in turn. The federal government is the most frequent and most distinctive participant in Supreme Court cases, and its role merits separate consideration.

Litigants

Every case that comes to the Supreme Court has at least two formal parties, or litigants, at least one on each side. For a case to reach the Court, one or more of the parties must have acted to initiate the litigation and move it upward through the court system.

Litigants in the Supreme Court are a diverse lot.[1] Of those who petition the Court to hear cases, the great majority are individuals, and most of these individuals are criminal defendants. Among respondents, the litigants who are brought to the Court by petitioners, the largest category includes the array of governments and government agencies from the federal level to the local level. Individuals are also respondents in many cases. Businesses frequently appear as petitioners or respondents. Other kinds of litigants, such as nonprofit groups and labor unions, participate in Court cases as well.

Perhaps the most important question concerning litigants is why they become involved in court cases and carry those cases to the Supreme Court. The motives of litigants can be thought of as taking two general forms, resulting in two "ideal types" of Supreme Court litigation. Some litigants fit one of these ideal types, while others have mixed motives.

The first type of case can be called ordinary litigation because of its relative frequency. Usually, parties bring cases to court or appeal unfavorable decisions because they seek to advance a direct personal or organizational interest. Plaintiffs file personal injury suits in court because they hope to obtain a monetary advantage from litigation. Similarly, litigants appeal court decisions because they believe that their potential gain from a successful appeal and the likelihood of success are sufficient to justify additional trouble and expense.

One example of ordinary litigation is *Rush Prudential HMO v. Moran* (2002).[2] Debra Moran, a resident of a Chicago suburb, was diagnosed with a condition that caused her severe shoulder pain. When physicians in her HMO's network could not relieve her condition, she sought to have surgery done by a Virginia physician who offered a promising treatment. The HMO refused to pay for the surgery, so Moran sued the HMO under

Debra Moran and her husband, Paul, at the Supreme Court after oral arguments in her case.

an Illinois statute that required HMOs to provide a medical service if an independent reviewing physician found it necessary. While the suit was pending, Moran and her husband borrowed money to pay the $95,000 cost of the surgery themselves. In court, the HMO argued that the state law was preempted by a federal statute and was therefore void. Ultimately, the case reached the Supreme Court, which decided there was no preemption. The Court's ruling was an important policy decision, but Moran initiated the case and carried it forward to treat her health problem and then to recover the substantial cost of what turned out to be successful treatment.

The second ideal type of case may be called "political" litigation. In these cases, litigants seek to advance policies they favor rather than their direct self-interest. Most often, political litigation is aimed at winning a judicial decision that supports the litigant's policy goals. For example, a group concerned with environmental protection might bring a suit to obtain a stringent interpretation of a statute that regulates air pollution. Someone who seeks to promote equality for disabled people may challenge a company practice on the ground that it violates protections of disabled workers stated in federal law. If groups initiate political litigation, they must have standing, a legal stake in the case, to act as litigants themselves; if not, they can recruit others who do have standing.

Brown v. Legal Foundation of Washington (2003) is a good example of political litigation.[3] The Washington Legal Foundation (WLF) and several individuals challenged state programs under which interest earned on money that lawyers hold for clients is used to fund legal services for low-income people. Their argument was that these programs take clients' money without compensation in violation of the Fifth Amendment. In practice, each challenger would gain little or nothing monetarily if they won the case. Their primary gain would be the satisfaction of eliminating a program they disliked. This was especially true of the WLF, a conservative group that had waged a long campaign against a program that it saw as financing litigation for liberal causes. As it turned out, the Court ruled against the challenge to the programs.

Many cases have large elements of both ordinary and political litigation. Individuals or companies may bring lawsuits to gain something directly, but along the way they become concerned with the larger policy issues that arise from their cases. In cases brought by government agencies, ordinary and political elements may be difficult to separate: prosecutors file criminal cases to advance the specific mission of their agencies, but that mission is linked to the broader political goal of attacking crime.

The proportion of cases that can be classified as fully or partly political increases with each step upward in the judicial system, so political litigation is most common in the Supreme Court. This pattern is not accidental. Ordinary litigation usually ends at a relatively early stage because the parties find it more advantageous to settle their dispute or even to accept a defeat than to fight on. In contrast, political litigants often want to get a case to the highest levels of the judicial system, where a victory may establish a national policy they favor. In addition, political litigation sometimes attracts the support of interest groups that help to shoulder the costs and other burdens of carrying a case through the judicial system.

Even so, the great majority of cases brought to the Supreme Court are best classified as ordinary litigation. A large proportion are criminal cases in which a convicted defendant who wants to get out of prison, or to stay out, seeks a hearing. Other cases come from business corporations whose economic stake in the outcome justifies a petition to the Court. Still other cases concern a variety of individual grievances, big or small; in these cases, the aggrieved party cannot resist going to the Supreme Court in one final effort to obtain redress.

Political litigation is more common in the cases that the Court agrees to hear, because those cases are more likely to concern the broad legal issues that interest the justices. Yet, as the *Moran* case illustrates, ordinary litigation is by no means absent from the cases that the Court hears. Even in the biggest cases, the ones that attract the attention of large numbers of interest groups, the chief motivation of the litigants is often their own direct interests.

Attorneys

Will K. Wright received his law degree at the University of Tulsa in 1994 and was admitted to the bar later that year. But as a Bostonian in Oklahoma, he had difficulty getting a job. He was contemplating a career change when he met Kristja Falvo. When Falvo asked his occupation, Wright responded, "I think I'm a lawyer but I haven't practiced in 18 months." Falvo asked him to check a legal question for her. Several years later, Falvo's legal question turned into a Supreme Court case on student privacy, and in November 2001 Wright found himself arguing before the Court.[4]

In the same month John G. Roberts Jr. argued before the Court on behalf of Toyota in a case involving interpretation of the Americans with Disabilities Act. Roberts was accustomed to the role of Supreme Court advocate: over the years he had participated in oral arguments more than thirty times, and he had helped to write briefs in a much larger number of cases. Much of his participation in Court cases occurred during four years as a member of the solicitor general's staff, serving as advocate for the federal government. In 1993 he joined a Washington, D.C., firm, and in that practice he represented a variety of clients with Supreme Court cases. In the Court's 2001 term Roberts presented oral arguments for three other clients besides Toyota: a government planning agency, a private university, and the HMO that opposed Debra Moran. In 2003 he was appointed to a federal court of appeals.

Will Wright and John Roberts illustrate the two kinds of lawyers who participate in Supreme Court litigation.[5] In the first group are attorneys who appear before the Court only on rare occasions; many of them appear only once. They typically become involved in a case at its inception, without any thought that it might go as far as the Supreme Court. When the Court does accept their case, they or their clients may be urged to give the case to a more experienced practitioner. One such lawyer reported that "within hours of the Court's order granting *certiorari,* several prestigious D.C. firms started calling on our client to peddle their services." But in this case, as in many others, the client decided to "stick with the same team that had ridden this case from the day the original lawsuit was filed."[6]

The second group includes the lawyers who are frequent participants in cases at the Court. Most prominent are members of the solicitor general's staff, who practice primarily in the Supreme Court. One member of the staff, Lawrence Wallace, had presented 157 oral arguments before his retirement in 2003.[7] Some attorneys work for interest groups that frequently become involved in Supreme Court cases. Others, like John Roberts, have private practices in which Supreme Court advocacy is a major specialty. Many of these lawyers served in the solicitor general's office or as law clerks in the Court, gaining experience that attracts clients when they move to the private sector.[8] The box on pages 78–79 describes several lawyers who are part of this "inner circle." Unlike other attorneys, those in this second group usually become involved in a case at the appellate level, often when it reaches the Supreme Court.

Of the two groups of lawyers who participate in Supreme Court cases, the first is by far the larger. As Table 3-1 shows, most attorneys who argued cases before the Court in its 2001 term were doing so for the first time. (One of those attorneys was making his first argument in *any* court.) [9] Of course, the lawyers who participate with some frequency are involved in a disproportionate number of cases. Indeed, the federal government with its experienced advocates participates in a majority of the cases decided on the merits. As a result, the "inner circle" plays an important part in shaping the arguments that the Court hears in the cases it decides each term.[10]

Complaints about the quality of advocacy before the Court focus on inexperienced attorneys. One example was the lawyer whom Chief Justice Rehnquist scolded during oral argument, saying that he had "made us gravely wonder . . . how well-prepared you are for this argument." [11] Indeed, Kevin McGuire found from his analysis of cases that the side whose lawyer had more experience before the Court enjoyed an advantage in winning a favorable decision.[12]

This advantage is not overwhelming. Inexperienced Supreme Court advocates sometimes perform very well. More important, the quality of lawyers' work is only one factor that helps to shape the Court's decisions, in part because the justices and their law clerks do their own close analysis of cases. It is hardly rare for a lawyer to secure a victory after arguing a case badly. One experienced advocate before the Court argued that "good lawyering can be a real plus" but "bad lawyering is not necessarily the death knell it is in other courts." [13]

In the legal system as a whole, a relationship exists between the wealth of an individual or institution and the quality of the legal services available to that party. To a considerable degree, this is true of the Supreme Court. The experienced Supreme Court advocates in private practice are most readily available to large corporations and other prosperous organizations that can afford their regular fees. Some "inner circle" lawyers charge clients more than $600 an hour.[14]

For parties without substantial resources, the picture is mixed. Some skilled attorneys who regularly argue cases before the Court represent

---

Some Lawyers Who Participate . . .

Carter G. Phillips. Phillips clerked for Chief Justice Warren Burger and served on the solicitor general's staff. He then joined the Washington office of a large law firm, and his work includes considerable activity in Supreme Court cases. He handles a wide range of cases for clients that include businesses, local governments, and professional groups. Over the past several years, he has presented oral arguments in an average of two cases a year, and he has achieved a familiarity with the Court that allows him to tell a justice about "the flaw in your analysis" during an argument

Laurence Gold. As general counsel of the AFL-CIO from 1981 to 1995, Gold was an active participant in Supreme Court litigation. He is currently associated with a Washington, D.C., law firm but continues to handle litigation in the Court. He has represented workers and unions in cases that raise a wide range of issues, from interpretation of federal labor laws to the power of the federal government to regulate state employment practices.

Eric Schnapper. Schnapper is a law professor at the University of Washington, and he previously taught for many years at Columbia Law School. Along with his teaching and research, for twenty-five years he served as counsel with

---

segments of society that are relatively poor or powerless. And Supreme Court specialists in private practice sometimes take cases for clients who have limited resources. On the other hand, the great majority of individual litigants lack access to such specialists.

A poor person who lacks the support of an interest group may have to petition the Court for a hearing without a lawyer's help, and this certainly constitutes a disadvantage. If the Court accepts such a case, it will appoint an attorney to represent the indigent litigant. Some of those lawyers have experience arguing cases before the Court. This is not a profitable duty; indeed, one lawyer who argued a case on behalf of a death row inmate in 2002 asked the Court to raise its cap of $5,000 in fees for such service on the ground that this amount was woefully inadequate. The Court turned him down.[15]

Lawyers are eligible to participate in cases if they join the Supreme Court bar, for which the most important requirement is that they have been admitted to practice in a state for three years. Lawyers who cannot meet this requirement, however, usually are allowed to argue cases they have brought to the Court. Only a minority of the lawyers who belong to

---

. . . *Frequently in Cases before the Supreme Court*

the NAACP Legal Defense and Educational Fund. Since then he has continued to work on civil rights cases. Over the years, he has helped to write briefs in several dozen Supreme Court cases. He has argued ten cases before the Court, primarily on the interpretation of federal statutes that prohibit discrimination.

Edwin Kneedler. Kneedler has worked for the federal government with the Office of the Solicitor General for nearly his entire legal career, dating back to the late 1970s. Like other lawyers in the solicitor general's office, he participates regularly in Supreme Court cases. Along with his work in other roles, he has presented oral arguments in more than seventy cases during his career. The subjects of his arguments reflect the diversity of cases in which the federal government participates, ranging from immigration to energy regulation.

Sources: Supreme Court decisions; biographical directories and sources. The quotation from Carter Phillips in oral argument is from *Correctional Services Corporation v. Malesko,* argued October 1, 2001, p. 11 of transcript (at Web site of the U.S. Supreme Court, www.supremecourtus.gov); see Dahlia Lithwick, "McJustice For All," in "Supreme Court Dispatches," October 2, 2001 (slate.msn.com).

---

the Supreme Court bar ever take cases before the Court; lawyers join primarily for the honor.

The Court routinely disbars lawyers after serious disciplinary action by their state bars. In 2001 Bill Clinton resigned from the Supreme Court bar to avoid that sanction after he had accepted suspension from the Arkansas bar.[16] A year earlier the Court disbarred another lawyer after he had submitted two petitions for certiorari. Among the issues he raised in the petitions were whether the federal court of appeals for the Second Circuit should be declared a "corrupt enterprise" under federal law and whether its "Chief Injustice" could be "brought to trial for racketeering." For a 5–4 majority of the justices, his invective against the court of appeals was sufficiently offensive to justify disbarment.[17]

Interest Groups

Interest groups are opportunists: they direct their efforts where they can have the greatest impact. For that reason, one good indicator of the importance of a government institution is the attention that interest groups give to that institution. It is not surprising that many groups give

TABLE 3-1

Prior Oral Arguments (1988–2000 terms) by Lawyers Arguing One or More Cases in the 2001 Term

Prior oral arguments	Lawyers		
	Total	*Solicitor general's office*	*Other*
0	93	0	93
1	12	2	10
2	8	1	7
3	7	0	7
4	3	0	3
5–9	10	4	6
10–14	6	3	3
15–19	3	2	1
20–24	2	1	1
25–29	1	1	0
30 or more	6	5	1
	151	19	132

Note: Each lawyer who argued one or more cases in the 2001 term is counted only once. Because oral arguments before the 1988 term are not counted, the table underestimates slightly the overall level of experience.

substantial attention to the Supreme Court, whose decisions establish significant policies on issues as diverse as antitrust and free speech. As a result, interest groups are important participants in the Court.

Forms of Group Activity. Groups that seek to influence congressional decisions try to communicate directly with individual members of Congress. In contrast, it is considered highly improper to lobby judges directly. Because of this norm, Supreme Court justices generally try to avoid contact with litigants and the groups that support them.

But interest groups can attempt to influence the Court in other ways. As described in chapter 2, some groups participate in the nomination and confirmation of justices. Groups on both sides of the abortion controversy conduct marches and demonstrations when the Court considers abortion cases, in part to put indirect pressure on the justices.

The primary route used to influence the Court is participation in the litigation process, participation that takes multiple forms. First, groups can initiate litigation or help bring it to the Court. Organizations that exist primarily as interest groups generally lack standing to bring suits in their own names. But other organizations that may be considered interest groups, especially businesses and governments, are often parties in Supreme Court cases.

A group that is not a party can "sponsor" a case on an issue that concerns it, providing attorneys' services and bearing the costs from the start. Sponsorship entails considerable expense and practical difficulties, and relatively few groups undertake it. Still, a substantial portion of the cases the Court agrees to hear are sponsored by interest groups. Sometimes groups engage in a kind of limited sponsorship of cases that have already been initiated, helping to bear the financial costs and supplying legal services and advice.

One recent example of sponsorship was *Board of Education v. Earls* (2002).[18] An Oklahoma school district required all students in grades seven through twelve to undergo tests for alcohol and illegal drugs before participating in extracurricular activities, some of which were linked to courses. Acting on behalf of two students, the American Civil Liberties Union (ACLU) sued the school district in federal court on the ground that the drug testing was an unconstitutional search. The ACLU's attorneys carried the case forward through a defeat in district court, a victory in the Tenth Circuit Court of Appeals, and ultimately a 5–4 defeat in the Supreme Court.

Whether or not it sponsors cases, a group can try to influence the Court's decisions to accept or reject cases and how to decide those that it accepts. If a group effectively controls a case, its attorneys submit a brief that asks the Court to grant or deny a writ of certiorari. If the case is accepted for decision on the merits, the group's attorneys submit new briefs and participate in oral argument.

When a group does not control the case, it still may submit arguments to the Court in what are called amicus curiae, or friend of the court, briefs. With the consent of the parties to a case or by permission of the Court, any person or organization may submit an amicus brief to supplement the arguments of the parties. (Legal representatives of government do not need to obtain permission.) Most of the time, the parties give their consent for the submission of amicus briefs. When the Court's consent is needed, it seldom is denied—only twenty-two times in the 1992–2001 terms. Amicus briefs can be submitted on whether a case should be heard or, after a case is accepted for hearing, directly on the merits.

An amicus can also participate in oral argument if invited or allowed by the Court. The federal government regularly plays this role, as it did twenty-nine times in the 2001 term. Lawyers for states argued as amicus in three cases in that term, reflecting the Court's increasing willingness to give this privilege to the states.

Amicus briefs are by far the most common means by which groups other than parties participate in litigation before the Court. As might be expected, amicus briefs are especially common in cases that the Court has accepted for consideration on the merits. In the 2001 term amicus briefs were submitted in more than 95 percent of the cases decided after oral argument, and half the cases had at least five briefs.[19] And because groups or individuals can join in submitting a brief, the number of participants is considerably larger than the number of briefs.

The popularity of amicus briefs has several sources.[20] First, although the costs of preparing them are substantial, they are considerably cheaper than case sponsorship. Second, the logistics of submitting an amicus brief are relatively simple. Third, many lawyers and other people believe that amicus briefs influence the Court's decisions. For this reason, parties to cases often encourage or even orchestrate supportive briefs, and groups whose interests are implicated by a case may feel that they need to have their say. Group leaders can also use amicus briefs as a concrete action with which to impress their members.

The Array of Groups in the Court. Interest group participation in Supreme Court litigation has increased dramatically in the past few decades.[21] Groups are sponsoring more cases, and amicus briefs have proliferated. To take one indicator, the average number of amicus briefs in cases with oral arguments was 0.63 in the 1956–1965 terms, rose to 4.23 in the 1986–1995 period, and was 5.47 in the 2001 term.[22] The growth in amicus briefs is symbolized by the record-breaking eighty-five that were submitted in the Court's 2003 case on affirmative action in law school admissions.[23] This growth has several sources. Throughout government, the number of active interest groups and the level of their activity have increased considerably. The apparent success of some groups in shaping the Supreme Court's policies has encouraged other groups to seek a similar impact. Indeed, "arms races" have developed between groups that compete to influence the Court's decisions in particular fields.[24]

With this growth, hundreds of interest groups participate in Supreme Court cases in some way. Among them are nearly all the groups that are most active in Congress and the executive branch. The box on page 84 provides a sampling of this participation by listing some of the groups that submitted amicus briefs in the 2002 term.

The groups that come to the Court can be placed in four broad categories. The largest category includes economic groups: individual businesses, trade associations, professional associations, labor unions, and farm groups. Economic groups predominate in the Court, as they do in

University of Michigan president Mary Sue Coleman and behind her Barbara Grutter and Jennifer Gratz, outside the Supreme Court after oral arguments in the cases challenging affirmative action in admissions to the university. The lawsuits by Grutter and Gratz were sponsored by the Center for Individual Rights.

the other branches, because they are numerous and well funded and because the Court does a great deal that they care about. In particular, the business community feels the effects of most of the Court's decisions. Nearly all the subjects that the justices address concern businesses in some way. Cases on state-federal relations often arise from state taxation or regulation of businesses. Civil rights cases frequently concern the enforcement of antidiscrimination laws against employers.

In the second category are groups that represent segments of the population defined by something other than economics. The most prominent of these groups is the NAACP Legal Defense and Educational Fund (sometimes called the NAACP Legal Defense Fund or simply the Fund).[25] The Fund was created by the NAACP as a separate litigating group in 1939, and it later became fully independent. It initiates litigation through its staff of about thirty lawyers, most of whom are in New York City, and a large network of cooperating attorneys throughout the United States. The Fund initially focused its efforts on securing voting rights for black citizens and desegregating schools in the South. It has also worked to challenge capital punishment and to obtain effective enforcement of federal laws against employment discrimination. The Fund's successes in the Court

A Sampling of Groups
Submitting Amicus Curiae Briefs
to the Supreme Court in the 2002 Term

Economic Groups: Businesses and Occupations

Chamber of Commerce of the United States
Motion Picture Association of America
Songwriters Guild of America
Ford Motor Company
Intel Corporation
Dr. Seuss Enterprises
Brotherhood of Locomotive Engineers
California District Attorneys Association

Noneconomic Interests

American-Arab Anti-Discrimination Committee
Asian American Legal Defense and Education Fund
National Gay and Lesbian Task Force
Lutheran Women's Caucus

Ideological Groups

Washington Legal Foundation
Criminal Justice Legal Foundation
People for the American Way
Americans United for Life
Religious Coalition for Reproductive Choice

Governments and Government Groups

United States
State of Kentucky
District of Columbia
Office of the Public Defender for the State of New Jersey
National League of Cities

have encouraged the development of similar organizations, such as the Mexican American Legal Defense and Educational Fund and several litigation groups representing women.

The groups in the third category represent broad ideological positions rather than the interests of a specific segment of society; the ACLU is an example.[26] Established in 1920 to protect civil liberties, the ACLU has always relied heavily on litigation. The ACLU involves itself in virtually every area of civil liberties law. It acts primarily on complaints of civil liberties violations that people bring to local ACLU affiliates, which provide volunteer attorneys for cases they perceive as meritorious. If those cases reach the Supreme Court, they are often handled by the national ACLU office. The ACLU also has created special projects to undertake concerted litigation campaigns in specific areas of concern such as women's rights, capital punishment, and national security. For example, the Drug Policy Litigation Project handled the student drug testing case that originated in Oklahoma. The ACLU frequently submits amicus briefs in cases that it does not sponsor.

The ACLU is one of many ideological groups that work to achieve liberal policy goals. Two others are the Sierra Club, which has a litigation arm devoted to environmental protection, and the Planned Parenthood Federation of America, for which abortion rights are a primary concern. In the 1960s Ralph Nader pioneered public interest law firms, which were established to handle cases that they perceived as serving the public interest from a liberal perspective. These firms initiate litigation on issues such as consumer rights, civil liberties, and the environment.

Ideological groups that favor conservative positions on legal issues were slower to involve themselves in litigation, but many such groups are now active. For example, Americans for Effective Law Enforcement supports narrow interpretations of the procedural rights of criminal defendants. Several public interest law firms act on behalf of conservative interests. As noted, the Washington Legal Foundation mounted a long-term campaign against the use of interest from lawyers' trust accounts for clients to fund legal services for low-income people. A similar campaign against affirmative action programs by another firm, the Center for Individual Rights, led to the Supreme Court's 2003 decisions on the use of affirmative action in college admissions.[27]

Several litigating groups represent conservative religious interests.[28] One is the American Center for Law and Justice (ACLJ), established by religious leader Pat Robertson in 1991.[29] The ACLJ gives some emphasis to assisting people who want to participate in religious activities in schools and other places. Another Christian group, the Rutherford Institute, handles a wide range of cases relating to religious expression and other issues. The Institute sponsored the 2001 case in which the Court ruled that a religious club for students must be allowed to meet in a public school building.[30] It also supported Paula Jones in the lawsuit against President Clinton that ultimately brought about Clinton's impeachment in 1998.

The final category consists of governments, which regularly appear as interest groups in the Court. The federal government is a special case, which is examined separately. State and local governments often come to the Court as litigants, and they file many amicus briefs. It has become standard practice for several states, sometimes a majority, to join in a brief to emphasize their strong shared interest in a case.

Group Strategies and Tactics. In *Brown v. Board of Education* (1954), the Supreme Court ruled that public school students cannot be segregated by race. *Brown* and the four cases that accompanied it were sponsored by the NAACP Legal Defense Fund, and the Fund's victory was the culmination of a long campaign to achieve desegregation. Under the leadership of Thurgood Marshall, the Fund had begun with challenges to blatant discrimination against black students in graduate and professional schools; its successes in those cases helped move the Court toward the far more sweeping decision in *Brown.*

The path to *Brown* was not as smooth as it appears in retrospect. The Fund's leaders struggled to raise the money needed for their litigation campaign, and they had to worry about coordinating cases they had not initiated. And the Fund's ultimate success resulted in large part from favorable circumstances. Still, that success underscored the value of careful planning by groups that undertake litigation.

Not all groups map out long-term litigation campaigns, but they all face strategic and tactical decisions.[31] At the strategic level, groups that are not set up solely to litigate must decide how much of their energy and resources to devote to litigation rather than other forms of political action. Groups must also decide what kinds of issues to emphasize in their litigation work and how to coordinate their efforts with other groups that have similar interests. At the tactical level, a group's lawyers consider whether initiating a specific case or supporting a litigant in an existing case would serve their goals. They sometimes have a choice among different regions in which to initiate cases or between federal and state courts. And like other lawyers, they have to choose which arguments to make in the cases in which they participate.

Many considerations affect these decisions, including the views of group members and the availability of resources. Perhaps the most fundamental consideration is a group's perceptions of the courts in general and the Supreme Court in particular. It is not surprising that conservative groups have become more active in Supreme Court litigation since the 1970s as the Court has become more receptive to conservative arguments. Similarly, choices of specific cases and arguments reflect judgments about potential responses from the justices.

The Significance of Interest Groups. Interest groups can affect what the Supreme Court does in several ways; here, I focus on their effect in determining whether cases get to the Court. In this respect, cases may be placed in three categories.

The largest category includes the cases that come to the Court without any participation by interest groups. For the most part, these cases constitute what I have called ordinary litigation. The issues in these cases are too narrow to interest any group. They reach the Court because the parties and attorneys have sufficient motivation of their own to seek a Supreme Court hearing and sufficient resources to finance the litigation. These conditions are met when businesses have substantial resources and a large financial stake in a case. They are also met when indigent criminal defendants face significant prison terms and need not pay lawyers' fees or most of the other expenses involved in getting a case to the Court.

The second category consists of cases that would have reached the Court without any interest group involvement, but in which groups are involved in some way. An interest group may assist one of the parties by providing attorneys' services or financing to ensure that the case does reach the Supreme Court and to gain some control over the position that the party takes. Far more often, a group submits an amicus brief supporting the petition for a hearing by the Court.

The third category includes cases that would not reach the Court without group sponsorship. There are many important legal questions in civil liberties that no individual litigant has the capability or sufficient incentive to take to the Supreme Court. For example, one parent or even several parents could hardly arrange and finance a school desegregation suit on their own, nor could most of the individuals whom the ACLU assists go to court without the group's legal assistance.

Because group sponsorship of cases in the Court is relatively rare, only a small proportion of cases brought to the Court fall in this third category. But groups are most likely to sponsor cases that have the potential to be heard by the Court and to produce major legal rulings. Indeed, much of the Court's expansion of legal protections for civil liberties during the twentieth century was made possible by interest group action.[32]

Groups can do more than get cases to the Court; they can help to determine whether those cases are heard and how the Court rules. That influence is discussed later in this chapter and in chapter 4.

The Federal Government as Litigant

Of all the litigants in the Supreme Court, the federal government appears most frequently. In the 2001 term it was a party in about two-fifths of the cases brought to the Court for consideration and in forty-two of the eighty-eight cases actually argued before the Court. It frequently participates as an amicus in other cases, as it did in thirty-three cases that were argued in the 2001 term. Altogether, then, the government played an official role in 85 percent of the cases in which the Court heard arguments during that term.[33] As a result of its frequent participation, the federal government is the most important interest group in the Court.

In turn, the group of lawyers that has the greatest impact on the Court is the set of about two dozen who work for the Office of the Solicitor General in the Justice Department. Those lawyers are primarily responsible for representing the federal government in the Supreme Court. They decide whether to bring federal government cases to the Court; only a few federal agencies can take cases to the Court without the solicitor general's approval. Lawyers in the solicitor general's office also do the bulk of the legal work in Supreme Court cases in which the federal government participates, including petitions for hearings, the writing of briefs, and oral arguments.

The solicitor general's office occupies a complicated position.[34] On the one hand, it represents the president and the executive branch, functioning as their law firm in individual cases. In this role, the office helps to carry out policies of the president and administrative agencies. But the office also has developed a unique relationship with the Supreme Court, one in which it serves as an adviser as well as an advocate. As Richard Pacelle put it, the solicitor general's office straddles the line "between law and politics."[35]

The unique relationship of the Office of the Solicitor General with the Court rests on the fact that it represents a unique litigant. For one thing, the executive branch and the Supreme Court are both part of the federal government. In addition, the executive branch is involved in far more potential Supreme Court cases and actual cases than any other entity. As a result, the solicitor general has the opportunity to build a mutually advantageous relationship with the Court.

One way the solicitor general does so is by exercising self-restraint in requesting that the Court hear cases. In the cases acted on by the Court in the 2001 term, the federal government filed 20 petitions for certiorari, while its opponents filed 3,407. Although the government loses fewer cases in the courts of appeals than do its opponents, the primary reason for this difference is the solicitor general's willingness to forgo possible petitions for certiorari. The solicitor general's office also seeks to maintain credibility by taking a less partisan stance than other litigants. For example, lawyers in the office try to ensure that the justices can rely on statements in their briefs. Further, the experience that those lawyers gain allows them to make high-quality arguments to the Court.

In response, the justices give considerable deference to the solicitor general. The office has an extraordinary success rate for its certiorari petitions. The Court frequently "invites" (in reality, orders) the solicitor general to file amicus briefs in cases that do not affect the federal government directly because the justices are interested in the government's views. And the solicitor general often participates in oral argument as amicus, a role that is uncommon for other litigants.

The office's special relationship with the Court leads to a degree of independence from the president and attorney general, who understand the value of maintaining that relationship. But the solicitor general usually is someone who shares the president's general point of view about legal policy; the office operates in a general climate created by the president and attorney general; and these superiors occasionally intervene in specific cases. As a result, an administration's policy views will be reflected in the overall pattern of positions that the office takes in litigation. Between 1965 and 2000, to take one example, Republican administrations took liberal positions about half the time in sex discrimination cases, Democratic administrations 80 percent of the time.[36]

These linkages between the solicitor general's office and the administration have strengthened in the last quarter century, beginning with the Reagan presidency. In effect, the political side of the solicitor general's work has become more prominent. In the Clinton administration, for example, solicitors general with liberal points of view took into account Clinton's less liberal views on most civil liberties issues and his desire to avoid being identified with unpopular positions.

This change is symbolized by George W. Bush's selection of Theodore Olson as solicitor general. Olson had been heavily involved in conservative causes, and he had argued for Bush in the Supreme Court in *Bush v. Gore*. Primarily because of this background, Olson was confirmed in the Senate by only four votes. As solicitor general, Olson has helped to formulate and carry out administration policies on prosecutions involving terrorism.

In the Bush administration, the political side of the solicitor general's work is evident in two controversial cases. In 2002, after debate within the Justice Department, the government reversed a long-standing position and supported the view of Attorney General John Ashcroft that the Second Amendment provides individuals with the right to possess guns.[37] President Bush himself resolved the 2003 debate over the government's position on affirmative action programs at the University of Michigan and announced the decision to file amicus briefs opposing those programs in a televised address.[38]

At the same time, the legal side of the solicitor general's work has remained strong. In some cases, the office has taken positions that run counter to the general tenor of Bush administration policy. And the federal government continues to benefit from the expertise of lawyers in the solicitor general's office—including Olson, who is highly respected for his skills as an advocate.

Deciding What to Hear: The Court's Role

In 1983 Calvin Burdine was tried for murder in Texas. Represented by a court-appointed lawyer, who slept during part of the trial, Burdine was convicted and sentenced to death. After years of legal battles in the case, in 1999 a federal district judge ruled that the lawyer's sleeping had violated Burdine's right to a fair trial. That decision was overturned by a panel of the federal court of appeals for the Fifth Circuit, a decision that was itself overturned by the full court of appeals. The state of Texas then petitioned the Supreme Court to hear the case.

By this time Burdine's case had gained national attention. Beyond its element of human interest, it became part of the growing debate over the fairness of trials that result in death sentences. Many people were eager to see how the Supreme Court would decide the case.

The Court decided nothing. In *Cockrell v. Burdine* (2002), it denied certiorari. Surprising as this action was to some observers, it is hardly unusual for the Court to turn aside high-profile cases. Earlier in the 2001 term, for example, the justices refused to hear Microsoft's appeal in the antitrust case in which the software company and the federal government battled over the structure of the computer industry.[39] Most petitioners who lacked such visibility fared no better in the 2001 term. Of the 8,023 cases that it considered, the Court granted certiorari and full consideration to only 88.[40] In nearly all of the rest, it simply left the lower court decision standing.

Options

In screening petitions for hearings, the Court makes choices that are more complicated than simply accepting and rejecting individual cases. To begin with, petitions are not always considered in isolation from one another. The justices may accept a case to clarify or expand on an earlier decision in the same policy area. They may accept several cases that raise the same issue to address that issue more fully than a single case would

Calvin Burdine, an inmate on death row in Texas. Burdine's claim that he had received inadequate counsel was successful when the Supreme Court refused to hear the state's petition for certiorari in his case.

allow them to do. They may reject a case because they are looking for a more suitable case on the same issue.

When the Court does accept a case, the justices can choose which issues they will consider. The Court often limits its grant of certiorari to one issue raised by the petitioner, and it sometimes asks the parties to address an issue that neither had raised. In 2001 it accepted a pair of cases but limited its consideration of them to one issue raised by the petitioner because the other issues were raised in a third case. When oral argument revealed a technical problem with the third case, the Court expanded its grant of certiorari in the first two cases to those other issues.[41] No matter what issues the parties raise and address, the Court retains the freedom to determine the issues it actually resolves in its opinion. In *Mapp v. Ohio* (1961), the Court made a landmark decision on police searches and seizures after the parties had argued the case as one about constitutional limits on the regulation of obscenity.

When the Court accepts a case, it also determines the kind of consideration it will give that case. It may give the case full consideration, which means that the Court receives a new set of briefs on the merits from the parties and holds oral argument, then issues a decision on the merits with a full opinion explaining the decision. Alternatively, it may give the case summary consideration. This usually means that the case is decided without new briefs or oral argument; the Court relies on the materials that the parties already submitted. A large minority of the cases that the Court accepts, nearly half in the 1999–2001 terms, receive summary consideration.[42]

In most summary decisions, the Supreme Court issues a "GVR" order—Granting certiorari, Vacating the lower court decision, and Remanding the case to that court for reconsideration. Most of these orders are issued because some event since the lower court decision, usually a Supreme Court decision, is relevant to the case. On the first day of the 2002 term, for example, the Court issued nine GVRs in light of decisions it had reached in the 2001 term.

In other summary decisions, the Court actually reaches a decision on the merits and issues an opinion of several paragraphs or even several pages. This opinion typically is labeled *per curiam,* meaning by the Court, rather than being signed by a justice, but it has the same legal force as a signed opinion.[43] When the Court takes this kind of action, justices sometimes complain that it should not have decided the case without getting full information from the parties through briefs that directly address the merits of the case and through oral argument.

Even after accepting a case, the Court can avoid a decision by issuing what is called a "DIG" for "Dismissed as Improvidently Granted." A DIG occurs a few times each term, when the parties' briefs on the merits or the oral arguments suggest to the justices that the case is inappropriate for a decision. *Adarand Constructors v. Mineta* (2001) looked like the vehicle for a significant decision on affirmative action when the Court accepted the case. By the time of oral argument, however, the justices realized that the case had procedural problems that prevented them from deciding the affirmative action issue. Some of the justices berated Adarand's lawyer for bringing them the case, passing over the fact that the Court had—as one commentator put it—"granted cert on a loser set of facts."[44] A month later the Court issued a DIG.

Congress caused a 2003 case to drop off the Court's agenda. The issue in *Department of Justice v. City of Chicago* was whether a Justice Department bureau must release certain information about gun sales and crimes. A few weeks before oral argument, Congress enacted a budget bill with a provision forbidding the agency from spending money to release the information, apparently to get the case out of the Court. The action was successful; the Court canceled the argument and sent the case back to a lower court for reconsideration.[45]

Screening Procedures

The Court uses a series of complex procedures to screen petitions for hearing, and these procedures are made more complex by two distinctions between types of cases. The first is between the certiorari cases, over which the Court's jurisdiction is discretionary, and the very small number of cases that the Court is required to decide, labeled appeals. Few appeals reach the Court—on average, about a dozen a term.[46] The Court retains, and uses, the option of deciding them without holding oral argument or issuing full opinions. The second distinction, between paid cases and paupers' cases, requires more extensive discussion.

Paid Cases and Paupers' Cases. Less than one-third of the requests for hearings that arrive at the Supreme Court are "paid" cases, for which the Court's filing fee of $300 has been paid and all required copies of materials have been provided. The remaining cases are brought *in forma pauperis* by indigent people for whom the fee and the requirement of multiple copies are waived. The great majority of the "paupers' cases" are brought by prisoners in federal and state institutions. (A person responding to a petition may also be given pauper status.)

Criminal defendants who have had counsel provided to them in the lower federal courts because of their low incomes are automatically entitled to bring paupers' cases in the Supreme Court. Other litigants must submit an affidavit supporting their motion for leave to file as paupers. The Court has never developed precise rules specifying when a litigant can claim pauper status. In recent years, however, it has denied a number of litigants the right to proceed as paupers in particular cases on the grounds that they were not truly paupers or that their petitions were frivolous or malicious. The Court has also gone further, issuing a general denial of pauper status to several litigants who had filed large numbers of paupers' petitions. Justice Stevens regularly dissents from such denials because of an experience he had before becoming a judge: he had found "unexpected merit" in the allegations of a repetitive and annoying litigant when he led an investigation of judicial corruption in Illinois in 1969.[47]

A very small proportion of paupers' petitions are accepted for full decisions on the merits—about one-tenth of 1 percent in the 2001 term, compared with 4.3 percent of the paid cases in the same term.[48] The lack of inherent merit in many of these cases and the fact that many litigants have to draft petitions without a lawyer's assistance help to account for the low acceptance rate. It may also be that the Court looks less closely at paupers' petitions than at the paid petitions. One former law clerk said that after clerks have served for several months, "they flip through" the paupers' petitions "pretty fast. I wouldn't want my case to be in that pile." [49]

But because there are so many paupers' petitions, even the small proportion that are accepted add up to a significant number of cases—an average of about a dozen a term in recent years—and they constitute an important part of the Court's work on issues of criminal procedure.

Prescreening: The Discuss List. Under its "rule of four," the Court grants a writ of certiorari and hears a case on the merits if at least four justices vote at conference to grant the writ. But petitions for hearings are considered and voted on at conference only if they are put on the Court's "discuss list." [50] The chief justice creates the discuss list, but other justices can and do add cases to it. Cases left off the discuss list are denied hearings automatically. This is the fate of a substantial majority of petitions.

The discuss-list procedure serves to limit the Court's workload. But this procedure also reflects a belief that most petitions do not require collective consideration, because they are such poor candidates for acceptance. A great many petitions raise only very narrow issues, and many others make very weak legal claims, so it is easy to reject them.

Action in Conference. In conference, the chief justice or the justice who added a case to the discuss list opens the presentation of views on the case. In order of seniority, from senior to junior, the justices then speak and usually announce their votes. If the discussion does not make the justices' positions clear, a formal vote is taken, also in order of seniority. Despite the prescreening of cases, a substantial majority of the petitions considered in conference are denied.

Most cases receive very brief discussion in conference. This has been especially true under Chief Justice Rehnquist. When the Court meets in late September to deal with the petitions that have accumulated during the summer, Rehnquist "insists that his colleagues come prepared and ready to vote in rapid succession, with a minimum of discussion." [51] As a result, the conference usually serves only as a place for individual votes to be added together.

Some cases receive more consideration, which sometimes extends beyond the initial discussion. In conference, any justice can ask that a case be "redistributed" for a later conference. This step might be taken to obtain additional information, such as the full record of the case in the lower courts. A justice also might ask for redistribution to circulate an opinion dissenting from the Court's tentative denial of a hearing and thereby try to change the Court's decision. As Justice Stevens once noted, such an opinion "sometimes persuades other Justices to change their votes and a petition is granted that would otherwise have been denied." [52] Cases can be redistributed more than once; *Eldred v. Ashcroft,* a 2003 copyright case, was redistributed three times.

When it accepts a case, the Court also decides whether to allow oral argument or to decide the case summarily on the basis of the available written materials. Four votes are required for oral argument. A case that is not given oral argument may be granted a hearing and decided on the merits at the same conference, so that the two stages of decision in effect become one.

The Court almost never issues an opinion to explain its acceptance or rejection of a case. Nor are individual votes announced. But justices occasionally record their dissents from denials of petitions for hearings. During the 2001 term, one or more justices announced dissents in four cases. Opinions accompanied two of the dissents. In a death penalty case in 2002, Justice Breyer wrote an opinion dissenting from the Court's denial of certiorari, Justice Thomas answered Breyer with an opinion supporting the denial, and Justice Stevens answered Thomas with a short opinion "to emphasize that the denial of a petition for a writ of certiorari does not constitute a ruling on the merits." [53]

Clerks' Role. One of the law clerks' major functions is to scrutinize requests for hearings.[54] Since 1990 every justice except Stevens has joined the "certiorari pool." Petitions and other materials on each case are divided among the clerks for these eight justices. The clerk who has responsibility for a case writes a memorandum, one that typically includes a summary of the case and a recommendation that the petition be granted or denied. Some justices then have their own law clerks examine and react to the memo for each case. Chief Justice Rehnquist reports that his clerks divide the memos among themselves, read them, "and, if necessary, go back to the petition and response in order to make a recommendation to me as to whether the petition should be granted or denied." [55]

Because of the press of time, the justices rely heavily on law clerks' analyses of cases. Some justices and other observers have expressed particular concern about the justices' collective reliance on the pool memo.[56] One recent law clerk has argued that this reliance is less problematic than it might appear: clerks typically write their pool memos with care, and justices frequently vote contrary to the memo's recommendation. "Still," he concluded, "any system that depends to a considerable degree on the views of a single novice lawyer is fairly subject to criticism." [57] Justice Stevens lessens this problem by staying out of the pool. But he delegates a good deal of responsibility to his own clerks, who write memoranda or refer petitions directly to him in only a minority of cases.

Still, the law clerks' impact on certiorari decisions should not be exaggerated. For one thing, the great majority of petitions would elicit the same reaction from any justice or clerk: an obvious denial. "I would guess," Chief Justice Rehnquist wrote, "that several thousand of the petitions for certiorari filed with the Court each year are patently without merit," so that no justice "would have the least interest in granting them." [58] And justices involve themselves most fully in the screening process at the point where individual judgments make the most difference—in selecting cases to hear from those on the discuss list.

Criteria for Decision

As noted earlier, the Court seldom offers an explanation when it accepts or rejects a case. In cases that the Court decides on the merits, its opinion often includes a rationale for accepting the case, but the rationale is usually brief and not very illuminating.

The Court's Rule 10 provides general guidance by specifying some of the conditions under which the Court will hear a case. The rule emphasizes the Court's role in ensuring the certainty and consistency of the law. The criteria for accepting a case cited in Rule 10 include the existence of important legal issues that the Court has not yet decided, conflict among courts of appeals on a legal question, conflict between a lower court's decision and the Supreme Court's prior decisions, and departure "from the accepted and usual course of judicial proceedings" in the courts below.

These criteria make sense, but they suggest a conception of the Court's function and of its members' interests that is unrealistically narrow. The Court's pattern of screening decisions and evidence from other sources indicate the significance of several considerations, only some of which are included in Rule 10.

Technical Criteria. The Supreme Court will reject a petition for hearing if it fails to meet certain technical requirements. Some of these requirements are specific to the Court. For example, paid petitions must comply with the Court's Rule 33, which establishes requirements on matters such as the size of print and margins used, type of paper, format and color of cover, and maximum length. In *Calderon v. Thompson* (1997), a litigant had to obtain special permission from the justices "to proceed with 8 1/2-by-11-inch paper." These requirements are relaxed for the paupers' petitions, but even paupers' petitions may be rejected if their deviation from the rules is extreme.

The Court also imposes the same kinds of technical requirements for the hearing of cases that other courts apply. One specific requirement is that petitions for hearing be filed within ninety days of the entry of judgment in the lower court, unless the time has been extended in advance. The Court routinely refuses to file petitions that are brought after the deadline.

More fundamental are the requirements of jurisdiction and standing. The Court cannot accept a case for hearing that clearly falls outside its jurisdiction. For example, the Court could not hear a state case in which the petitioner raised no issues of federal law in state court.

The rule of standing holds that a court may not hear a case unless the party bringing the case is properly before it. The most important element of standing is the requirement that a party in a case have a real and direct legal stake in its outcome. This requirement precludes hypothetical cases, cases brought on behalf of another person, "friendly suits" between parties that are not really adversaries, and cases that have become "moot" (in effect, hypothetical) because the parties can no longer be affected by the outcome. For this reason, the Court must dismiss a case if the parties have reached a settlement, as it did in 2000 in two important cases involving the federal statute that prohibits discrimination against disabled people.[59] In 2003 the Court dismissed a case involving the same statute even though the parties had failed to reach a settlement; lawyers for the state of California, the petitioner, wanted to withdraw the case because it was creating political problems for the governor and state attorney general.[60]

The technical requirements sometimes are easy to apply. But their application can be more ambiguous, arousing disagreement among the justices. Those disagreements often reflect views about the underlying merits of cases. For example, the justices who are most likely to grant standing to environmental groups are generally the ones most favorable to the policy positions of those groups. As this example indicates, the rules of jurisdiction and standing are not only requirements imposed on the Court but means by which the Court itself can regulate access to its judgments in accordance with its members' goals.

The technical criteria serve as preliminary screening devices by which some cases are eliminated. But most cases meet these criteria, and the Court must use others to choose among them.

Conflict Between Courts. Justice Breyer heartily agrees with Rule 10 on the importance of conflict among lower courts as a basis for accepting cases. "If the lower courts are in agreement," he asked, "why us?"[61] Other justices have expressed the same view. Justice Ginsburg said that "the overwhelming factor" in the granting of certiorari "is the division of opinions in the Circuits."[62]

The depictions of case selection by Breyer and Ginsburg have considerable accuracy.[63] The existence of legal conflict greatly increases the chances that a case will be accepted. In the 1997–2001 terms, 39 percent of the Court's majority opinions cited lower court conflict as a reason (usually the only reason) for accepting the case.[64] Conflict exists in other cases in which the Court does not cite it, and one expert estimates that 80 percent of the cases that the Court accepts involve conflicts between federal courts of appeals.[65]

The Court does not accept all conflict cases. Indeed, the justices reject substantially more such cases than they accept. In choosing among the conflict cases, they take into account the extent of the conflict and the seriousness of its effects. The Court emphasized the latter criterion in 1995 when it revised its Rule 10 by inserting the word "important" in three places, indicating that it was inclined to hear conflict cases only if they involved important matters or legal questions. But the Court occasionally accepts a case to resolve a conflict even though only two courts are in conflict on a seemingly minor issue. In contrast, the Court sometimes turns down cases involving fairly serious conflicts among several courts. Eventually, however, the Court is likely to resolve a conflict that is persistent and troublesome.[66]

Importance of the Issues. Whether or not a case involves conflict between lower courts, the significance of the issues has considerable influence on the Court's willingness to accept the case. Rule 10 emphasizes this consideration for good reason: the best way for the Court to maximize its impact is to decide the cases that affect the most people and that raise the most important policy issues.

This consideration in itself eliminates most petitions for certiorari. The "questions presented" at the beginning of these petitions are narrow and limited in their impact. Frequently, they ask only whether the case was wrongly decided. The petitioners in these cases may have suffered an injustice, but the justices typically see little reason to address an issue that will have little or no impact beyond the litigants themselves.

Whether a case has sufficient importance for the Court to hear is in part a subjective matter. The justices look for cases in which a decision would have broad effects on courts, government, or society as a whole. In some of the cases that meet this criterion, the issues have an obvious importance. These are the cases that attract widespread attention when they are argued and when the Court reaches its decision. Such cases are in the minority; a former law clerk has said that "the Supreme Court decides an awful lot of boring cases." But he added that these boring cases can involve important legal issues.[67]

Just as the Court rejects some cases with conflicts between lower courts, it rejects some important cases as well. The primary reason is the same: the number of meritorious cases is considerably larger than the number the Court is willing and able to hear. Justices may have more specific reasons to vote against cases with significant issues. To take two examples, they may agree with the lower court decision or want to delay before tackling a difficult issue.

Policy Preferences. Rule 10 does not mention justices' personal conceptions of good policy as a criterion for accepting or rejecting cases, but those conceptions are quite weighty in guiding the Court's choices. Because case selection is such an important part of the Court's policymaking, members of the Court could scarcely resist use of the agenda-setting process as a way to advance their policy goals.

Justices could act on their policy goals primarily in two ways. First, they might vote to hear cases because they disagree with the lower court decision that they are reviewing: seeing what they believe was an error by the lower court, they want to correct it. Second, they might act strategically by voting to hear cases when they think the policy they favor would gain a majority if the Court decided those cases on the merits.

In 1984 Justice Rehnquist attested to the justices' use of the first approach: "The most common reason members of our Court vote to grant certiorari is that they doubt the correctness of the decision of the lower court." [68] As the Court has reduced the number of cases it accepts, this may no longer be true. Justice Souter said in 1998 that it was "axiomatic that this Court cannot devote itself to error correction." [69] Still, a belief that the lower court has erred inclines the justices to accept cases. In the 2001 term, the Court affirmed lower courts in only 23 percent of the cases that it decided with full opinions, [70] a proportion far lower than the rate in appellate courts that must hear all the cases they receive. Inevitably, the justices' evaluations of lower court decisions reflect their ideological positions. If a lower court has reached a conservative decision, a liberal justice is more likely to view it as wrongly decided and vote to hear the case than is a conservative colleague.

The second, strategic, approach requires justices to predict how the Court would decide a case if it were accepted. Such predictions often can be made with some confidence because the justices have a good sense of each other's positions on legal issues. Considerable evidence suggests that justices engage in this prediction process. One study demonstrated that justices are much more likely to vote to grant certiorari when the Court's decision could be expected to reflect their ideological leanings rather than to run contrary to those leanings. [71]

The practice of voting not to hear a case when a justice fears that the Court would make the "wrong" decision is so well established that justices and clerks routinely refer to "defensive denials" of certiorari. [72] Defensive denials are especially appealing to the members of the Court's ideological minority at any given time (such as liberals on the Rehnquist Court) because they have the most reason to fear the Court's prospective decisions.

It is uncertain how these two ways of acting on policy preferences fit together, but research on this question indicates that each is important. Justices respond to both their evaluations of lower court decisions and their expectations about the Court's decision if a case is accepted.[73] And it is clear that justices' preferences, expressed in these ways, have considerable effect on their choices of cases.

Identity of the Petitioner. During its 2001 term, the Supreme Court considered twenty petitions for certiorari filed by the federal government. It granted hearings in seventeen of the twenty cases. The government also filed nine amicus briefs supporting petitions for certiorari; the Court accepted all nine cases. Thus, the solicitor general's office secured hearings in twenty-six cases for a success rate of 90 percent. Of the thousands of other petitions it considered, the Court granted certiorari in about sixty, less than 1 percent.[74]

The federal government did unusually well in the 2001 term, but its success rate is consistently higher than 50 percent. What accounts for this impressive record? It can be ascribed chiefly to the advantages of what Marc Galanter calls a "repeat player"—a litigant engaged in many related cases over time.[75] This status provides the government with at least three advantages.

First, the solicitor general's staff chooses cases to bring to the Court from a large pool of cases that are eligible for Court consideration. As a result, the staff can select those that are the most likely to be accepted. Almost any litigant who could be so selective would enjoy a fairly high rate of success in the Supreme Court.

Second, the solicitor general's selectivity earns some gratitude from the Court and builds credibility as well. If the federal government brought petitions at the high rates that other litigants bring them, the Court's caseload would be much heavier than it is. The justices reciprocate for this restraint by viewing the government's petitions in a favorable light. Further, the justices know that the government takes to the Court only the cases that its lawyers deem most worthy, so the justices are also inclined to view those cases as worthy.

Third, the attorneys in the solicitor general's office handle a great many Supreme Court cases, and they develop an unusual degree of expertise in dealing with the Court. Few other lawyers learn as much about how to appeal to the Court's interests. As a result, the government can do more than most other litigants to make cases appear worthy of acceptance.

It helps that the solicitor general represents the federal government, a litigant with unique status. This status is reflected in the Court's treatment of the solicitor general's office as something of a partner. But it is primarily the advantage of the repeat player that accounts for the remarkable record of the solicitor general as a petitioner for certiorari.

Some other litigants and interest groups also enjoy advantages in securing hearings from the Court. As noted earlier, large corporations can hire experts in Supreme Court litigation, and lawyers who handle litigation for interest groups such as the AFL-CIO often develop that expertise. These lawyers—and certain interest groups—may develop credibility with the Court. But no other litigant or group has anything like the full set of advantages that account for the solicitor general's success.

Avoiding Problematic Cases. Undoubtedly, every member of the Supreme Court recognized the danger of intervening in the legal dispute over the outcome of the 2000 presidential election. Whatever the Court ruled, a good many people in and out of government would be unhappy with its ruling. Moreover, if the Court's decision was perceived as the product of partisanship, the Court's prestige might suffer considerably. Indeed, according to one report, the justices who eventually dissented in *Bush v. Gore* were "startled" when the majority accepted the first of the two cases it decided in the election controversy.[76] Yet the Court did intervene.

Two years later, the Court was faced with another election dispute. The Democratic candidate for the U.S. Senate from New Jersey had dropped out of the race a month before the election, and the Democrats sought to replace his name on the ballot with that of another candidate. Interpreting an ambiguous state law, the New Jersey Supreme Court, like the Florida Supreme Court in 2000, ruled in favor of the Democrats. The state Republican Party asked the U.S. Supreme Court to intervene. The Court denied a stay of the New Jersey decision, thereby turning the case away.[77]

The election cases of 2000 and 2002 were unusual, but they are examples of litigation that can pose problems for the Court. Sometimes, as in these cases, accepting a case might embroil the Court in a partisan dispute. More frequently, a legal issue involves so much controversy that a decision on either side would produce considerable unhappiness.

Quite often, as in the Florida cases in 2000, at least four justices are willing to face those problems; after all, the Court regularly addresses issues as controversial as the legality of abortion and religious observances in public schools. But sometimes the justices pass up cases that might embroil the Court in controversy, and the goal of avoiding controversy can play a part in the rejection. This may have been true of the New Jersey case in 2002, especially because the Court's intervention in the 2000 presidential election had been criticized so heavily.[78]

A good example is the Court's refusal to rule on whether it was constitutional for the United States to participate in the war in Vietnam without a declaration of war. Few issues brought to the Court have been so important, but the Court refused to hear the cases that raised this question between 1967 and 1972. Undoubtedly, some justices wanted to avoid injecting the Court into the most important and most disputed issue of national policy.

Occasionally, it is a specific case rather than an issue that seems problematical. In 1961 members of the Court had resolved that they would establish the right of indigents to a free attorney in felony cases. Then, with the assistance of their law clerks, the justices searched for a case with the appropriate facts to establish that principle. They rejected a large number of cases before accepting Clarence Gideon's petition. One attractive feature of his case was that he had been convicted of the relatively minor felony of breaking and entering a poolroom with intent to commit a misdemeanor. A reversal of Gideon's conviction would provoke less public wrath than the reversal of a conviction for a violent offense.[79]

Often the Court's refusal to address a difficult issue is only temporary. It may accept a case later, after the issue has been allowed to "percolate" in the lower courts. If an issue recurs often enough and has considerable importance, the justices may have little choice but to address it at some point.

Summary. When Supreme Court justices vote on petitions for hearings by the Court, their choices reflect their goals and perspectives. Each justice acts on a complex set of considerations. Inevitably, justices with different priorities and perspectives respond differently to petitions. Some give a higher priority to resolving conflicts among lower courts than others. They assess the importance of cases in various ways. And they act on quite different sets of policy preferences.

It follows that the Court's selection of cases to decide fully, like everything else it does, is affected by its membership at any given time. Most cases are unlikely to be accepted no matter who is on the Court. But the composition of the cases the Supreme Court actually accepts in a term strongly reflects the identities of the justices who serve during that term.

Caseload Growth and the Court's Response

The 7,924 cases that litigants brought to the Supreme Court during the 2001 term constituted a record number. That record symbolizes the huge increase in the number of filings in the past several decades. The Court had never received even two thousand cases in a term until 1961, and 1979 was the first term in which it received as many as four thousand. The growth in the Court's caseload over the years can be seen in the "total petitions" line in Figure 3-1.

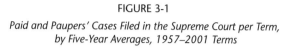

FIGURE 3-1

*Paid and Paupers' Cases Filed in the Supreme Court per Term,
by Five-Year Averages, 1957–2001 Terms*

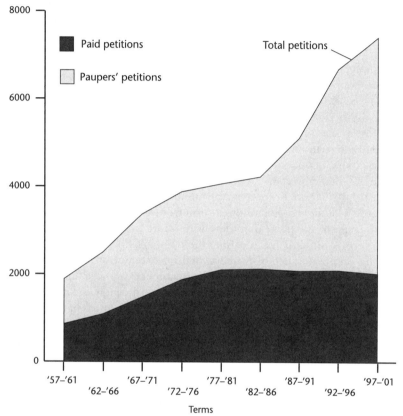

Sources: Gerhard Casper and Richard A. Posner, *The Workload of the Supreme Court* (Chicago: American Bar Foundation, 1976), 34; "Statistical Recap of Supreme Court's Workload During Last Three Terms," *United States Law Week,* various years.

The long-term growth in caseload reflects two quite different processes in two different periods. The first was a general growth that culminated in the 1960s. In part, this growth reflected broad developments in American society: a larger population, an apparent increase in "rights consciousness" that led people to bring more legal claims, and the development of interest groups that assist litigants in carrying cases through the courts.

Meanwhile, massive growth in the activities of the federal government produced new laws and legal questions.

The Court contributed to this trend by allowing indigent litigants to file paupers' petitions without meeting all the ordinary requirements for filing cases. In addition, the Court showed considerable sympathy for claims that government actions violated civil liberties. This sympathy encouraged those who felt their rights had been violated, whether they were criminal defendants or members of racial minority groups, to bring cases to the Court.

The caseload grew slowly in the 1970s and early 1980s, but since then a second period of rapid growth has taken place: the 7,924 cases filed in 2001 represented an 87 percent increase over the average of 4,227 in the 1982–1986 terms. As Figure 3-1 shows, this new rise in cases is entirely in the paupers' petitions. The numbers of paid petitions per term have remained remarkably stable at between 1,800 and 2,200 in all but two years since the 1975 term. In contrast, the numbers of paupers' petitions, which hovered around two thousand per term from the early 1970s to the mid-1980s, grew to the point that there were more than six thousand in the 2001 term—more than three times the number of paid petitions.

The preponderance of paupers' petitions come from prisoners, and the number of inmates who were serving sentences of more than one year in prison tripled between 1984 and 2001. Not surprisingly, the numbers of challenges to convictions by prisoners in the federal courts have grown a great deal during the same period.[80] This trend accounts for most if not all of the increase in paupers' cases. Indeed, this growth has occurred even though other factors that affect criminal petitions have worked in the opposite direction. The Court has become much less favorable to the claims brought by criminal defendants since the 1960s, and more recently both Congress and the Court have limited the use of habeas corpus actions to challenge criminal convictions.

After the growth that culminated in the 1960s, observers of the Court and the justices themselves argued that the larger number of cases had created problems for the Court and for federal law. For the Court, the perceived problem was that the justices' ability to do their work well was compromised by the increased volume of work. For federal law, the concern was that the Court by necessity was accepting a smaller proportion of petitions as their numbers grew, so that important issues were going unresolved.

Caseload growth has been a recurring feature of the Court's history, and in earlier eras Congress gave the Court relief from its burdens by increasing its power to reject cases. The Court of Appeals Act of 1891 created a new set of intermediate appellate courts and gave the Court discretionary jurisdiction over a large minority of cases for the first time. The

Judiciary Act of 1925 expanded that discretionary jurisdiction by requiring that most cases come to the Court as requests for writs of certiorari, which the Court could reject without reaching any decision on the merits, rather than as appeals, which the Court could not. The 1925 statute changed the Court as an institution by giving it more freedom to determine the scope of its activity, the kinds of issues it would address, and its role as a policymaker.

In the 1970s and 1980s, there were several proposals to create a new court between the courts of appeals and the Supreme Court as a way to address the problems resulting from caseload growth. Depending on the proposal, this new court would help the Supreme Court to screen petitions for hearings or it would actually decide some cases in place of the Court. Although some justices favored these proposals, the support for them on the Court and elsewhere in government was insufficient for Congress to make such a major change in the structure of the judicial branch.

Beginning in the late 1980s, the Court acted on its own to make an unofficial but major change. After William Rehnquist became chief justice in 1986, the Court began to accept fewer cases. Between the mid-1980s and the late 1990s, the number of decisions with full, signed opinions dropped from 140 per term to 80. Since then the Court has maintained these lower caseloads.

If the Court of the 1970s suffered from a workload problem, that problem apparently has been solved. Because the number of paid petitions for hearings has not risen in the past thirty years, the justices have had ample time to adjust to that number. The continuing growth in paupers' petitions has little impact on the justices, as so few are considered seriously. Meanwhile, the work involved in reaching decisions on the merits has been cut essentially in half in the Rehnquist Court.

If the Court of the 1970s was failing to resolve important issues in federal law, its acceptance of fewer cases today is likely to aggravate that problem. As long ago as 1987, Chief Justice Rehnquist said that the Court was failing to hear some cases involving important legal questions that it would have heard thirty years earlier.[81] If his perception was accurate then, it would seem to be even more accurate when the Court is deciding only half as many cases. Some justices and commentators disagree. In 2003 Justice Kennedy said that the number of cases heard by the Court "frankly, is too low" but added that the Court was deciding the cases that merited its review.[82] Still, the Court almost surely bypasses more significant legal questions today than it did two decades ago.

In any event, the difficulty of gaining a hearing in the Supreme Court has become greater than before. In its 1985 term, the Court accepted about one in twelve of the paid petitions filed with it; in the 2001 term that rate dropped to one in twenty-three. For paupers' petitions the decline was even more precipitous, from an already low 1 in 108 in 1985 to a spectacularly low 1 in 1,022 in 2001.[83] As one disgruntled lawyer said when the Court rejected a seemingly promising case in 1998, "I don't think I'd ever advise anyone to file a pauper case again."[84]

Conclusion

A central theme of this chapter is the Supreme Court's ability to set its own agenda. Congress and litigants play an important part in shaping that agenda, but the Court largely controls what cases it hears. From the wide variety of legal and policy questions brought to the Court, the justices can choose the few that they will address fully. They can also choose which issues in a case they will decide. And the Court affects the choices of lawyers and interest groups through its opinions by suggesting the kinds of legal claims that it will view favorably in future cases.

The Court has been criticized for the ways it uses its agenda-setting powers, but the justices employ these powers rather well to serve their purposes. They accept and reject cases on the basis of individual and collective goals such as avoiding troublesome issues, resolving legal conflicts, and establishing policies that the justices favor. The justices' selection of cases for full decisions helps them shape the Court's role as a policymaker. They also use that process to limit their workloads.

After the Court selects the cases to be decided, it then makes the decisions. In the next chapter, I examine the process by which the Court makes its decisions.

NOTES

1. This summary of the distribution of litigants across categories is based in part on Gregory A. Caldeira and John R. Wright, "Parties, Direct Representatives, and Agenda-Setting in the Supreme Court" (Paper presented at the annual meeting of the Midwest Political Science Association, Chicago, April 1989).
2. The description of the *Moran* case is based on court briefs and opinions and on Judy Peres, "HMO Arbitration Case Heads to Top Court," *Chicago Tribune,* January 13, 2002, sec. 1, p. 10.
3. The description of the *Brown* case is based on court briefs and opinions and on press reports, including Tony Mauro, "Escrow Fight: Is it Principle or Politics?" *Legal Times,* December 2, 2002, 1, 8.
4. Marcia Coyle, "'Spiritual' Journey From Okla. to the High Court," *National Law Journal,* December 3, 2001, A6. The case was *Owasso Independent School District v. Falvo* (2002).
5. This discussion is based in part on Kevin T. McGuire, *The Supreme Court Bar: Legal Elites in the Washington Community* (Charlottesville: University Press of Virginia, 1993).

6. Christine Hogan, "And May It Please the Court? A North Dakota Lawyer Reflects on a Supreme Experience," *For the Defense* 42 (October 2000): 9.
7. "Recognition of Service of Deputy Solicitor General Wallace," 154 L. Ed. 2d ii (2002).
8. See Kevin T. McGuire, "Lobbyists, Revolving Doors, and the U.S. Supreme Court" (Paper presented at the annual meeting of the Midwest Political Science Association, Chicago, April 23–25, 1998).
9. Marcia Coyle, "'Brief Writer's' Triumph," *National Law Journal,* December 23–December 30, 2002, A10. The case was *Atkins v. Virginia* (2002).
10. Kevin T. McGuire, "The Supreme Court Bar and Institutional Relationships," in *The Supreme Court in American Politics: New Institutionalist Interpretations,* ed. Howard Gillman and Cornell Clayton (Lawrence: University Press of Kansas, 1999), 115–132.
11. Quoted in Barbara A. Perry, *The Priestly Tribe: The Supreme Court's Image in the American Mind* (Westport, Conn.: Praeger, 1999), 109. The case was *Shalala v. Whitecotton* (1995).
12. Kevin T. McGuire, "Repeat Players in the Supreme Court: The Role of Experienced Lawyers in Litigation Success," *Journal of Politics* 57 (February 1995): 187–196.
13. Marcia Coyle, "High Court Bar's 'Inner Circle,'" *National Law Journal,* March 3, 1997, A16.
14. Joan Biskupic, "Lawyers Emerge as Supreme Court Specialists," *USA Today,* May 16, 2003, 6A.
15. Marcia Coyle, "Lawyer Wrestles with High Court over Low Fees," *National Law Journal,* October 14, 2002, A7. The case was *Bell v. Cone* (2002).
16. *In the Matter of Clinton* (2001).
17. *In the Matter of Disbarment of Moore* (2000). The quotations are from the petitions for certiorari in *Brown v. New York City Police Department* (2000) and *Spencer v. New York City Transit Authority* (2000). This episode is discussed by Tony Mauro in "Free Speech at the Bar," *Legal Times,* June 26, 2000, 10.
18. The discussion of this case is based in part on information at the ACLU's website, *www.aclu.org.*
19. Figures on amicus briefs in the 2001 term were compiled from docket sheets on the Supreme Court Web site at *www.supremecourtus.gov.*
20. The discussion in this paragraph is based in part on Marcia Coyle, "Court Hears Many Voices in One Case," *National Law Journal,* May 1, 2000, A1, A12, A13.
21. See Andrew Jay Koshner, *Solving the Puzzle of Interest Group Litigation* (Westport, Conn.: Greenwood Press, 1998).
22. The pre-2001 figures are from Joseph D. Kearney and Thomas W. Merrill, "The Influence of Amicus Curiae Briefs on the Supreme Court," *University of Pennsylvania Law Review* 148 (January 2000): 754 n.26.
23. *Grutter v. Bollinger* (2003).
24. Kearney and Merrill, "Influence of Amicus Curiae Briefs," 821–824.
25. This paragraph is based in part on Stephen L. Wasby, *Race Relations Litigation in an Age of Complexity* (Charlottesville: University Press of Virginia, 1995), esp. 61–64.
26. See Samuel Walker, *In Defense of American Liberties: A History of the ACLU,* 2d ed. (Carbondale: Southern Illinois University Press, 1999).

27. *Grutter v. Bollinger* (2003); *Gratz v. Bollinger* (2003). See Shira Kantor, "Conservative Crusaders Target Affirmative Action in Court," *Chicago Tribune,* January 19, 2003, sec. 1, p. 10.
28. Steven P. Brown, *Trumping Religion: The New Christian Right, the Free Speech Clause, and the Courts* (Tuscaloosa: University of Alabama Press, 2002).
29. James H. Andrews, "Religious Right Fights for Rights," *Christian Science Monitor,* February 7, 1994, 14; Tim Stafford, "Move Over ACLU," *Christianity Today,* October 25, 1993, 20–24.
30. The case was *Good News Club v. Milford Central School* (2001). The case is discussed in Marcia Coyle, "Faith-Based Journey," *National Law Journal,* March 26, 2001, A18.
31. See Wasby, *Race Relations Litigation in an Age of Complexity.*
32. Charles R. Epp, *The Rights Revolution: Lawyers, Activists, and Supreme Courts in Comparative Perspective* (Chicago: University of Chicago Press, 1998), 44–70.
33. Data on the 2001 term discussed here and later in this section were provided by the Office of the Solicitor General.
34. This discussion is based in part on Richard L. Pacelle Jr., *Between Law and Politics: The Solicitor General and the Structuring of Civil Rights, Gender, and Reproductive Rights Litigation* (College Station: Texas A & M University Press, 2003).
35. Ibid.
36. Ibid., 202. See Stephen S. Meinhold and Steven A. Shull, "Policy Congruence Between the President and the Solicitor General," *Political Research Quarterly* 51 (June 1998): 527–537.
37. Brief for the United States in Opposition to Certiorari, *Haney v. United States* (2002). See Tony Mauro, "Behind the U.S. Switch on Gun Rights," *National Law Journal,* May 13, 2002, A1, A17.
38. Neil A. Lewis, "President Faults Race Preferences as Admission Tool," *New York Times,* January 16, 2003, A1, A24. The cases were *Grutter v. Bollinger* (2003) and *Gratz v. Bollinger* (2003).
39. The case was *Microsoft Corporation v. United States* (2001).
40. "Statistical Recap of Supreme Court's Workload During Last Three Terms," *United States Law Week*, July 16, 2002, 3080.
41. *Verizon Maryland Inc. v. Public Service Commission* (2001, 2002).
42. "Statistical Recap of Supreme Court's Workload."
43. On per curiam opinions in general, see Stephen L. Wasby, Steven Peterson, James Schubert, and Glendon Schubert, "The Per Curiam Opinion: Its Nature and Functions," *Judicature* 76 (June–July 1992): 29–38.
44. Dahlia Lithwick, "Little Court of Horrors," *Slate,* at *slate.msn.com,* October 31, 2001.
45. Nick Anderson, "New Law Hurts Chicago Case in Gun Industry Suit," *Los Angeles Times,* February 27, 2003, A17.
46. This figure is taken from data provided by the Office of the Solicitor General.
47. John Paul Stevens, "Foreword," in Kenneth A. Manaster, *Illinois Justice: The Scandal of 1969 and the Rise of John Paul Stevens* (Chicago: University of Chicago Press, 2001), xi.
48. "Statistical Recap of Supreme Court's Workload."
49. Tony Mauro, "'Pauper' Petitions a Long Shot," *USA Today,* December 23, 1998, 10A.

50. This examination of the discuss list and of the conference are based in part on H. W. Perry Jr., *Deciding to Decide: Agenda Setting in the United States Supreme Court* (Cambridge: Harvard University Press, 1991), 43–51, 85–91.

51. David G. Savage, "'Long Conference' Pared Down," *Los Angeles Times,* September 26, 2001, A28.

52. *Singleton v. Commissioner of Internal Revenue,* 439 U.S. 940, 945–946 (1978).

53. *Foster v. Florida* (2002).

54. This discussion of the clerks' roles is drawn in part from Perry, *Deciding to Decide,* 51–84; Dan T. Coenen, review of Perry, *Deciding to Decide,* in *Constitutional Commentary* 10 (winter 1993): 180–193; and Sean Donahue, "Behind the Pillars of Justice: Remarks on Law Clerks," *The Long Term View* 3 (spring 1995): 79–80.

55. William H. Rehnquist, *The Supreme Court,* new ed. (New York: Alfred A. Knopf, 2001), 233.

56. Tony Mauro, "Ginsburg Plunges into the Cert Pool," *Legal Times,* September 6, 1993, 8.

57. Donahue, "Behind the Pillars of Justice," 80.

58. Rehnquist, *The Supreme Court,* 233.

59. *Alsbrook v. Arkansas* (2000); *Florida v. Dickson* (2000). See Joan Biskupic and Al Kamen, "2 Appeals Involving Disabilities Act Voided," *Washington Post,* March 2, 2000, A10.

60. Charles Lane, "On Second Thought," *Washington Post,* April 11, 2003, A25. The case was *Medical Board of California v. Hason* (2003).

61. Tom Miller, "Breyer Speaks to Bar Convention," *Alaska Bar Rag,* May-June 2001, 10.

62. "Judicial Conference, Second Judicial Circuit of the United States," 178 *Federal Rules Decisions* 210, 282 (1997).

63. This discussion draws from Arthur D. Hellman, "Never the Same River Twice: The Empirics and Epistemology of Intercircuit Conflicts," *University of Pittsburgh Law Review* 63 (fall 2001): 81–157.

64. This figure was calculated from data in the Supreme Court Database, compiled by Harold Spaeth.

65. Thomas Goldstein, "One Plugged, Thousands to Go," *Legal Times,* November 18, 2002, 68.

66. See Arthur D. Hellman, "Light on a Darkling Plain: Intercircuit Conflicts in the Perspective of Time and Experience," in *The Supreme Court Review 1998,* ed. Dennis J. Hutchinson, David A. Strauss, and Geoffrey R. Stone (Chicago: University of Chicago Press, 1999), 247–302.

67. Neil M. Richards, "The Supreme Court Justice and 'Boring' Cases," *The Green Bag* 4 (summer 2001): 402, 406. The quotation is from p. 402.

68. William H. Rehnquist, "Oral Advocacy: A Disappearing Art," *Mercer Law Review* 35 (1984): 1027.

69. *Calderon v. Thompson,* 523 U.S. 538, 569 (1998).

70. "The Supreme Court, 2001 Term," *Harvard Law Review* 116 (November 2002): 460.

71. Gregory A. Caldeira, John R. Wright, and Christopher J. W. Zorn, "Sophisticated Voting and Gate-Keeping in the Supreme Court," *Journal of Law, Economics, and Organization* 15 (October 1999): 549–572.

72. Perry, *Deciding to Decide,* 198–207. The quotation is on p. 200.

73. Caldeira, Wright, and Zorn, "Sophisticated Voting and Gate-Keeping"; Charles M. Cameron, Jeffrey A. Segal, and Donald Songer, "Strategic Au-

diting in a Political Hierarchy: An Informational Model of the Supreme Court's Certiorari Decisions," *American Political Science Review* 94 (March 2000): 101–116; Sara C. Benesh, Saul Brenner, and Harold J. Spaeth, "Aggressive Grants by Affirm-Minded Justices," *American Politics Research* 30 (May 2002): 219–234.

74. These data were provided by the Office of the Solicitor General.
75. Marc Galanter, "Why the 'Haves' Come Out Ahead: Speculations on the Limits of Legal Change," *Law and Society Review* 9 (fall 1974): 97–125.
76. Linda Greenhouse, "Election Case a Test and a Trauma for Justices," *New York Times,* February 20, 2001, A18.
77. *Forrester v. New Jersey Democratic Party* (2002).
78. David G. Savage, "Justices Allow Switch on N.J. Ballot," *Los Angeles Times,* October 8, 2002, A13.
79. Nathan Lewin, "Helping the Court with Its Work," *New Republic,* March 3, 1973, 18. The case was *Gideon v. Wainwright* (1963).
80. Kathleen Maguire and Ann L. Pastore, eds., *Sourcebook of Criminal Justice Statistics 2000,* at *www.albany.edu/sourcebook/,* Tables 5.61, 6.27, accessed November 24, 2002.
81. "Chief Justice Urges National Appeals Court, Repeal of Court's Mandatory Jurisdiction," *The Third Branch,* July 1987, 1, 5.
82. "U.S. Representative Frank Wolf (R-Va) Holds Hearing on FY 2004 Supreme Court Budget Request," FDCH Political Transcripts, April 9, 2003, *accessed at http://web.lexis-nexis.com.* See Tony Mauro, "Money Matters and Mandatory Minimums," *Legal Times,* April 14, 2003, 14.
83. These figures are based on data in "Statistical Recap of Supreme Court's Workload During Last Three Terms," *United States Law Week,* various years.
84. Mauro, "'Pauper' Petitions a Long Shot," 10A.

Chapter 4

Decision Making

The Supreme Court exists to make decisions. The appointment of justices and the Court's selection of cases are important because they shape what the Court does as a decision maker, and its choices as a decision maker give it an impact on the nation and its people. This chapter examines how and why the Court makes its decisions on the merits.

Components of the Court's Decision

A Supreme Court decision on the merits has two components: the immediate outcome for the parties to the case and a statement of general legal rules. In cases that the Court fully considers, it nearly always presents the two components in an opinion. In the great majority of cases, at least five justices subscribe to this opinion, so that it constitutes an authoritative statement by the Court.

The Court's opinions vary in form, but they usually begin by describing the background of the case. The opinion then turns to the legal issues in the case, discussing the opposing views on those issues and indicating the Court's conclusions about the issues. The outcome for the parties is summarized at the end of the opinion.

Except in the few original jurisdiction cases the Court hears, the outcome is expressed in relation to the lower court decision the Court has reviewed. The Court can affirm the lower court decision, leaving undisturbed that court's treatment of the parties. Alternatively, it can modify or reverse the lower court decision. The terms *modify* and *reverse* are imprecise. In general, a reversal overturns the lower court decision altogether or nearly so, and modification is a more limited, partial overturning. The Court may also vacate (make void) the lower court decision, an action whose effect is similar to that of reversal.

When the Court does disturb a lower court decision, it sometimes makes a final judgment. More often, it remands the case to the lower court, sending it back for reconsideration. The Court's opinion provides guidance on how the case should be reconsidered. For example, the opinion in a tax case may say that a court of appeals adopted the wrong interpretation of the federal tax laws and that the court should reexamine the case on the basis of a different interpretation. The Court's opinion in a 2002 case used typical language: "The judgment of the Court of Appeals for the Sixth Circuit is therefore reversed, and the case is remanded for further proceedings consistent with this opinion." [1]

The outcome for the parties in *Bush v. Gore* affected the whole country. In most cases, however, the outcome has little impact beyond the parties themselves. Rather, what makes most decisions consequential is the statement of general legal rules that apply to the nation as a whole. When the Court's opinion resolves the legal issues in a case, it is not just providing guidance to a specific lower court in a specific case. It is also laying down rules that any court must follow in a case to which they apply and that can affect the behavior of people outside of court.

As a result, decisions that directly affect only a few people may have a substantial indirect effect on thousands or even millions of other people. In *Board of Education v. Earls* (2002), the Court ruled against one student's challenge to a school district policy that required drug testing for students who wanted to participate in any extracurricular activities. But this decision established a rule that permits any school district to test all secondary school students who engage in extracurricular activities.

The Court has choices about the general legal rules that it establishes, just as it does about the outcome for the parties. A ruling for one of the parties often could be justified on any of several grounds, and the ground chosen by the Court helps to determine the long-term impact of its decision. If the Court overturns the death sentence for a particular defendant, it might base that decision on an unusual type of error in the defendant's trial. This decision would have a narrow impact. Or the Court could declare that the death penalty is unconstitutional under all circumstances and thereby make a fundamental policy change.

The Decision-Making Process

When the Court accepts a case for a decision on the merits, it initiates the decision-making process for that case. That process varies from case to case, but it typically involves several stages.

Presentation of Cases to the Court

The written briefs that the Court receives when it considers whether to hear a case often touch on the merits of the case. Once a case has been accepted for oral argument and decision, attorneys for the parties submit new briefs that focus on the merits. In the preponderance of cases that reach this stage, interest groups submit amicus curiae briefs stating their own arguments on the merits.

Most of the material in these briefs concerns legal issues. The parties muster evidence to support their interpretations of relevant constitutional provisions and statutes. In their briefs they frequently offer arguments about policy as well, seeking to convince the justices that support for their position constitutes not only good law but good public policy.

Material in the briefs is supplemented by attorneys' presentations in oral argument before the Court. Attorneys for the parties to a case sometimes share their time with the lawyer for an amicus, usually the federal government. In most cases, each side is provided half an hour for its argument. Occasionally, the Court grants more time, and in 2003 the parties in the constitutional challenges to the McCain-Feingold campaign finance law were given a total of four hours for argument.[2] When time expires a red light goes on at the attorneys' lectern. The rule is strictly applied. Once, when the red light went on, an attorney asked, "May I finish my sentence?" "Yes," Chief Justice Rehnquist responded, "assuming it's a short one." [3] An attorney in another case stood up to use the time he had left himself for rebuttal of the opposing attorney's argument. Rehnquist announced, "You have 10 seconds remaining, we'll round down, this case is submitted." Not realizing what had happened, the attorney tried to say something, only to watch the justices leave the courtroom.[4]

Oral argument allows attorneys to supplement and highlight the material in their briefs. More important, it allows the justices to probe issues that concern them by questioning the lawyers. Presentations by lawyers are interrupted with great frequency by questions and comments from members of the Court, even more today than in past eras, and it is the justices who control the flow of argument.

Justices differ in how much they participate in the give-and-take of oral argument. Some justices, such as Antonin Scalia and Ruth Bader Ginsburg, are quite active. At the other end of the spectrum, Clarence Thomas seldom asks a question. One reason, he has said, is that "these people only have 30 minutes. Let them talk a little bit. We're not there to debate with them." [5] But when Thomas intervened in a 2002 argument to speak at length about the evils associated with cross-burning, he changed the whole course of the argument.[6]

Justices ask questions to clarify issues for themselves, but they also use questions to shape their colleagues' perceptions of a case. Justice Stevens has said that "you have a point in mind that you think may not have been brought out . . . but you want to be sure your colleagues don't overlook that so . . . you'll ask a question to bring it out." [7] This use of the argument time makes sense. As Rehnquist points out, this is the only time before the conference discussion of a case "when all of the judges are expected to sit on the bench and concentrate on one particular case." [8]

Justice Scalia stands out for his efforts to control the direction of the argument. "Often," one observer noted, "if an attorney fails to make the argument Scalia favors, the Justice simply intervenes and takes over the argument." [9] Reporter Dahlia Lithwick wrote after one argument that her

choice for best oral advocate *ever* to appear before the U.S. Supreme Court is Associate Justice Antonin Scalia. While Scalia is a distinguished jurist, I'm not sure he always gets the credit he deserves on those days, like today, when he actually finds himself both hearing and arguing a case at the same time.

After describing Scalia as "co-counsel" to one of the lawyers in a case, Lithwick reported that at one point the lawyer "actually begins to look toward Scalia for backup before responding" to a question.[10]

We might expect oral arguments to be exciting and dramatic, and some are. But many are surprisingly dull. Lithwick reported on the first day of the 2002 term that "the deathly boringness of the first case argued today was almost mystically eclipsed by the arcane hypertechnicality of the second one." [11] On occasion, justices fall asleep during argument.

Tentative Decisions

After oral argument the Court discusses each case in one of its conferences later the same week. The conference is a closed session attended only by the justices. The discussion is fairly structured.[12] The chief justice presides and begins by summarizing the case, then states personal views on the case and usually a vote on the decision. The associate justices, starting with the most senior member (in terms of service on the Court, not age) and ending with the most junior, then present their own views and votes. According to Justice Breyer, "No one speaks twice until everyone has spoken once." [13] Speaking by seniority puts junior justices at a disadvantage; as Justice Blackmun said of Justice Ginsburg when she was the most junior member, "By the time she speaks just about everything has been said." [14] Typically, little or no additional discussion follows this presentation of positions. According to Justice Scalia, "To call our discussion of a case a conference is really something of a misnomer, it's much more a statement of the views of each of the nine Justices, after which the totals are added and the case is assigned." [15]

One might expect a more freewheeling discussion of cases, with justices speaking at length and arguing back and forth. But the Court's workload creates time pressures that preclude extended discussions. Just as important, the justices usually bring to the conference fixed views on the cases. They have already read the written materials and listened to oral argument, and often they have discussed the case with their law clerks. In addition, their views on cases are influenced by their own, frequently strong, attitudes about policy. As a result, Chief Justice Rehnquist reported, "it is very much the exception" for justices' minds to be changed in conference. In his view, extended discussion ordinarily would have little impact on the justices' positions.[16]

After each two-week sitting, the writing of the Court's opinion in each case is assigned to a justice. If the chief justice voted with the majority, the chief assigns the opinion. In other cases, the most senior justice in the majority makes the assignment. Because so many conference votes are lopsided, the chief justice is usually among the majority. If the Court is divided, the senior justice in the minority assigns the primary dissenting opinion.

Reaching Final Decisions

The justice who was assigned the Court's opinion writes an initial draft, guided by the views expressed in conference. The justice's clerks may do much of the drafting. Once this opinion is completed and circulated, justices in the original majority usually sign on to it.[17] Sometimes, however, they hold back, either because they have developed doubts about their original vote or because they disagree with some of the language in the draft opinion. Members of the original minority also read the draft opinion for the Court. Some might decide to sign on to the opinion because their view of the case has changed, or they might see a possibility of signing on if the opinion is modified.

Justices who do not immediately sign on often let the assigned justice know about the reasons for their doubts, indicating that they would be willing to sign on if certain changes are made. Justices who voted with the majority are especially likely to ask for changes. Their memos initiate a process of explicit or implicit negotiation in which the assigned justice tries to gain the support of as many colleagues as possible. At the least, that justice wants to maintain the original majority for the outcome supported by the opinion and to win a majority for the language of the opinion, so that it becomes the official statement of the Court. As Justice Blackmun put it, "Sometimes one says what he'd prefer not to say in order to get that fifth vote." [18]

In this effort, the justice who was assigned the Court's opinion often competes with other justices who write alternative opinions supporting the opposite outcome or arguing for the same outcome with a different rationale. Most of the time, assigned justices succeed in winning a majority for their opinions, although sometimes with very substantial alterations. More often than not, however, they fail to win the unanimous support of their colleagues. Table 4-1, which lists several characteristics of the

TABLE 4-1
Selected Characteristics of Supreme Court Decisions, 2001 Term

Characteristic	Number	Percentage
Number of decisions	80	—
Vote for Court's decision[a]		
Unanimous	32	40
Nonunanimous	48	60
Support for Court's opinion		
Unanimous for whole opinion	22	28
Unanimous for part of opinion	5	6
Majority but not unanimous	49	61
Majority for only part of opinion	2	3
No majority for opinion	2	3
Cases with		
Dissenting opinions[b]	48	60
Concurring opinions[c]	30	38
Total number of		
Dissenting opinions	64	—
Concurring opinions	46	—

Note: The decisions included are decisions on the merits that are listed in the front section of *Supreme Court Reports, Lawyer's Edition.*

a. "Decision" refers to outcome for the parties. Partial dissents are not counted as votes for the decision.

b. Opinions labeled "concurring and dissenting" are treated as dissenting opinions.

c. Some concurring opinions are in full agreement with the Court's opinion.

Court's decisions in the 2001 term, shows that such unanimity was achieved only 28 percent of the time.

Occasionally, no opinion gains the support of a majority. Table 4-1 shows that this occurred twice in the 2001 term, and in two other cases no opinion had majority support in its entirety. Without a majority opinion, there is no authoritative statement of the Court's position on the legal issues in the case. The opinion on the winning side with the greatest support—the "plurality opinion"—may, however, specify the points for which majority support exists.

Concurring and Dissenting Opinions

In most cases, an opinion gains a majority but lacks unanimous support. Disagreement with the majority opinion can take two forms. First, a justice may cast a dissenting vote, which expresses disagreement with the result reached by the Court as it affects the parties to a case. If a criminal conviction is reversed, for example, a justice who believes it should have been affirmed will dissent. Second, a justice may concur with the Court's decision, agreeing with the result in the specific case but differing with the rationale expressed in the Court's opinion. Both kinds of disagreement are common. Dissenting votes are especially common, appearing in a majority of decisions.

A justice who disagrees with the majority opinion generally writes or joins in a dissenting or concurring opinion. Because they are individual expressions rather than statements for the Court, both types of opinions can vary a great deal in form and tone. For the same reason, they usually reveal more about the author's views, and often express those views in more colorful language, than do majority opinions.

When a justice writes a dissenting opinion after conference, one aim often is to persuade enough colleagues to change their positions that a minority becomes a majority. After the Court reaches its final decision, this aim is no longer relevant, but issuing a dissenting opinion can serve several purposes.

For one thing, dissenting opinions give justices who disagree with the result in a case the satisfaction of expressing unhappiness with that result and justifying their disagreement. Justice Scalia has said that the right to dissent "makes the practice of one's profession as a judge more satisfying." [19]

Dissenting opinions sometimes have more concrete purposes as well. Through their arguments, dissenters may try to set the stage for a later Court to adopt their view. This may be one reason why the majority opinion sometimes responds to the arguments made by a dissenter. In the short term, a dissenting opinion may be intended to subvert the Court's decision by pointing out how lower courts can interpret it narrowly or by urging Congress to overturn the Court's reading of a statute.

When more than one justice dissents, the dissenters usually join in a single opinion—most likely the opinion originally assigned by the senior dissenting justice. But often there are multiple dissenting opinions, each expressing its own view although sometimes indicating agreement with another opinion.

One type of concurring opinion disagrees with the majority opinion, taking the position expressed by Harry Blackmun in one case: "I concur in the result the Court reaches in this case, but I cannot follow the route the Court takes to reach that result." [20] Sometimes this disagreement on doctrine is virtually total. Sometimes it is more limited—at the extreme, refusing only to accept a potentially significant footnote.

Another type of concurring opinion is written by justices who join the majority opinion, indicating that they agree with both the outcome for the litigants and the legal rules that the Court establishes. Under those circumstances, why would justices write separate opinions? Most often, they do so to influence reactions to the Court's decisions by interpreting the majority opinion for lower courts and other audiences. Occasionally, a concurring opinion is aimed at refuting a dissenting opinion. One example was Justice O'Connor's concurrence in *Zelman v. Simmons-Harris* (2002), in which the Court upheld the use of school vouchers to pay tuition for religious schools; O'Connor devoted one section to her disagreement with Justice Souter's dissent.

Announcing the Decision

The decision-making process for a case ends when all the opinions have been put in final form and all justices have determined which opinions they will join. The decision is then announced in open court.

Typically, the justice who wrote the majority opinion reads a portion of the opinion. Occasionally, the authors of dissenting opinions also read their opinions, and sometimes their unhappiness with the outcome is clearly expressed. Justice Scalia responded to the Court's decision in *Atkins v. Virginia,* a 2002 decision that limited use of the death penalty, by describing the decision as a "raw assumption of power." [21]

The length of time required for a case to go through all the stages from filing in the Court to the announcement of a decision can vary a good deal. The cases that the Court decided after full consideration in June 2002 were filed as early as December 2000 and as late as November 2001.

After the Court decides a case—or declines to hear it—the losing party may petition for a rehearing. Such petitions are rarely granted.

Influences on Decisions: Introduction

Perhaps the most important thing to understand about the Supreme Court is why the Court reaches the decisions that it hands down. Cases present the justices with choices: which party to support, what rules of law to establish. How can these choices be explained?

This question is very difficult to answer. Like policymakers elsewhere in government, Supreme Court justices act on the basis of several intermixed considerations. It is not surprising that people who study the Court offer quite different explanations for the Court's decisions.

The rest of this chapter is devoted to this question. No conclusive answer is possible, but some insight into the bases for the Court's decisions can be gained by looking at four broad forces that shape those decisions: the state of the legal rules the Court interprets, the justices' personal values, interaction among the justices, and the Court's political and social environment. The sections that follow consider each of these forces.

The State of the Law

Every case requires the Supreme Court to interpret the law, usually in the form of constitutional provisions or federal statutes. In this sense a justice's job is very different from that of a legislator: justices interpret existing law rather than write new law. For this reason, the state of the existing law is a good starting point for explanation of the Court's decisions.

The Law's Significance in Decisions

To what extent does the state of the law explain the Court's decisions? One possible position is that the law is the *only* explanation of what the Court does, that its decisions simply reflect the provisions of law it is called upon to interpret. In 1999 Justice Thomas told a group, "I just follow the law, so it doesn't make any difference what my opinions are." [22] But that position does not accord with two realities about the Court.

One reality is what might be called the legal ambiguity of the cases the Supreme Court decides. The Court chooses to hear cases that almost always involve situations in which the proper interpretation of the Constitution or a federal statute is uncertain. A justice who intended only to interpret the law properly would still have to make choices.

A second reality is that justices care about more than the law. In particular, they often hold strong preferences about the policy issues involved in cases. Understandably, they would be happier if their position in a case was consistent with their policy preferences than if their position conflicted with their conception of good policy.

Justices may act consciously to make good policy. Justice Breyer said, "If you see the result is going to make people's lives worse, you'd better go back and rethink it. The law is supposed to fit together in a way that makes the human life of people a little bit better." [23] The legal ambiguity of cases allows such justices to provide legal justification for the decisions they prefer. Even if justices consciously seek only to interpret the law properly, their "rooting interests" tend to steer them toward the interpretation that is most consistent with their policy preferences. Thus, it is understandable that in most decisions the justices disagree about the outcome for the litigants, the appropriate legal rules, or both. In those decisions the ambiguity of the law causes justices with different preferences to reach different conclusions.

This does not mean that the state of the law is irrelevant to the justices. Even if decisions on either side could be justified under the law, the law may weigh more heavily on one side than the other. If the justices care about making good law, they would be drawn toward the side that seems to have a stronger legal argument.

And there is excellent reason to think that justices do care about making good law. They have been trained in a tradition that emphasizes the law as a basis for judicial decisions. They are evaluated informally by a peer group of judges and legal scholars who care about their ability to reach well-founded interpretations of the law. Perhaps most important, they work in the language of the law. The arguments they receive in written briefs and oral arguments are primarily about the law. The same is true of arguments they make to each other in draft opinions and memoranda.[24]

It is impossible to specify just how much the state of the law affects justices, and scholars have heated disagreements about this issue.[25] But the law does exert an influence. This influence is clearest when justices take positions that seem to conflict with their conceptions of good policy. Sometimes the justices in the majority are sufficiently unhappy with their interpretation of a statute that they ask Congress to consider rewriting the statute to override their decision—to establish a policy that they feel powerless to adopt themselves because of their reading of the law.[26]

Means of Interpretation

Judges can use a complex array of techniques to interpret provisions of law, but most of these techniques fit into a few broad approaches. Discussion of those approaches provides a way to consider the role of law in the Court's decisions.

"Plain Meaning."   In the most basic approach, judges analyze the literal meaning of the words in the law. Nearly everyone agrees that interpretation of a legal provision should begin with a search for plain meaning, and many possible interpretations of the law are ruled out because they are inconsistent with plain meaning. For example, the Twenty-second Amendment to the Constitution states, "No person shall be elected to the office of the President more than twice." It is difficult to imagine how the Supreme Court could justify a ruling that a twice-elected person can be elected to a third term.

The Court seldom faces such easy issues, however. Most of the Court's decisions involve ambiguous provisions such as the Fourteenth Amendment's protection of "due process of law," which has no plain meaning. And even a provision that may seem to have a plain meaning can be interpreted in multiple ways. The First Amendment states that "Congress shall make no law . . . abridging the freedom of speech," but justices and commentators have disagreed about the meaning of "freedom of speech" and even of "speech." As legal scholar Cass Sunstein wrote, "On so many of the central constitutional questions . . . the Constitution's words tell us much less than we need to know."[27]

Federal statutes typically are less vague, but even they often leave large gaps. One commentator complained that Congress "cannot or will not be specific." [28] And even specific language can be quite ambiguous. One statute requires at least five years' imprisonment for someone who "during and in relation to any crime of violence or drug trafficking crime . . . uses or carries a firearm." [29] But the meaning of both "uses" and "carries" can be uncertain. Has someone used a gun by offering to trade it for cocaine? Does keeping a gun in the trunk of a car constitute using or carrying the gun? The Court has wrestled with these and other questions involving the language of this statute, and more often than not the justices have disagreed about the answers.[30]

Intent of Framers or Legislators. When the plain meaning of a legal provision is unclear, justices can seek to ascertain the intentions of those who wrote the provision. Evidence concerning legislative intent can be found in congressional committee reports and floor debates, which constitute what is called the "legislative history" of a statute or a constitutional amendment. For provisions of the original Constitution, similar evidence is found in records of the Constitutional Convention of 1787.

Sometimes the intent of Congress or the Framers of the Constitution is fairly clear. Frequently, however, it is not. The body that adopted a provision may not have spoken on an issue; the members of Congress who wrote the broad language of the Fourteenth Amendment could hardly indicate their intent concerning all the issues that have arisen under that amendment. And evidence about intent may be contradictory, in part because of conflicting efforts to influence the courts. Some evidence of legislative intent comes from sources such as committee reports that may represent the views of congressional staff more than those of the members.

The use of intent in constitutional interpretation has long been the subject of controversy. Some people argue that the Court should adhere to the intent of the Framers of each provision as closely as possible; others believe it should interpret the Constitution in terms of the current meaning of its language and its underlying values. To a considerable extent this is an ideological debate, with liberals wanting the freedom to adopt broad interpretations of constitutional rights. For example, some conservative justices point to evidence that the writers of the Eighth Amendment did not view capital punishment as "cruel and unusual," while some liberals argue that the Court should interpret the Eighth Amendment in light of changing standards about punishments.

In recent years justices have debated the use of legislative intent in interpreting statutes. The leading opponent is Justice Scalia, who does not refer to legislative history himself and sometimes distances himself from its use by his colleagues. In *Moseley v. V. Secret Catalogue* (2003), for example, he joined the majority opinion except for its discussion of legislative history. Scalia views legislative history as illegitimate; it is the laws, not the intentions of legislators, that govern. Further, he sees it as an uncertain guide to congressional intent, highly susceptible to being used as justification "for decisions arrived at on other grounds." [31]

Scalia has gained some support on the Court, primarily from other conservatives. But other justices—most vocally, Justice Stevens—continue to favor the use of legislative history. In a 2001 dissent, Stevens argued that ignoring evidence of legislative intent "may produce a result that is consistent with a court's own views of how things should be, but it may also defeat the very purpose for which a provision was enacted." [32]

Precedent. The Supreme Court's past decisions, its precedents, provide another guide to decision making. A basic doctrine of the law is *stare decisis* (let the decision stand). Under this doctrine a court is bound to adhere to the rules of law established by courts that stand above it. No court stands above the Supreme Court, but *stare decisis* also includes an expectation that courts will generally adhere to their own precedents.

Technically, a court is expected to follow not everything stated in a relevant precedent but only the rule of law that is necessary for decision in that case—what is called the holding. As Justice Souter said in a 1999 case, "a line of argument unnecessary to the decision of the case remains dictum," [33] and "dictum" has no legal force. In a 2001 decision, the majority opinion said that "we hold that medical necessity is not a defense to manufacturing and distributing marijuana," the activities involved in the case. The Court also suggested that medical necessity would not provide a defense for a user of marijuana and, more broadly, questioned whether the general defense of "necessity" applied to the federal criminal law. The suggestion was almost surely dictum, and the question undoubtedly was dictum.[34]

The rule of adhering to precedent would not eliminate ambiguity in legal interpretation even if the justices followed it strictly. Most cases before the Supreme Court concern issues that are at least marginally different from those decided in past cases, so precedents do not lead directly to a particular outcome. Indeed, justices often "distinguish" a precedent, holding that it does not govern the current case. They may also narrow a precedent without overturning it altogether. Through both methods, the Burger and Rehnquist Courts have limited the reach of major Warren Court decisions on the rights of criminal defendants.

When the Court distinguishes or narrows a precedent, dissenters sometimes complain that it has ignored or implicitly abandoned the precedent. In a 2001 case, Justice Breyer said that the case differed from a precedent that the Court had distinguished only in that "it involves mushrooms rather than fruit." In a 2000 case, Justice Stevens charged that "the Court has effectively overruled" two prior decisions.[35]

The Court explicitly abandons some precedents, and it has done so at an unusually high rate since 1960. Depending on the count, the Court has overturned an average of three or four precedents a year in this period.[36] This record is reflected in the frequency with which litigants ask the Court to overturn a precedent—sixty-seven times in the 1985–1994 terms.[37]

Inevitably, justices' reactions to precedents are affected by their evaluations of those precedents as legal policy. Most of the time, justices continue to reject a precedent that they opposed when it was originally established.[38] In one such instance in 2000, Justice Stevens wrote on behalf of three colleagues, "Despite my respect for *stare decisis,* I am unwilling to accept *Seminole Tribe* as precedent." [39] Moreover, the Court is most likely to overturn precedents after changes in its membership shift its collective point of view.[40] Many of the precedents overturned by the Rehnquist Court had been issued by the more liberal Warren and Burger Courts that preceded it.

All this may suggest that precedents carry no weight. Yet justices have a degree of reluctance—some more than others—to overturn precedents directly. To take one example, Justice Scalia certainly does not regard precedents as sacred, but in a 2001 case he followed a precedent on review of punitive damages awards while reiterating his disagreement with that precedent.[41] The Court as a whole adheres to a good many precedents that no longer accord with the majority view among the justices.

Thus, if *stare decisis* does not control the Court's decisions, it does structure and influence them. The same is true of the law in general: it channels the justices' choices, often in subtle ways, but it also leaves them considerable freedom in making those choices.

Justices' Values

In 1971 President Richard Nixon nominated Assistant Attorney General William Rehnquist to the Supreme Court. Rehnquist had a long record of conservative positions on political and legal issues—views that he had expressed as a Supreme Court law clerk, a participant in Arizona politics, and a member of the Nixon administration. Rehnquist's nomination drew opposition from liberals who expected that his conservative views would be reflected in his votes and opinions on the Court. Rehnquist told the Senate Judiciary Committee, however, that "my fundamental commitment, if I am confirmed, will be to totally disregard my own personal belief." [42]

Yet Rehnquist's record on the Court has confirmed the expectations of his opponents in 1971. For the most part, his votes and opinions have

The Stanford Law School class of 1952. Sandra Day O'Connor (first row), despite finishing near the top of her class, could not get a job as an attorney with a law firm because she was a woman. William Rehnquist is at the far left of the back row.

been strongly conservative, especially on civil liberties issues. His stance on the rights of criminal defendants has basically followed the lines of a memorandum he wrote on the subject in 1969.[43] On a specific issue concerning the use of involuntary confessions in trials, he took the same position as a law clerk in 1952 and as chief justice in 1991.[44]

The Influence of Policy Preferences

Clearly, Rehnquist's "personal belief" has had a good deal of impact on his record as a justice. And the same is true of his colleagues on the Court. There has been less consistency between the pre-Court records of some other justices and their votes and opinions on the Court, but careful observers who attempt to predict the general stance that a nominee will take on the Court have been fairly successful.[45] And when justices express their personal views on policy issues outside the Court, their positions in cases are usually consistent with those views. To take one example, the conservative values that Justice Thomas has expressed in his speeches and writings are reflected in his votes and opinions as a justice.[46]

This should not be surprising. Because the state of the law leaves justices with considerable discretion, their choices must be based largely on other considerations. Because the Court has considerable freedom from external pressures, the most powerful of these other considerations are the justices' policy preferences.

Some scholars argue that the justices' policy preferences are essentially a complete explanation of the Court's decisions.[47] In contrast, I think that the justices' preferences exert their effects in combination with other important forces, such as the political environment—and, for that matter, the law. But policy preferences certainly provide the best explanation for differences in the positions that the nine justices take in the same cases, because no other factor varies so much from one justice to another.

Justices' attitudes on policy issues result from the same influences that shape political attitudes generally. In the case of Justice O'Connor, for example, her family's experiences with federal regulation of their ranch and her own service as a state official undoubtedly help to explain her support for state powers vis à-vis those of the federal government. Similarly, her personal experiences with sex discrimination are reflected in her positions on that issue as a justice.[48] Because justices have different backgrounds and learn different things from those backgrounds, each brings a particular set of attitudes to the Court.

The justices' behavior on the Court could reflect their policy preferences in two different ways. Justices might simply take the positions that best reflect their views of good policy. Or they might act strategically, adjusting their positions to achieve the best results. In chapter 3, I discussed strategy in decisions whether to accept cases: to a degree, justices vote whether to hear cases on the basis of their predictions about how the Court would rule on those cases. In decisions on the merits, strategic justices might write opinions that do not fully reflect their own views to win the support of other justices. Or the Court collectively could modify its position on an issue to reduce the chances that Congress will override the Court's decision and substitute a policy that most justices greatly dislike.

It is not clear to what extent the justices behave strategically and what forms their strategies take.[49] But it appears that strategic considerations seldom move justices very far from the positions they most prefer. For this reason, the impact of justices' policy preferences can be considered initially without taking strategy into account. In the next two sections, I consider strategy aimed at other justices and at the Court's political environment.

The Ideological Dimension

Liberal and Conservative Positions. Justices' preferences, and the votes and opinions that reflect those preferences, may be understood in ideological terms. On most issues that come to the Supreme Court, opposing positions can be labeled as liberal and conservative. The labeling of positions is straightforward on most civil liberties issues: the position more favorable to legal protection for liberties is considered liberal. Some civil liberties issues involve the right to equal treatment by government and private institutions under the Constitution and federal statutes. The liberal position on these issues is more sympathetic toward challenges to inequality than is the conservative position. Similarly, the liberal position gives greater weight to procedural rights, such as those protecting criminal defendants, and substantive rights, such as freedom of expression and privacy. In contrast, the conservative position gives greater weight to values that compete with these rights, such as the capacity to fight crime effectively.

On economic issues, liberal and conservative positions are more difficult to define. But the liberal position is basically more favorable to economic "underdogs" and to government policies that are intended to benefit underdogs. For example, the conservative position is more positive toward businesses in conflicts with labor unions and toward efforts by businesses to limit government regulation of their practices.

Some cases that come before the Supreme Court, such as boundary disputes between two states, do not have obvious liberal and conservative sides, nor do cases in which two civil liberties conflict. On the whole, ideological lines in American society and thus in the Court have become more complicated. Still, most issues that the Court decides do have clearly defined conservative and liberal sides.

Ideology and Decisions. If opposing positions in most cases can be identified as liberal or conservative, the justices' voting patterns can be described in terms of the frequency with which they support the conservative side and the liberal side. Table 4-2 shows the ideological patterns of votes for the justices in the 2000 and 2001 terms. As the table shows, every justice cast a good many votes on both sides. But the justices also differed considerably in their ideological tendencies: Justice Stevens supported the liberal side more than twice as often as his three most conservative colleagues.

As I have suggested, the votes that justices cast and the opinions they write reflect the influence of several different forces. Even though a majority of Justice Souter's votes supported liberal positions, he should not necessarily be labeled a liberal. With a different mix of cases and under different circumstances, Souter might have cast a majority of conservative votes. But because differences in justices' positions reflect primarily differences in their policy preferences, it is appropriate to conclude—at least if these two terms are typical—that Souter is more conservative than

TABLE 4-2
*Percentages of Liberal Votes
Cast by Justices, 2000 and 2001 Terms*

Justice	Liberal votes
Stevens	64.2
Souter	60.2
Ginsburg	60.2
Breyer	57.9
O'Connor	42.6
Kennedy	39.2
Rehnquist	31.3
Thomas	30.7
Scalia	27.3

Source: U.S. Supreme Court Database, compiled by Harold Spaeth, Michigan State University.

Note: Cases are included if they were decided on the merits with full opinions; 168 cases are included. Criteria for classifying votes as liberal or conservative are those used in the database.

Stevens and substantially more liberal than Justice Scalia. Indeed, the relative positions of the justices tend to remain fairly stable from term to term. That stability underlines the importance of policy preferences in shaping the positions that justices take.

It is reasonable to describe the justices in terms of their overall liberalism or conservatism, because there is considerable ideological consistency in their positions across issues. A justice who is strongly conservative on the issue of privacy is also likely to be quite conservative on conflicts between business and labor. In this respect, the justices are similar to other policymakers. This consistency, however, is far from absolute. A justice who takes liberal positions on economic issues may be conservative on civil liberties issues. Some members of the current Court give considerably more support to freedom of expression than they do to the rights of criminal defendants.

Within specific areas of policy, the degree of consistency is somewhat greater. The degree of consistency can be measured by what is called a scalogram. If the nine justices can be ranked from most liberal to most conservative in the same way for all the issues that arise in a category such as criminal cases, the result would be a distinctive pattern of votes on cases in that category. Each time the most conservative justice votes for the liberal position in a case, every other justice should do so as well; each time the second most conservative justice casts a liberal vote, the seven more liberal justices should also do so; and so on. Any deviation from that

FIGURE 4-1
Scalogram of Justices' Votes in Nonunanimous Decisions Arising from Criminal Prosecutions, 2001 Term

Case citation[a]	Justices' votes									Liberal votes
	St	Gi	So	Br	O'C	Ke	Re	Th	Sc	
153-556	+	+	+	+	-	+	-	+	+	7
151-856	+	+	+	+	+	+	+	-	-	7
151-820	+	+	+	+	+	-	+	-	-	6
153-335	+	+	+	+	+	+	-	-	-	6
153-666	+	+	+	+	+	+	-	-	-	6
151-670	+	+	+	+	+	-	-	-	-	5
152-888	+	+	+	+	+	-	-	-	-	5
153-260	+	+	+	+	+	-	-	-	-	5
151-597	+	+	+	+	-	-	-	-	-	4
152-291	+	+	+	+	-	-	-	-	-	4
153-47	+	+	+	+	-	-	-	-	-	4
153-524	+	+	+	-	-	-	-	+	-	4
153-242	+	+	+	-	-	-	-	-	-	3
152-914	+	-	-	-	-	-	-	-	-	1
Total liberal votes	14	13	13	11	7	4	2	2	1	

Note: Cases are those arising from criminal prosecutions, including cases involving the rights of criminal defendants in a prison setting. Liberal votes (favoring defendants) are designated +; conservative votes (opposing defendants) are designated -. The stepped vertical line divides votes into two groups according to conventional rules of scalogram analysis; - signs to the left of the line and + signs to the right of the line may be interpreted as votes inconsistent with the ideological ordering of the justices.

Key: St=Stevens, Gi=Ginsburg, So=Souter, Br=Breyer, O'C=O'Connor, Ke=Kennedy, Re=Rehnquist, Th=Thomas, Sc=Scalia

a. Numbers refer to volumes and pages of citations in United States Supreme Court Reports, Lawyers' Edition.

pattern represents an ideological inconsistency. Scalograms, limited to nonunanimous decisions, lay out the actual pattern of liberal and conservative votes to show how closely they follow this expected pattern.

A scalogram depicting a high level of ideological consistency is presented in Figure 4-1, which shows votes in criminal cases during the Court's 2001 term. The justices varied a good deal in their support for criminal defendants, from Stevens at the liberal end of the spectrum (that is, most supportive of defendants) to Scalia at the conservative end. The

scalogram shows that to a considerable extent the divisions among the justices in individual cases followed the same ideological lines as the overall
rankings of justices. For example, in each of the three cases in which the
Court divided 5–4 in a liberal direction, the dissenters were Kennedy,
Rehnquist, Thomas, and Scalia. There were only a few exceptions to perfect ideological consistency.

The scalogram in Figure 4-1 is not typical. Criminal cases involve unusually sharp ideological divisions, and more substantial deviations from
ideological consistency would be found in other areas. Ideological consistency of the sort that scalograms measure is typically high but well short
of perfect.

The inconsistencies revealed by scalograms result chiefly from the
complexity of justices' attitudes. Justice Thomas might have a view on a
specific issue of criminal procedure that departs from his overall attitude
toward defendants' rights. Sympathies toward particular litigants sometimes come into play as well. In *Bush v. Gore,* conservative justices supported George W. Bush's equal protection claim and their liberal colleagues rejected it, even though the Court's liberals usually are more
favorable toward these claims. The best explanation for this lineup is that
the justices on both sides had strong rooting interests in the outcome of
the presidential election—rooting interests that outweighed their general attitudes toward equal protection.

Patterns of Agreement. Analysis of patterns of agreement among justices
provides another perspective on the Court's ideological divisions. For
each pair of justices who served in the 2000 and 2001 terms, Table 4-3
shows the average percentage of the time that they supported the same
opinion in the two terms. While Figure 4-1 focuses on votes, Table 4-3 focuses on doctrine; justices who voted for the same outcome but who could
not support the same opinion are treated as disagreeing.

The table shows that some pairs of justices agreed with each other
much more often than other pairs. Not surprisingly, the rates of agreement were highest between pairs of justices who are ideologically close to
each other. The four most liberal justices (Stevens, Souter, Ginsburg, and
Breyer) all agreed with each other more than 80 percent of the time, and
the same was true of the three strongest conservatives (Rehnquist, Scalia,
and Thomas). For the same reasons, the lowest rates of agreement were
between justices at opposite ends of the ideological spectrum. The four
most liberal justices each agreed with Thomas and Scalia less than half the
time. The positions of Kennedy and O'Connor in the middle of the Court
highlight their importance in casting "swing votes," that is, votes that determine whether the Court's decision will be liberal or conservative. Their
higher rates of agreement with the justices on their right underscore the

TABLE 4-3

Average Percentage of Cases in Which Pairs of Justices
Supported the Same Opinion, 2000 and 2001 Terms

| Justice | Justice | | | | | | | |
	Br	Gi	So	O'C	Ke	Re	Th	Sc
Stevens	82	81	81	59	57	52	45	41
Breyer		85	82	67	61	57	47	44
Ginsburg			89	65	62	56	47	44
Souter				72	64	57	46	47
O'Connor					76	77	65	67
Kennedy						86	77	76
Rehnquist							81	81
Thomas								86
Scalia								

Sources: "The Supreme Court, 2000 Term," Harvard Law Review 115 (November 2001): 540;
"The Supreme Court, 2001 Term," Harvard Law Review 116 (November 2002): 454.

Note: Numbers are averages, for the two terms, of the percentages of cases in each term in
which a pair of justices agreed on an opinion. Unanimous and nonunanimous cases are included.

Court's recent tendency to reach conservative decisions in cases that divide the justices along ideological lines.

One should be careful not to make too much of the overall patterns of
agreement. The justices do not always line up in expected ways; in *Archer
v. Warner* (2003), for example, Clarence Thomas and John Paul Stevens
joined in dissent from an opinion on which the rest of the justices agreed.
More important, patterns of agreement do not necessarily reflect self-
conscious alliances or blocs of justices. Certainly, the justices are aware of
general patterns of agreement among themselves. And like-minded justices sometimes do work together closely, as Earl Warren and William
Brennan did during the 1960s. But ideological allies do not always form
close working relationships, and those who agree most often in cases do
not necessarily have the closest personal relationships. When alliances do
develop, they are chiefly the result of agreement about judicial issues
rather than the source of that agreement. Shared preferences, not concerted action, best explain the tendency for certain justices to agree on
opinions.

Preferences and Policy Change

The process of policy change in the Supreme Court is difficult to analyze
systematically, because the issues before the Court constantly change. A
decline in the proportion of decisions favorable to labor unions might re-

flect a change in the Court's policies on labor law or simply a change in the kinds of labor cases that the Court decides, and it is not always easy to distinguish between the two possibilities. Still, at times it is clear that the Court's collective position in a policy area or a set of policy areas such as civil liberties has changed.

Such changes can occur for many reasons. But shifts in the preferences of the justices as a group are the primary source of policy change in the Court. These shifts could come from change in the views of people already serving on the Court or from change in the Court's membership. In practice, both are significant.

Changes in Views. Close observers of the Supreme Court often try to predict how the Court will decide a pending case; typically, they do rather well in their predictions. The primary reason is that individual justices tend to take stable positions on the issues that arise in various policy areas, positions that reflect their policy preferences. The views that a justice expressed in past cases about when cars can be searched or when mergers of companies violate the antitrust laws are a good guide to the justice's stance in a future case. In turn, the Court's collective position on such issues generally remains stable so long as its membership remains unchanged.

But as members of the Court, justices are exposed to new influences and confront issues in new forms. As a result, the policy preferences they express in their votes and opinions may shift. Small changes are common, and occasionally more fundamental changes occur.

A justice who serves on the Court for several years is likely to shift positions on some specific issues, usually because of experience with cases that concern those issues. In his opinion in a 2000 case, Justice Souter took the position that a city seeking to prohibit nude dancing establishments must provide evidence of negative "secondary effects" to meet its burden under the First Amendment. "Careful readers," Souter said,

will of course realize that my partial dissent rests on a demand for an evidentiary basis that I failed to make when I concurred in [a 1991 decision]. I should have demanded the evidence then, too, and my mistake calls to mind Justice Jackson's foolproof explanation of a lapse of his own, when he quoted Samuel Johnson, "'Ignorance, sir, ignorance.'" I may not be less ignorant of nude dancing than I was nine years ago, but after many subsequent occasions to think further about the needs of the First Amendment, I have come to believe that a government must toe the mark more carefully than I first insisted. I hope it is enlightenment on my part, and acceptable even if a little late.[50]

Individual issues aside, most justices retain the same basic ideological position throughout their career. A justice who begins as a liberal, such as Thurgood Marshall, generally remains a liberal; the same is usually true of a conservative such as William Rehnquist. When a justice's position shifts relative to that of the Court as a whole, it is usually because new appointments have shifted the Court's ideological center, while the justice has retained the same general views. According to law professor Dennis Hutchinson, John Paul Stevens "has stayed in the center as the court has moved to the right." [51]

Justice Harry Blackmun is one of the few justices whose basic views seemed to shift fundamentally. Blackmun came to the Court in 1970 as a Nixon appointee, and early in his tenure he aligned himself chiefly with the other conservative justices. He and Chief Justice Warren Burger, boyhood friends from Minnesota, were dubbed the "Minnesota Twins." In the 1973 term, Blackmun agreed with Burger on opinions in 84 percent of the decisions, and with liberal William Brennan in only 49 percent.[52] Blackmun gradually moved toward the center of the Court, and from the 1980 term on he usually had higher agreement rates with Brennan than with Burger—in 1985, Burger's last term, 30 percentage points higher. In the last few terms before his 1994 retirement, Blackmun had become one of the two most liberal justices on the Court.

This shift to the Court's left resulted in part from the replacement of liberal colleagues with conservatives, but Blackmun's own positions clearly became more liberal. Although the reasons for this change are uncertain, it appears that his experiences in dealing with cases that came to the Court—particularly *Roe v. Wade*, in which he wrote the Court's opinion—were important. And it also seems that Blackmun wanted to help maintain an ideological balance on the Court as it grew more conservative.[53]

Perhaps more common than individual ideological shifts are changes in the views of the justices as a group on a particular issue. These shifts typically result from developments in American society that shape the views of the justices along with other groups.

One example concerns the legal status of women. The liberal Warren Court gave unprecedented support to the goal of equality under the law, but it did not strike down legal rules that treated women and men differently. In contrast, the more conservative Burger and Rehnquist Courts have handed down a series of decisions promoting legal equality for men and women. Today, even the most conservative justices use a fairly rigorous standard to evaluate laws that treat women and men differently, a standard that might have been unthinkable in the 1960s.[54] The most fundamental cause of this change seems to be the direct and indirect impact of the feminist movement on the Court's agenda and, even more, on justices' views about women's social roles. In any event, this example underlines the potential for significant changes in justices' collective views on policy issues.

Membership Change. Although shifts in the positions of sitting justices can produce major policy changes in the Court, membership change is probably the most important source of policy change in the Court. If Supreme Court policies are largely a product of the justices' preferences, and if those preferences tend to be stable, then change will come most easily through the replacement of one justice with a successor who has a different set of policy preferences.

Change in the Court's membership often alters its positions on specific issues. As discussed earlier, the overturning of a recent precedent usually results from the replacement of justices who helped create that precedent with others who disagree with it. Even when the Court maintains a precedent, a critical shift in membership may ensure that it is extended no further.

More broadly, shifts in the Court's overall ideological position through new appointments typically lead to change in the general content of its policies. The Court's civil liberties policies since the 1950s demonstrate this effect of membership change. Table 4-4 shows the proportions of decisions favorable to parties with civil liberties claims during successive periods in the 1958 to 2001 terms. Because changes in the content of civil liberties cases can make these proportions misleading, the table also shows civil liberties support with an adjustment for the content of cases based on a statistical technique.

The early Warren Court was closely divided between liberals and conservatives; from 1958 until 1961 there was a relatively stable division between a four-member liberal bloc and a moderate to conservative bloc of five. By the standards of the 1920s and 1930s, the Court's decisions were quite liberal, but the table shows that parties with civil liberties claims won only a little more than half their cases between 1958 and 1961.

President Kennedy's 1962 appointments created a liberal majority; a law clerk during the 1962 term referred to it as "a turning point in the modern history of the Supreme Court."[55] The Johnson appointments later in the decade maintained that majority. The years from 1962 to 1968 were probably the most liberal in the Court's history. The Court established strikingly liberal positions in a variety of policy areas, and the proportion of pro–civil liberties decisions increased substantially.

Between 1969 and 1992, every appointment to the Court was made by a Republican president, and all but Ford sought to use their appointments to make the Court more conservative. Thus, the Court gained a distinctly more conservative set of justices. The impact of these membership changes on the Court's civil liberties policies was somewhat ambiguous. The Court adhered to some policies of the Warren Court and even took new liberal directions on issues such as women's rights. Yet, on the whole,

TABLE 4-4
Proportions of Supreme Court Decisions Favoring Parties with Civil Liberties Claims and Changes in Court Membership, 1958–2001 Terms

Terms	Proportions of pro–civil liberties decisions		New justices (appointing presidents) and justices leaving the Court
	Actual	*Adjusted*[a]	
1958–1961	60.1	60.1	—
1962–1968	75.3	77.6	*New:* White, Goldberg (Kennedy); Fortas, Marshall (Johnson). *Leaving:* Whittaker, Frankfurter, Goldberg, Clark.
1969–1974	48.8	55.9	*New:* Burger, Blackmun, Powell, Rehnquist (Nixon). *Leaving:* Warren, Fortas, Black, Harlan.
1975–1980	42.0	51.6	*New:* Stevens (Ford). *Leaving:* Douglas.
1981–1985	40.0	51.5	*New:* O'Connor (Reagan). *Leaving:* Stewart.
1986–1989	42.4	46.1	*New:* Scalia, Kennedy (Reagan). *Leaving:* Burger, Powell.
1990–1992	42.7	35.4	*New:* Souter, Thomas (Bush). *Leaving:* Brennan, Marshall.
1993–2001	44.7	40.9	*New:* Ginsburg, Breyer (Clinton). *Leaving:* White, Blackmun.

Source: Based on data in U.S. Supreme Court Database, compiled by Harold Spaeth of Michigan State University.

Note: Percentages for the same periods differ from those in the 7th edition of this book because civil liberties cases are defined somewhat differently in the sources used in the two editions.

a. Adjusted using a statistical technique to control for changes in the content of civil liberties cases decided by the Court. The technique is described in Lawrence Baum, "Measuring Policy Change in the U.S. Supreme Court," *American Political Science Review* 82 (September 1988): 905–912.

the Burger Court was distinctly less supportive of civil liberties than was the Court of the 1960s, and the early Rehnquist Court was even less supportive than the Burger Court.

Table 4-4 shows the impact of these Republican appointments on the proportion of decisions favorable to civil liberties. The Nixon appointments reduced that proportion from about three-quarters to about one-half. The replacement of the highly liberal William Douglas with the moderately liberal John Paul Stevens further reduced the level of support for civil liberties. If the content of cases is taken into account, another major decline in support occurred after David Souter and Clarence Thomas replaced the Court's two remaining strong liberals in the early 1990s.

Ruth Bader Ginsburg and Steven Breyer were the first appointees of a Democratic president since 1967, but they have had little impact on the Court's ideological balance. They are best characterized as moderate liberals, and taken together they are not very different from the two justices they succeeded. The proportion of pro–civil liberties decisions has increased only slightly since they joined the Court, and the Court's doctrinal positions continue to be conservative in most respects.

Thus, the Court continues to reflect the impact of the Republican appointments from the late 1960s through the early 1990s. These appointments have not had the revolutionary effects that might have been expected, a fact that cautions against exaggerating the impact of membership change. The change in policies that has occurred is still noteworthy, however, and strongly suggests that appointments are the most important mechanism by which the Court's policies can be altered.

Role Values

Policy preferences are not the only values that can affect the Court's decisions. Justices may also be influenced by their role values, their views about what constitutes appropriate behavior for the Supreme Court and its members. In any body, whether it is a court or a legislature, members' conceptions of how they should carry out their jobs structure what they do and affect their policy decisions.

A variety of role values can shape the justices' behavior. Their views about the desirability of unanimous decisions help determine the extent of dissent in the Court's decisions. Their judgments about the legitimacy of "lobbying" colleagues on decisions may determine the outcomes of some cases. But the most important role values concern the considerations that justices take into account in reaching their decisions and the desirability of judicial activism.

It is clear that several different forces shape the justices' votes and opinions in significant ways. The relative weight of these forces depends in part on what justices think they ought to do. In particular, justices have to create a balance between their strong policy preferences on many issues and the expectation that they will decide cases by making accurate interpretations of the law.

Some evidence suggests that justices differ in the relative weight they give to these legal and policy considerations.[56] However, these differences are not as sharp as they sometimes appear. For example, at any given time, some justices are considerably more willing than others to uproot some of the Court's precedents. But their attitudes toward precedent as such may be less important than their attitudes toward the policies embodied in particular precedents. In the 1960s, the Court overturned conservative precedents on civil liberties in thirty-two cases, but it overturned liberal precedents only once. In the 1980s and 1990s, in contrast, the Court overturned twenty-two liberal precedents and only six conservative precedents in civil liberties.[57] Not surprisingly, it was conservatives in the 1960s and liberals in the 1980s and 1990s who adhered most strongly to the Court's precedents.

The heart of judicial activism is making significant policy changes. Because activism has overtones of illegitimacy, justices often emphasize the value of judicial restraint—the avoidance of activism. But this view has not been unanimous; some justices, such as William Brennan, have made strong defenses of activism. Commentators often label some justices as activists and others as proponents of restraint.

Here, too, historical patterns are illuminating. During the 1920s and early 1930s, the laws that the Court struck down were primarily government regulations of business practices. Conservative justices were the most willing to strike down such laws, while liberals on the Court and elsewhere argued for judicial restraint. In contrast, in the 1960s and 1970s, the Court struck down primarily laws that conflicted with civil liberties. Liberals were most likely to act against these laws, while conservatives called for judicial restraint. And since the 1980s the Court has overturned a mix of the two types of laws, with liberals taking the lead in civil liberties and conservatives in economic policy.[58] This history suggests that positions on activism and restraint serve chiefly as justifications of policy choices rather than determining those choices themselves.

This is not to say that the justices' views about activism and other role values have no impact on their behavior. Undoubtedly, such values help to structure the ways in which justices perceive their jobs. But justices' conceptions of good public policy have a more fundamental impact on their choices.

Group Interaction

In the preceding section, I treated the justices as individuals who act on their own. But when justices make choices, they do so as part of a Court that makes collective decisions and as part of American government and society. As I noted, justices who seek to make good policy might act strategically by taking their colleagues and other institutions into account. Whether justices act strategically or not, what they do can be influenced in a variety of ways by other justices and by their political and social environment. This section examines the Court as a group, and the next section considers the Court's environment.

A Quasi-Collegial Body

In historical accounts of the Supreme Court, some of the most dramatic events concern the interaction among justices in major cases. Newly appointed chief justice Earl Warren, engaging in what Justice Douglas called "a brilliant diplomatic process," moved the Court from sharp division to a unanimous decision in *Brown v. Board of Education* (1954).[59] Members of the Court competed over a period of several months to influence the outcome in *Roe v. Wade* (1973).[60] And the Court's adherence to most of the tenets of *Roe* in *Planned Parenthood v. Casey* (1992) reflected the close collaboration among three justices on a joint opinion that determined the Court's position.[61]

Yet depictions of the Court by justices and people close to them paint a quite different picture. Chief Justice Rehnquist, for example, has said that the Court is dominated chiefly "by centrifugal forces, pushing toward individuality and independence." [62] One legal scholar, a former law clerk, wrote that

it's really nine separate courts. The Justices lead separate, even isolated lives. They deal with each other only in quite formalized settings. They vote the way they want to and then retreat to their own chambers.[63]

Contradictory though they may seem, both of these depictions of the Court are accurate: they simply portray different aspects of the same reality. For one thing, the limited personal interaction among justices does not mean that they ignore each other when working out their positions in cases. Rather, the justices now exchange views primarily in writing. According to Justice Breyer, "Things take place in writing because that is a mode through which appellate judges are most comfortable communicating." [64]

More fundamentally, the justices do influence each other, but that influence occurs within constraints—constraints that result from their strongly held views on many issues. When they apply their general positions on an issue to a specific case, the resulting judgment about that case may be too firm for colleagues to sway. As Rehnquist wrote, when justices who have prepared themselves "assemble around the conference table on Friday morning to decide an important case presenting constitutional questions that they have all debated and written about before, the outcome may be a foregone conclusion." [65]

Yet the justices also have powerful incentives to work with each other, even if doing so requires that they adopt positions that depart from those they most prefer. One reason is institutional: justices want to achieve opinions that at least five members endorse, so that the Court is laying down authoritative legal rules. And, to give more weight to the Court's decisions, they generally would like to reach greater consensus. According to Justice O'Connor, "Neither my colleagues nor I make a practice of joining opinions with which we do not agree." Unanimity "does not overwhelm our other goals." Still, "we all greatly prefer the Court to be unanimous or almost so whenever possible, and we work to make that happen." [66]

The justices' interest in the legal rules that the Court collectively establishes is an even stronger incentive to work together. Justices would like to win the support of colleagues for the rules they prefer, so they have good reason to engage in efforts at persuasion. They also have reason to be flexible in the stances they take in cases, because flexibility may help them to win colleagues' support for rules that are at least close to the ones they prefer.

These incentives are reflected in the negotiation described in the first section of this chapter.[67] The most common course of events in a case is for a justice to write a draft opinion for the Court and then gain the support of a majority for that opinion without serious complications. But a draft opinion frequently attracts requests from colleagues for changes in the opinion, and most of the time justices who make these requests indicate that they cannot join the opinion unless the changes are made. The opinion author usually makes these changes. During the seventeen years of the Burger Court, requests for changes in the draft opinion occurred in 32 percent of all cases, and more often in important cases. Seventy percent of the time, the opinion was modified to make the requested change.[68]

Whether or not colleagues request changes in opinions for the Court, those opinions frequently are revised during the decision process. In the Burger Court, slightly more than half of all cases had at least three drafts of the Court's opinion circulated by the author.[69] While successive drafts may differ only on minor matters, they sometimes differ substantially— and occasionally with important consequences for legal policy.[70]

Beyond the content of opinions, the votes of individual justices on the case outcome can shift during the decision process. During the seventeen years of the Burger Court, 7.5 percent of the justices' individual votes to reverse or affirm shifted from one side to the other, and at least one such shift occurred in 37 percent of the cases. Most vote shifts increase the size of the majority, as the Court works toward consensus. During the Burger Court, the justices who initially voted with the majority switched their votes 5 percent of the time, while those who initially voted with the minority switched 18 percent of the time.[71] Occasionally, however, shifts of position turn an initial minority into a majority. This occurred in about 7 percent of the cases decided by the Burger Court.[72]

The effects of interactions among the justices should not be exaggerated. In the great majority of cases, the side that won in the Court's first vote on the merits of the case wins in the final vote as well. Most of the majority opinions that the Court issues look similar to the original drafts of those opinions. But votes and opinions do change; the Court's decisions are often more than simply an adding together of the positions with which each justice begins.

The group life of the Court has effects on its decisions that are broader and more subtle than shifts of position in individual cases. Interactions among the justices create general patterns of influence within the Court, and the Court's ability to reach consensus is affected by the extent of conflict among its members. Both of these effects merit consideration.

Patterns of Influence

Felix Frankfurter and William O. Douglas both joined the Supreme Court in 1939. Frankfurter was a Harvard law professor, one of the most renowned legal scholars in the United States. Douglas, who had been a law professor at Columbia and Yale, was widely regarded as brilliant. Each would serve a long time on the Court—Frankfurter for twenty-two years, Douglas for a record thirty-six years. Each has been included in lists of the greatest justices. But neither exerted a great deal of influence over his colleagues on the Supreme Court.

When William Brennan came to the Court in 1956, his work as a lawyer and state judge had given him a reputation for competence, but he was hardly regarded as a great legal thinker. Yet during most of his thirty-four years on the Court, Brennan was probably the most influential justice—even more influential than the chief justices with whom he served. In this sense at least, Brennan was a more successful justice than either Frankfurter or Douglas. How can this result be explained?

In the case of Douglas, the best explanation is a straightforward one: he had only a limited interest in exerting influence over his colleagues. Certainly, he devoted some efforts to winning support for his positions, especially in the cases that concerned him most. But in contrast with some other justices, whom he called "evangelists," [73] he generally preferred to go his own way. According to Chief Justice Rehnquist, "At the Court conferences we sometimes had the impression that he was disappointed to have other people agree with his views in a particular case, because he would therefore be unable to write a stinging dissent." [74]

Frankfurter is a more complicated case. He came to the Court expecting to play a major leadership role, and he was one of Douglas's "evangelists." But these efforts suffered because of his weak interpersonal skills. Justice Potter Stewart said that Frankfurter "courted" him, but "Felix was so unsubtle and obvious that it was counterproductive." [75]

Further, Frankfurter's arrogance caused him to lecture to colleagues, and he reacted sarcastically to opinions with which he disagreed. His behavior alienated several colleagues, with an inevitable impact on his influence within the Court.

Brennan differed from Douglas and Frankfurter in crucial ways. Unlike Douglas, he devoted enormous effort toward influencing his colleagues. He worked hard to gain support from more conservative colleagues, both in individual cases and over the long term. For example, he engaged in what one of Justice Blackmun's law clerks called a "courtship" of Blackmun.[76] In his commitment to winning support from his colleagues and his careful consideration of how to do so, Brennan was among the most strategic-minded justices ever to sit on the Court.[77]

Frankfurter was also strategic, but Brennan was far better suited to win support from his colleagues. Most important, he had the advantage of a personal style that was much warmer than Frankfurter's. "Everybody got along with him," according to one observer, "even those who bitterly opposed him from a doctrinal view." [78] Brennan was also perceptive about how to win majorities; one commentator said that he could "accurately judge his colleagues and figure out what is doable." [79]

Brennan's commitment and skills were reflected in the results. As a member of the Warren Court, working closely with Warren, he helped to forge a liberal majority for expansion of civil liberties. In the Burger and early Rehnquist Courts, he did much to shape the Court's decisions and thereby to limit its conservative shift.

These three justices illustrate the wide range of roles that justices can play in the Court's decision making. None of the current justices stand out to the same degree, but at least two are distinctive. John Paul Stevens is the most like Douglas in his individualism. One observer concluded that Stevens "makes little effort to win over other members of the Court." [80] Stevens acts on his belief that a justice who disagrees with the majority should dissent openly rather than going along; as a result, "I do clutter up the U.S. Reports with more separate writing than most lawyers have either time or inclination to read." [81] Yet the genial Stevens appears to have much better relationships with his colleagues than did the very irascible Douglas.

Antonin Scalia bears some resemblance to Frankfurter, but with important differences. He seems to share with Frankfurter a sense of superiority and a tendency to lecture colleagues. In oral argument he is highly active, sometimes domineering. His communications with colleagues during the decision process sometimes have a hard edge. When Justice Kennedy shifted away from Scalia's side in *Planned Parenthood v. Casey* (1992), in which the Court reaffirmed *Roe v. Wade*, it was reported that Scalia "walked over to Kennedy's nearby house . . . to upbraid him." [82]

Scalia reportedly responded to a reference to racial discrimination in Justice Ginsburg's draft opinion in *Bush v. Gore* with a strongly worded memorandum attacking her for raising race as an issue. According to this report, Ginsburg then eliminated the reference.[83]

Scalia's concurring and dissenting opinions sometimes criticize other justices' opinions in harsh tones. In 2002 the Indiana Supreme Court suspended a lawyer from practice for a strongly worded attack on the opinion from which he was appealing. To make his point that judges sometimes use equally strong language to attack each other, a justice who did not think the lawyer should be suspended quoted two Scalia opinions.[84]

Scalia's behavior sometimes creates frictions with other justices.[85] Yet he is a gregarious person who has close relationships with some colleagues. More important, his intellectual power gives him considerable influence. One example is the support he has attracted for his view that the Court should give no weight to legislative history in interpreting statutes. And federal judge Alex Kozinski, who is close to Scalia, has argued that Scalia "sets the terms of the debate" on issues before the Court and that he is creating a foundation for long-term influence over development of the law.[86] In this way, Scalia may be engaging in a patient but effective long-term strategy within the Court.

As the discussion so far suggests, justices differ in their influence over the Court's collective decisions. But these differences should not be exaggerated. For one thing, no justice can dominate the strong-minded people who serve on the Court. Under highly unfavorable conditions, even the most influential justice will lose most of the time. Brennan enjoyed a surprising degree of success as the Court became more conservative in the 1970s and 1980s, but he lost more and more battles as new appointments moved the Court further from his views. And every justice has considerable power simply by holding one of only nine votes. No matter how unskilled or unpopular a justice might be, that justice still can vote to affirm or reverse, to support one opinion or another.

The Chief Justice

The chief justice is formal head of the Supreme Court, but the chief's capacity to influence the Court has significant limits. One limitation stems from administrative duties, which reduce the time that the chief can spend on cases. More fundamental is the difficulty of leading colleagues who strongly resist control. As Chief Justice Rehnquist wrote, the chief "presides over a conference not of eight subordinates, whom he may direct or instruct, but of eight associates who, like him, have tenure during good behavior, and who are as independent as hogs on ice. He may at most persuade or cajole them." [87] But the chief holds significant formal powers, powers that provide considerable potential for leadership.

Chief Justice Rehnquist presiding at the impeachment trial of President Clinton. By all accounts, Rehnquist has been an effective leader of the Court.

The Chief Justice's Powers. The chief presides over the Court in oral argument and in conference. In conference the chief can direct discussion and frame alternatives, which can shape the outcome of the discussion. Most important, the chief ordinarily speaks first on a case in conference. Another power involves the discuss list, the set of petitions for hearing that the Court considers fully. The chief, aided by clerks, makes up the initial version of the discuss list. This task gives the chief the largest role in determining which cases are set aside without group judgment.

Opinion Assignment. The power to assign opinions is important and complicated. By custom, the chief justice assigns the Court's opinion whenever the chief is in the majority on the initial vote in conference. (In other cases, the senior justice in the majority makes the assignment.) As a result, the chief justice assigns the great majority of opinions, a little over 80 percent in the period from 1953 to 1990.[88]

In making assignments, chief justices balance different considerations.[89] Administrative considerations relate to spreading workload and opportunities among the justices. Chief justices generally assign about the same number of opinions to each colleague, taking into account assignments from senior associate justices and the workload of opinion writing that a justice already faces at a given time. These considerations have been especially important to Chief Justice Rehnquist. He wrote in 2001, "As the term goes on I take into consideration the extent to which the various justices are current in writing and circulating opinions that have previously been assigned." [90]

Other considerations relate to the substance of the Court's decisions. The legal rules proclaimed by the Court may depend in part on who writes its opinion. For this reason, chief justices tend to favor themselves and colleagues who have similar ideological positions when assigning opinions in important cases.

The selection of the opinion writer may help to determine whether the initial majority remains a majority. When the initial majority is slim, the chief justice is likely to assign opinions to a relatively moderate member of that majority, even if the assigned justice is ideologically distant from the chief. This practice stems from the belief that a moderate typically has the best chance to write an opinion that will maintain the majority and perhaps win over justices who were initially on the other side.

Because chief justices favor ideological allies in assigning important opinions, in effect they reward the justices who vote with them most often. They might also use the assignment power more directly to reward and punish colleagues, as Chief Justice Burger apparently did. Justice Blackmun said that a justice who was "in the doghouse" with Burger might be assigned one of the "crud" opinions "that nobody wants to write." [91]

Under any chief justice, the assignment power gives other justices something to think about. Asked why he joins Rehnquist in singing carols at the Court's Christmas party, David Souter said, "I have to. Otherwise I get all the tax cases." [92] Souter was joking, but he touched on an important reality.

Variation in Leadership. What particular chief justices make of their formal powers and the strength of their leadership varies a good deal. These differences result from several conditions, including the chief's interest in leading the Court, the chief's skill as a leader, and the willingness of the associate justices to be led.

The two chief justices who preceded William Rehnquist—Earl Warren and Warren Burger—are of particular interest. Earl Warren could not compete with some colleagues as a scholar. He presided over a Court that had several skillful and strong-minded members, such as Douglas and Frankfurter, and that was closely divided between liberals and conservatives during most of his tenure. Under these conditions, Warren hardly could dominate the Court.

But Warren possessed excellent leadership skills, a product of his personality and his experience as a political leader. He had a good sense of how to build majorities for his positions, and he was effective at persuasion: several of his colleagues told one observer "how hard it had been to withstand the Chief Justice when he was able to operate in a one-on-one setting." [93] These attributes gave Warren considerable influence on the Court's direction.

Warren Burger was ambitious for leadership. He achieved some success in securing administrative changes in the federal courts and procedural changes in the Court itself. Simply by being chief justice, he exerted considerable influence over the Court's decisions. But he was far less effective than Earl Warren.

To a considerable extent, Burger's limited impact on the Court's decisions stemmed from his own qualities and predilections. Colleagues chafed at what they considered a poor style of leadership in conference, and they disliked Burger's practice, apparently unique to him, of casting "false" votes in conference for strategic purposes. "All too damned often," said one justice, "the Chief Justice will vote with the majority so as to assign the opinion, and then he ends up in dissent." [94] He was also accused of bullying his colleagues. One scholar concluded that Potter Stewart "loathed" Burger,[95] and other colleagues also disliked his leadership style. Apparently, they were not alone; Justice Marshall's messenger said that when Burger retired, "it was just like Christmas morning." [96]

But Burger also faced obstacles that were beyond his control. Perhaps most important, as a strong conservative he had the disadvantage of standing near one end of the Court's ideological spectrum. In any case, his example shows that even a chief justice who wants to be a powerful leader does not always achieve that goal.

William Rehnquist became chief justice in 1986 after serving on the Court for fifteen years. He brought important strengths to the position, especially his well-respected intellectual abilities and an affable personal style. For these reasons, his promotion was welcomed by colleagues and other Court personnel.[97]

Rehnquist appears to be a very effective chief justice. Reflecting his preferences, the Court's discussions of cases at conference are shorter and tighter than in the recent past. His leadership is one source of the sharp decline in the number of cases accepted by the Court. In decision making he enhances his influence by taking strong positions with an affable style. As a journalist wrote in 2002, he "puts his dissents on paper and leaves it at that: no railing, no personal attacks, no effort to draw the limelight." [98]

During Rehnquist's tenure as chief justice, the Court's positions on issues such as federalism and the death penalty have moved closer to his own positions. The primary reason is not his leadership but the series of appointments that have given the Court a more conservative viewpoint. As Rehnquist himself has underlined, the chief's impact on the Court's direction is limited. Within those limits, however, Rehnquist's skills and his desire to influence the Court's direction have allowed him to exert considerable impact.

Harmony and Conflict

According to a legal scholar in 2002, "It is abundantly clear that the Rehnquist Court is divided into hostile blocs; that the blocs do not trust each other; that there is at times a good deal of anger and vitriol on all sides." [99] Someone who reads the Court's opinions is likely to gain a similar impression. During the 1999 term, the justices "accused each other of hypocrisy, hostility, and flat-out stupidity." [100] In the last month of the 2001 term, dissenting opinions criticized an opinion's "meandering attempt to justify its unprecedented departure from a rule that has been settled since the days of John Marshall," ridiculed a majority opinion for its "nightmarish images of out-of-control flatware, livestock run amok, and colliding tubas," and awarded "the Prize for the Court's Most Feeble Effort to fabricate 'national consensus.'" [101]

The justices themselves depict the Court very differently. They usually emphasize how well they get along with each other despite their disagreements about legal policy. Justice Breyer, for example, told an audience in 2001, "I've never heard one of my colleagues make a snide remark about another." [102]

The reality lies somewhere between these two impressions of the Court. The high stakes that justices have in many of the Court's decisions, combined with the pressures under which they work, seem certain to produce personal conflicts. And all the sources of strife that exist in other groups can operate in the Court as well. Personal conflicts are likely to become deeper when justices serve together for many years. It is hardly surprising, for example, that the Court's decision in *Bush v. Gore* exacerbated frictions among the justices.[103]

At the same time, the justices have strong incentives to limit such frictions. Harmony makes the Court a more pleasant place to work and facilitates achieving consensus in decisions. And justices who seek the support of colleagues for the positions they favor want to maintain good relations with those colleagues. Thus, they work at minimizing personal conflict, and they achieve some success in this effort.

It is difficult to assess the balance between harmony and conflict from outside the Court. It seems clear that significant conflicts exist among the current justices, but signs of conflict such as bitter statements in opinions may mean less than some observers think. One conclusion is safe: the current Court is more harmonious than past Courts in which some pairs of justices were actually unable to work with each other.[104]

The Court's Environment

As members of Congress do their work, they constantly deal with people who want something from them: constituents who seek help from the government, reporters who look for good stories, lobbyists who argue for the positions of interest groups, and executive branch officials who want to build support for their legislative proposals. Members could try to ignore all these people. But they do not, because their ability to stay in office and their effectiveness as legislators depend on building favorable relationships with constituents, interest groups, and others in their political environment.

The Supreme Court is a very different kind of institution. The justices make their decisions in relative isolation from people outside the Court. This isolation stems in part from norms associated with courts in general and the Supreme Court in particular, norms that create some distance between the Court and those who seek to influence its decisions. Unlike members of Congress, the justices do not interact with lobbyists while they consider issues. More important, their lifetime appointments free the justices from worries about maintaining their positions. Popular or unpopular, they can continue to do their work on the Court.

But the Court is not completely insulated from its political and social environment. For one thing, people outside the Court care about its decisions, and some of them try to influence those decisions. Interest groups submit amicus briefs in cases. Law professors write articles about legal issues that they hope the justices (or their law clerks) will notice. Members of Congress offer their judgments about issues before the Court.

The views of people and institutions outside the Court sometimes do affect the Court's decisions. One reason may be strategic. Justices who want to enhance the Court's impact may feel they can do so by accommodating Congress or the general public. Strategy aside, justices simply may feel better if their actions get positive responses from the legal community or the mass media or other audiences that are important to them. If Justice Ginsburg is "unusually sensitive to public criticism," as a reporter concluded, she is hardly unique in caring about what people think of her work.[105] And the Court's environment surely affects the justices' thinking about cases and issues. For these reasons, the various elements of the Court's environment merit examination.

Mass Public Opinion

In the Court's opinion in a 2002 case, Justice Scalia wrote:

These cases present the question whether federal district courts have jurisdiction over a telecommunication carrier's claim that the order of a state utility commission requiring reciprocal compensation for telephone calls to Internet Service Providers violates federal law.[106]

It is doubtful that much of the public knew of this case or would have cared about the Court's decision had they known of it. This case was not unique; on many issues that come before the Court, there is no public opinion to speak of.

But many other Court decisions address issues that concern a large share of the public, such as crime and civil rights. And some individual decisions, such as the Court's major rulings on abortion, are highly visible and controversial. On these issues and cases, it is possible that public opinion or potential public reactions influence the justices.

Such influence may seem unlikely, because the justices do not depend on public approval to keep their jobs. But justices, like other people, may enjoy popularity for its own sake. Justices also see public support for the Court as a resource, strengthening its position in conflicts with the other branches and improving compliance with its decisions. For these reasons, at least some justices pay attention to the public; Justice Blackmun, for example, "read and pondered his mail." [107] In turn, public opinion might have an impact on the Court.

Such impact is least likely when the public is closely divided on an issue. The five justices who voted to end the Florida recount in *Bush v. Gore* knew that their decision would arouse strong negative reactions from a large share of the public. But they also knew that an equal portion of the public would applaud their decision. Under the circumstances, they could feel free to make the decision they favored. Indeed, the Court's public standing suffered no serious damage after the decision.[108]

Even when a strong majority of the public favors one side of an issue, the Court does not necessarily go along with the majority. Examples of highly unpopular decisions include the Court's rulings limiting religious exercises in public schools, striking down state and federal laws against flag burning, and holding that states could not establish term limits for members of Congress.

In other instances, the Court *has* joined a strong majority. One example is public concern about illegal drugs. Over the last two decades, the Court has addressed a wide range of cases involving conflicts between the government's interest in controlling illegal drugs and civil liberties. With some noteworthy exceptions, it has approved the government policies in question. A typical example was its 2002 decision upholding mandatory drug testing for public school students who participate in extracurricular activities.[109] This line of decisions undoubtedly has several sources. In part, it simply reflects the Court's growing conservatism on civil liberties issues. But it also reflects the widespread perception of illegal drugs as a major national problem. In one dissent, Justice Thurgood Marshall charged that the majority had been "swept away by society's obsession with stopping the scourge of illegal drugs." [110]

If Marshall was correct, it is uncertain why the Court was "swept away." Perhaps some justices sought to take positions that were popular with the general public and with the other branches of government. But it may be that the justices had simply come to share the concern about drugs that pervaded American society as a whole. This shared concern could still be considered the influence of public opinion, but influence of an indirect sort.

Beyond specific issues, the Court might follow general tides of public opinion. As the public moves to the political left or right, so may the Court. Scholars have disagreed about the extent to which the Court follows ideological trends among the public, but it is at least plausible that the Court does so.[111]

In any case, public opinion has much less influence on the Court than it does on Congress, primarily because the justices do not face elections. But the public's views do affect the Court to some degree, and Chief Justice Rehnquist has explained why that impact is inevitable:

Judges, so long as they are relatively normal human beings, can no more escape being influenced by public opinion in the long run than can people working at other jobs. And if a judge on coming to the bench were to decide to hermetically seal himself off from all manifestations of public opinion, he would accomplish very little; he would not be influenced by current public opinion, but instead would be influenced by the state of public opinion at the time he came to the bench.[112]

Elite Opinion: Mass Media and the Legal Community

Aside from general public opinion, the opinions of particular groups in society may influence justices who pay attention to them and who care about what they think or say. Two groups whose opinions are potentially relevant to all of the justices are the mass media and the legal community.

As they do with interest groups, the justices typically maintain a degree of distance from the news media. They interact with reporters less than do their counterparts in the other branches of government, and they give relatively few on-the-record interviews about their work.

Still, the mass media are important to the Court. They are the justices' primary source of information on public opinion and the views of other policymakers. By the same token, the media are the public's primary source of information about the Court. For these reasons, it is not surprising that justices sometimes react to stories about the Court and even try to influence media coverage. Justice Scalia, for example, wrote an angry letter to the editor of a legal newspaper after it reported that he was seeking to end a ban on paid public appearances by federal judges.[113]

The attention paid to the mass media suggests that they can influence what the justices do. Coverage of issues in the media might shape justices' perceptions of those issues, and an interest in favorable coverage might influence justices' positions in cases. Some conservatives believe that the media have a more pervasive effect. In their view, Supreme Court reporters are primarily liberals who praise justices for taking liberal positions. As a result, some justices are tempted to move to the left to win approval in the short term and a favorable image in history. Conservative commentators who believe in this impact have labeled it the "Greenhouse Effect," after Linda Greenhouse, longtime Court reporter for the *New York Times*. One commentator suggested that Justice Kennedy had become more liberal in his positions because of the Greenhouse Effect.[114]

The legal community is important as a professional reference group. Justices draw many of their acquaintances from this community. Most justices interact a good deal with practicing lawyers, law professors, and lower court judges. Lawyers are also the primary source of expert evaluation of the Court, especially through articles in the law reviews that law schools publish. Scrutiny by the legal community helps to make legal considerations important to the justices in reaching decisions. And if a particular view of legal issues is dominant among lawyers or in a segment of the bar that is important to a justice, that justice may be drawn toward the dominant view.

The law reviews can have another kind of impact as well. Because law review articles are often discussed in briefs and read by justices and law clerks, they constitute one source of the information that enters into the Court's decisions. Justices frequently cite law review articles in support of their positions, and on occasion articles may help to determine their positions. For their part, members of the Court sometimes write law review articles to influence the legal community. By doing so, they underline the importance of that community to them.

Litigants and Interest Groups

Simply by bringing cases to the Supreme Court, litigants and interest groups have an effect on the Court's policies. Once the Court has accepted a case, litigants and interest groups may influence its decision on the merits. Because communications to the Court must go through formal channels, any such influence comes primarily through advocacy in written briefs and oral arguments.

Certainly, justices pay attention to the material provided by litigants and interest groups. Opinions for the Court address the arguments raised by the parties to the case. Among the cases with amicus briefs in the 1986 to 1995 terms, in more than one-third a justice's opinion referred to an amicus brief.[115] When justices question lawyers closely during oral argument, they are often looking for responses to strong arguments by the other side. Therefore, the way lawyers frame arguments in a case can affect the justices' thinking and ultimately their decisions.

More broadly, as discussed in Chapter 3, the quality of advocacy on the two sides of a case has an impact. Once again, the federal government provides a good example. In the Court's full decisions on the merits in its 2001 term, the government had a 75 percent success rate, a fairly typical figure.[116] One source of that success is the expertise of the experienced advocates in the solicitor general's office.[117]

Justices may react to the identities of the litigants or amici in themselves rather than just the arguments they present. Another source of success for the federal government in the Court might be the justices' sympathies for the other branches, and individual justices may have positive or negative attitudes toward groups such as the ACLU or toward particular companies. In the 2003 cases on affirmative action in university admissions, what one commentator called "the range and sheer weight of the establishment voices on the affirmative action side" may have influenced some justices.[118] On the whole, however, the justices care much more about the legal and policy issues they decide than about the litigants that bring those issues to them. In any event, responses to the litigants' identities reflect the justices' attitudes more than they reflect any influence exerted by those litigants. As a former solicitor general has pointed out, even the federal executive branch can have little impact on a Court that has five justices who are committed to a particular direction in policy.[119]

Congress and the President

Several sets of policymakers affect the Court and its policies. For example, lower courts and some administrative agencies implement the Court's decisions. In turn, the justices may take those policymakers into account when they reach decisions. The president and Congress are especially important to the Court, so they have the greatest potential for influence on the Court's decisions.

Congress. Congressional powers over the Court range from reversing the Court's interpretations of statutes to control over salary increases for the justices. Because of this array of powers, the justices have good reason to think about congressional reactions to their decisions. Relations with Congress can affect their prestige and their comfort. And justices who think strategically in a broad sense, who care about the ultimate impact of the Court's policies, want to avoid congressional actions that undercut those policies.

If the justices do act strategically toward Congress, the most likely form of strategy involves decisions that interpret federal statutes. These decisions are more vulnerable than the Court's interpretations of the Constitution because Congress and the president can override them simply by enacting a new statute. Indeed, such overrides are fairly common.

For this reason, justices might try to calculate whether their preferred interpretation of a statute would be sufficiently unpopular in Congress to produce an override. If so, justices would modify their interpretation to avoid that result. By making this implicit compromise with Congress, the justices could get the best possible result under the circumstances: not the interpretation of a statute that they favor most, but one that is closer to their preferences than the new statute that Congress would enact to override the Court's decision.

It may be, however, that most justices do not care that much whether Congress overrides their decisions. Or justices might find it so difficult to predict overrides and their content that there is little to be gained by trying to make those predictions. In any case, it is not yet clear how often justices pursue this strategic approach.[120]

Occasionally, the Court gets into conflicts with Congress that go much deeper than disagreement over the meaning of statutes. During a few periods in the Court's history, its general line of policy aroused so much dissatisfaction in Congress that it generated a serious threat of concrete action against the Court itself. In those periods, at least some justices some of the time have acted to reduce that threat.

The first such period was the early nineteenth century, when John Marshall's Court faced congressional attacks because of its activist policies. Marshall, as the Court's dominant member, was careful to limit the frequency of decisions that would further anger its opponents.[121] As discussed in chapter 1, the Court's shift from opposition to support of New Deal legislation in the late 1930s probably reflected the effort by one or two justices to avoid a serious confrontation with the other branches. In the late 1950s, members of Congress reacted to the Court's expansions of civil liberties by seeking to override its policies and limit its jurisdiction; the Court reversed some of its own positions and thereby helped to quiet congressional attacks on the Court.

There have been no clear retreats of this sort since the 1950s. Indeed, the Court has exhibited considerable resistance to congressional pressures. Members of Congress have attacked the Court for its positions on a variety of civil liberties issues, including school desegregation, legislative districting, abortion, school prayer, and flag burning. On each of these issues, members have tried to overturn the Court's decisions, to limit its jurisdiction over the issue, or both. Yet in the face of these attacks, the Court has adhered to many of its unpopular policies, and it changed others only when new appointments made the Court more conservative. Recent history is thus a reminder that the justices do not automatically shy away from decisions that create conflict with Congress.

The President. Presidents have multifaceted relationships with the Supreme Court, and these relationships provide several sources of potential influence. Two of these sources, discussed in earlier chapters, are the power to appoint justices and the government's major role in Supreme Court litigation. The appointment power gives presidents considerable ability to determine the Court's direction. The president helps to shape the federal government's litigation policy and affects the Court's decisions through appointment of the solicitor general and occasional intervention in specific cases.

Presidents may have other ways to exert more direct influence over the justices. One stems from personal relationships between justices and presidents. Some members of the Court were close associates of the presidents who later selected them. Justices may also interact with presidents while serving on the bench. A few, such as Abe Fortas with President Johnson, have been frequent visitors to the White House for advisory or social purposes. Such relationships hardly compel justices to support the president's position in litigation, but they might affect a justice's responses to cases with which the president is concerned.

Second, justices could seek to curry favor with the president in the hope of promotion to chief justice when a vacancy arises. After George W. Bush won the presidency, Anthony Kennedy was thought to be a possible successor to Chief Justice Rehnquist. Some people speculated that some of Kennedy's actions as a justice and his collaboration in an education program with first lady Laura Bush were motivated in part by an interest in Rehnquist's position.[122] But in some cases Kennedy has taken positions that would hurt rather than help his prospects to become chief justice,[123] and it is not clear that his actions or those of any other justice have been influenced by the hope of promotion.

Finally, presidents can affect both the public's view of the Court and responses by Congress and other institutions to the Court's decisions. For this reason, justices have an incentive to keep the peace with the president just as they do with Congress. As a result, presidents undoubtedly exert a subtle influence on the Court's policy choices.

That influence is greatest when the president has strong support elsewhere in government and in the public. In the next few years, the Court is likely to hear challenges to government policies aimed at preventing terrorist acts. In deciding these cases, the justices will feel considerable pressure from the president's administration to rule against those challenges, and that pressure will be strengthened by the strong concern with terrorism in Congress and the general public. The justices' own concern with terrorism also will affect their decisions. As suggested earlier, the influence of the Court's environment is often difficult to separate from that of the justices' own attitudes.

Conclusion

Of all the considerations that may influence the Supreme Court's decisions, I have given primary emphasis to the justices' policy preferences. The application of the law to the Court's cases is usually ambiguous, and constraints from the Court's environment are generally weak. As a result, the justices have considerable freedom to take positions that accord with their own conceptions of good policy. For this reason, the Court's membership and the process of selecting the justices have the greatest impact on the Court's direction.

If justices' preferences explain a great deal, they do not explain everything. The law and the political environment rule out some possible options for the Court, and they influence the justices' choices among the options that remain. The group life of the Court affects the behavior of individual justices and the Court's collective decisions. In particular, the justices regularly adjust their positions to win support from colleagues and help build majorities. These forces are reflected in results that might seem surprising: strikingly liberal decisions from a seemingly conservative Court and the maintenance of precedents even when most justices no longer favor the policies they embody.

Thus, what the Court does is a product of multiple, intertwined forces. These forces can be discussed one at a time, but ultimately they operate together in complicated ways to shape the Court's decisions. Those who want to understand why the Court does what it does must accept the complexity of the process by which justices make their choices.

NOTES

1. *BE&K Construction Company v. National Labor Relations Board,* 536 U.S. 516, 537 (2002).
2. *McConnell v. Federal Election Commission* (2003).
3. Joan Biskupic, "The Quirks of the Highest Order," *Washington Post,* May 3, 1999, A23.

4. Dahlia Lithwick, "Corn Porn," *Slate*, at *slate.msn.com*, October 4, 2001.
5. Charles Lane, "A Private Hearing, of Sorts, for Anti-War Activists," *Washington Post*, May 6, 2002, A19.
6. Linda Greenhouse, "An Intense Attack by Justice Thomas on Cross-Burning," *New York Times*, December 12, 2002, A1, A27. The case was *Virginia v. Black* (2003).
7. Joan Biskupic, "Supreme Court Film Offers Glimpse Behind Justices' Closed Doors," *Washington Post*, June 17, 1997, A15.
8. William H. Rehnquist, *The Supreme Court*, new ed. (New York: Alfred A. Knopf, 2001), 244.
9. David Savage, "Hate Speech, Hate Crimes, and the First Amendment," in *A Year in the Life of the Supreme Court*, ed. Rodney A. Smolla (Durham: Duke University Press, 1995), 195.
10. Dahlia Lithwick, "Nino's Chain Gang," *Slate*, at *slate.msn.com*, April 17, 2002.
11. Dahlia Lithwick, "Tell Me Why I Don't Like First Mondays," *Slate*, at *slate.msn.com*, October 7, 2002.
12. This discussion of the conference is based in part on Rehnquist, *The Supreme Court*, 256–258.
13. Tom Miller, "Breyer Speaks to Bar Convention," *Alaska Bar Rag*, May-June 2001, 10.
14. Philippa Strum, "Change and Continuity on the Supreme Court: Conversations with Justice Harry A. Blackmun," *University of Richmond Law Review* 34 (March 2000): 292.
15. Bernard Schwartz, *Decision: How the Supreme Court Decides Cases* (New York: Oxford University Press, 1996), 42.
16. Rehnquist, *The Supreme Court*, 258.
17. The process of responding to draft majority opinions is described in Forrest Maltzman, James F. Spriggs II, and Paul J. Wahlbeck, *Crafting Law on the Supreme Court: The Collegial Game* (New York: Cambridge University Press, 2000), 62–72.
18. Strum, "Change and Continuity on the Supreme Court," 288.
19. Antonin Scalia, "The Dissenting Opinion," *Journal of Supreme Court History*, 1994, 42.
20. *U.S. Department of Justice v. Reporters Committee for Freedom of the Press*, 489 U.S. 749, 780 (1989).
21. Tony Mauro, "Key Rulings on Death Penalty, Free Speech," *Legal Times*, June 24, 2002, 8.
22. Leah Garchik, "Freedom of Conversation," *San Francisco Chronicle*, October 25, 1999, E11.
23. Tony Mauro, "Solicitor General Has Subpar Season," *Legal Times*, September 4, 1995, 9.
24. Walter Murphy, *Elements of Judicial Strategy* (Chicago: University of Chicago Press, 1964), 44 n.*. See Jack Knight and Lee Epstein, "The Norm of *Stare Decisis*," *American Journal of Political Science* 40 (November 1996): 1018–35.
25. Jeffrey A. Segal and Harold J. Spaeth, *The Supreme Court and the Attitudinal Model Revisited* (New York: Cambridge University Press, 2002), chap. 2; Howard Gillman, "What's Law Got to Do With It? Judicial Behavioralists Test the 'Legal Model' of Judicial Decision Making," *Law & Social Inquiry* 26 (spring 2001): 465–504; Robert M. Howard and Jeffrey A. Segal, "An Original Look at Originalism," *Law & Society Review* 36 (2002): 113–138.

26. Lori Hausegger and Lawrence Baum, "Inviting Congressional Action: A Study of Supreme Court Motivations in Statutory Interpretation," *American Journal of Political Science* 43 (January 1999): 162–185.

27. Cass R. Sunstein, "The Spirit of the Laws," *New Republic*, March 11, 1991, 32.

28. Fred Barbash, "Congress Didn't, So the Supreme Court Did," *Washington Post*, July 5, 1998, C1.

29. 18 U.S.C., sec. 924(c)(1). See Carlos E. Gonzales, "Reinterpreting Statutory Interpretation," *North Carolina Law Review* 74 (March 1996): 588–590.

30. *Smith v. United States* (1993); *Bailey v. United States* (1995); *Muscarello v. United States* (1998).

31. *Thunder Basin Coal Co. v. Reich*, 510 U.S. 200, 219 (1994). See Antonin Scalia, *A Matter of Interpretation: Federal Courts and the Law* (Princeton: Princeton University Press, 1997), 14–37.

32. *Circuit City Stores, Inc. v. Adams*, 532 U.S. 105, 133 (2001).

33. *Reno v. American-Arab Anti-Discrimination Committee*, 525 U.S. 471, 511 (1999).

34. *United States v. Oakland Cannabis Buyers' Cooperative* (2001). The dicta are discussed in Justice Stevens's concurring opinion.

35. *United States v. United Foods, Inc.*, 533 U.S. 405, 420 (2001); *Smith v. Robbins*, 528 U.S. 259, 289 (2000).

36. The lower count is based on Congressional Research Service, *The Constitution of the United States of America: Analysis and Interpretation* and *2000 Supplement* (Washington, D.C.: Government Printing Office, 1996, 2000), and the higher count on Saul Brenner and Harold J. Spaeth, *Stare Indecisis: The Alteration of Precedent on the Supreme Court, 1946–1992* (New York: Cambridge University Press, 1995), 112–121, both supplemented by the lists in the annual *Supreme Court Yearbook*, written by Kenneth Jost and published by CQ Press.

37. Jeffrey A. Segal and Robert M. Howard, "How Supreme Court Justices Respond to Litigant Requests to Overturn Precedent," *Judicature* 85 (November-December 2001): 152.

38. Harold J. Spaeth and Jeffrey A. Segal, *Majority Rule or Minority Will: Adherence to Precedent on the U.S. Supreme Court* (New York: Cambridge University Press, 1999).

39. *Kimel v. Florida Board of Regents*, 528 U.S. 62, 97 (2000).

40. James F. Spriggs II and Thomas C. Hanford, "Explaining the Overruling of U.S. Supreme Court Precedent," *Journal of Politics* 63 (November 2001): 1091–1111.

41. *Cooper Industries, Inc. v. Leatherman Tool Group, Inc.* (2001).

42. Quoted in Alpheus Thomas Mason, *The Supreme Court from Taft to Burger* (Baton Rouge: Louisiana State University Press, 1979), 293.

43. John W. Dean, *The Rehnquist Choice* (New York: Free Press, 2001), 268–269.

44. David G. Savage, *Turning Right: The Making of the Rehnquist Supreme Court* (New York: Wiley, 1992), 381–382. The 1991 case was *Arizona v. Fulminante*.

45. Jeffrey A. Segal and Albert D. Cover, "Ideological Values and the Votes of U.S. Supreme Court Justices," *American Political Science Review* 83 (June 1989): 557–565; Jeffrey A. Segal, Lee Epstein, Charles M. Cameron, and Harold J. Spaeth, "Ideological Values and the Votes of Justices Revisited," *Journal of Politics* 57 (August 1995): 812–823.

46. Scott Douglas Gerber, *First Principles: The Jurisprudence of Clarence Thomas* (New York: New York University Press, 1999).

47. A good example is Segal and Spaeth, *Supreme Court and the Attitudinal Model Revisited.*

48. On O'Connor's family experiences, see Sandra Day O'Connor and H. Alan Day, *Lazy B: Growing Up on a Cattle Ranch in the American Southwest* (New York: Random House, 2002), esp. 264–265. On sex discrimination, see Sandra Day O'Connor, *The Majesty of the Law: Reflections of a Supreme Court Justice* (New York: Random House, 2003), part 4.

49. See Lee Epstein and Jack Knight, *The Choices Justices Make* (Washington, D.C.: CQ Press, 1998); and Jeffrey A. Segal, "Separation-of-Powers Games in the Positive Theory of Congress and Courts," *American Political Science Review* 91 (March 1997): 28–44.

50. *City of Erie v. Pap's A. M.* (2000). A case citation is omitted from the opinion excerpt, but Souter was referring to *Barnes v. Glen Theatre, Inc.,* 501 U.S. 560 (1991).

51. David G. Savage, "Stevens, Souter: Supremely Vexing to GOP," *Los Angeles Times,* June 10, 2001, A22.

52. Figures on agreement between Blackmun and his colleagues are taken from the annual statistics on the Supreme Court term in the November issues of *Harvard Law Review,* vols. 85–100 (1972–1987). See also "The Changing Social Vision of Justice Blackmun," *Harvard Law Review* 96 (1983): 717–736.

53. Joseph F. Kobylka, "The Judicial Odyssey of Harry Blackmun: The Dynamics of Individual-Level Change on the U.S. Supreme Court" (Paper presented at the annual meeting of the Midwest Political Science Association, Chicago, April 1992); Stephen L. Wasby, "Justice Harry A. Blackmun: Transformation from 'Minnesota Twin' to Independent Voice," in *The Burger Court: Political and Judicial Profiles,* ed. Charles M. Lamb and Stephen C. Halpern (Urbana: University of Illinois Press, 1991), 63–99.

54. *United States v. Virginia* (1996).

55. Richard A. Posner, "A Tribute to Justice William J. Brennan, Jr.," *Harvard Law Review* 104 (November 1990): 13.

56. Spaeth and Segal, *Majority Rule or Minority Will,* 290–301.

57. "Civil liberties" is defined broadly. These figures were calculated by the author from the lists of overturnings in Congressional Research Service, *The Constitution of the United States of America: Analysis and Interpretation* (Washington, D.C.: Government Printing Office, 1996), 2250–6, and *1998 Supplement* (Washington, D.C.: Government Printing Office, 1999), 127, updated from Kenneth Jost, *The Supreme Court Yearbook, 1998–1999* (Washington, D.C.: CQ Press, 2000), 24. These lists differ somewhat from that in Brenner and Spaeth, *Stare Indecisis.*

58. See Segal and Spaeth, *Supreme Court and the Attitudinal Model Revisited,* 415–416.

59. See Richard Kluger, *Simple Justice: The History of Brown v. Board of Education and Black America's Struggle for Equality* (New York: Knopf, 1976), 582–699. The quotation is from William O. Douglas, *The Court Years, 1939–1975: The Autobiography of William O. Douglas* (New York: Random House, 1980), 115.

60. See David J. Garrow, *Liberty and Sexuality: The Right to Privacy and the Making of Roe v. Wade* (New York: Macmillan, 1994), 473–599.

61. David G. Savage, "The Rescue of Roe vs. Wade," *Los Angeles Times,* December 13, 1992, A1, A28, A29.

62. Rehnquist, *The Supreme Court,* 222.
63. Linda Greenhouse, "Name-Calling in the Supreme Court: When the Justices Vent Their Spleen, Is There a Social Cost?" *New York Times,* July 28, 1989, B10.
64. Institute of Governmental Studies, "Justice Stephen Breyer Visits IGS for an Informal Talk About the Supreme Court," *Public Affairs Report* 38 (Berkeley: University of California, May 1997), 10.
65. William H. Rehnquist, "Chief Justices I Never Knew," *Hastings Constitutional Law Quarterly* 3 (summer 1976): 647.
66. O'Connor, *Majesty of the Law,* 119.
67. See Maltzman, Spriggs, and Wahlbeck, *Crafting Law on the Supreme Court.*
68. Sandra L. Wood, "Negotiating on the Burger Court" (Paper presented at the annual meeting of the Midwest Political Science Association, Chicago, April 1999), 22–23.
69. Paul J. Wahlbeck, James F. Spriggs II, and Forrest Maltzman, "Marshalling the Court: Bargaining and Accommodation on the U.S. Supreme Court" (Paper presented at the annual meeting of the Western Political Science Association, San Francisco, March 1996), 18–19.
70. Bernard Schwartz, *The Unpublished Opinions of the Burger Court* (New York: Oxford University Press, 1988); Schwartz, *The Unpublished Opinions of the Rehnquist Court* (New York: Oxford University Press, 1996).
71. Forrest Maltzman and Paul J. Wahlbeck, "Strategic Policy Considerations and Voting Fluidity on the Burger Court," *American Political Science Review* 90 (September 1996): 587.
72. Segal and Spaeth, *Supreme Court and the Attitudinal Model Revisited,* 286.
73. Douglas, *The Court Years,* 18.
74. Rehnquist, *The Supreme Court,* 225–226.
75. James F. Simon, *The Antagonists: Hugo Black, Felix Frankfurter and Civil Liberties in Modern America* (New York: Simon & Schuster, 1989), 249.
76. Ruth Wedgwood, "Constitutional Equity," *Yale Law Journal* 104 (October 1994): 33.
77. Hunter R. Clark, *Justice Brennan: The Great Conciliator* (New York: Birch Lane Press, 1995); Kim Isaac Eisler, *A Justice for All: William J. Brennan, Jr., and the Decisions That Transformed America* (New York: Simon & Schuster, 1993).
78. Alexander Wohl, "What's Left," *American Bar Association Journal* 77 (February 1991): 42.
79. Nina Totenberg, "A Tribute to Justice William J. Brennan, Jr.," *Harvard Law Review* 104 (November 1990): 37.
80. Bernard Schwartz, *A History of the Supreme Court* (New York: Oxford University Press, 1993), 318.
81. John Paul Stevens, "Foreword," in Kenneth A. Manaster, *Illinois Justice: The Scandal of 1969 and the Rise of John Paul Stevens* (Chicago: University of Chicago Press, 2001), xii.
82. Jeffrey Rosen, "The Agonizer," *The New Yorker,* November 11, 1996, 87.
83. Jeffrey Toobin, *Too Close to Call: The Thirty-Six Day Battle to Decide the 2000 Election* (New York: Random House, 2001), 266–267.
84. *In the Matter of Wilkins,* 777 N.E. 2d 714, 720 (Ind. Sup. Ct. 2002).
85. John C. Jeffries Jr., *Justice Lewis F. Powell, Jr.* (New York: Scribner's, 1994), 534.

86. Alex Kozinski, "My Pizza with Nino," *Cardozo Law Review* 12 (June 1991): 1583–91. The quotation is on page 1588.
87. Rehnquist, "Chief Justices I Never Knew," 637.
88. Forrest Maltzman and Paul J. Wahlbeck, "Hail to the Chief: Opinion Assignment on the Supreme Court" (Paper presented at the annual meeting of the American Political Science Association, Chicago, August–September 1995), 11.
89. This discussion of criteria for opinion assignment is based largely on the findings for the 1953–1990 period in Maltzman and Wahlbeck, "Hail to the Chief"; and Maltzman and Wahlbeck, "May It Please the Chief? Opinion Assignments in the Rehnquist Court," *American Journal of Political Science* 40 (May 1996): 421–443.
90. Rehnquist, *The Supreme Court,* 260.
91. Ruth Marcus, "Alumni Brennan, Blackmun Greet Harvard Law Freshmen," *Washington Post,* September 6, 1986, 2.
92. Tony Mauro, "The Highs and Lows of the 1992 Court," *Legal Times,* December 28, 1993, 14.
93. Bernard Schwartz, *Behind Bakke: Affirmative Action and the Supreme Court* (New York: New York University Press, 1988), 99.
94. Bernard Schwartz, *The Ascent of Pragmatism: The Burger Court in Action* (Reading, Mass.: Addison-Wesley, 1990), 14.
95. Garrow, *Liberty and Sexuality,* 558.
96. Jeffries, *Justice Lewis F. Powell, Jr.,* 545.
97. This discussion of Rehnquist is based in part on Schwartz, *A History of the Supreme Court,* 364–367; Savage, *Turning Right;* David G. Savage, "The Rehnquist Court," *Los Angeles Times Magazine,* September 29, 1991, 12–16, 38, 40; David J. Garrow, "The Rehnquist Reins," *New York Times Magazine,* October 6, 1996, 65–71, 82, 85; and Sue Davis, "The Chief Justice and Judicial Decision-Making: The Institutional Basis for Leadership on the Supreme Court," in *Supreme Court Decision-Making: New Institutionalist Approaches,* ed. Cornell W. Clayton and Howard Gillman (Chicago: University of Chicago Press, 1999), 141–149.
98. Joan Biskupic, "After 30 Years, Chief Sees a Court More Like Him," *USA Today,* June 28, 2002, 4A.
99. Lawrence M. Friedman, "The Rehnquist Court: Some More or Less Historical Comments," in *The Rehnquist Court: A Retrospective,* ed. Martin H. Belsky (New York: Oxford University Press, 2002), 146.
100. Joan Biskupic, "High Court's Uncommon Bond," *USA Today,* June 30–July 2, 2000, 1A.
101. The quotations are from, respectively, *McKune v. Lile,* 536 U.S. 24, 55 (2002) (Stevens); *Board of Education v. Earls,* 536 U.S. 822, 852 (2002) (Ginsburg); and *Atkins v. Virginia,* 536 U.S. 304, 347 (2002) (Scalia).
102. Miller, "Breyer Speaks to Bar Convention," 11.
103. Joan Biskupic, "Election Still Splits Court," *USA Today,* January 22, 2001, 1A, 2A.
104. See Phillip J. Cooper, *Battles on the Bench: Conflict Inside the Supreme Court* (Lawrence: University Press of Kansas, 1995).
105. Jeffrey Rosen, "The New Look of Liberalism on the Court," *New York Times Magazine,* October 5, 1997, 65.
106. *Verizon Maryland Inc. v. Public Service Commission of Maryland,* 535 U.S. 635, 638 (2002).

107. Harold Hongju Koh, "A Tribute to Justice Harry A. Blackmun," *Harvard Law Review* 108 (November 1994): 20.
108. James L. Gibson, Gregory A. Caldeira, and Lester Kenyatta Spence, "The Supreme Court and the U.S. Presidential Election of 2000: Wounds, Self-Inflicted or Otherwise?" *British Journal of Political Science,* forthcoming; Stephen P. Nicholson and Robert M. Howard, "Framing Support for the Supreme Court in the Aftermath of *Bush v. Gore,*" *Journal of Politics* 65 (August 2003): 676–695.
109. *Board of Education v. Earls* (2002). See Bob Egelko, "Supreme Court Justices Touchy About Drugs," *San Francisco Chronicle,* March 31, 2002, A4.
110. *Skinner v. Railway Labor Executives' Association,* 489 U.S. 602, 654 (1989).
111. See William Mishler and Reginald S. Sheehan, "The Supreme Court as a Countermajoritarian Institution? The Impact of Public Opinion on Supreme Court Decisions," *American Political Science Review* 87 (March 1993): 87–101; Helmut Norpoth and Jeffrey A. Segal, "Popular Impact on Supreme Court Decisions: Comment," *American Political Science Review* 88 (September 1994): 711–716; and Roy B. Flemming and B. Dan Wood, "The Public and the Supreme Court: Individual Justice Responsiveness to American Policy Moods," *American Journal of Political Science* 41 (April 1997): 468–498.
112. William H. Rehnquist, "Constitutional Law and Public Opinion" (Talk presented at Suffolk University School of Law, Boston, April 10, 1986), 40–41.
113. Antonin Scalia, "Scalia: Article Off Base," *Legal Times,* October 2, 2000, 85.
114. Terry Eastland, "The Tempting of Justice Kennedy," *American Spectator* 26 (February 1993): 32–37. See also Thomas Sowell, "Blackmun Plays to the Crowd," *St. Louis Post Dispatch,* March 4, 1994, 7B; and Robert H. Bork, "Again, a Struggle for the Soul of the Court," *New York Times,* July 8, 1992, A19.
115. Joseph D. Kearney and Thomas W. Merrill, "The Influence of Amicus Curiae Briefs on the Supreme Court," *University of Pennsylvania Law Review* 148 (January 2000): 757.
116. This proportion is based on decisions on the merits, with opinions, in which the federal government or one of its agencies was a party, excluding a summary reversal.
117. Kevin T. McGuire, "Explaining Executive Success in the U.S. Supreme Court," *Political Research Quarterly* 51 (June 1998): 505–526; see Corey A. Ditslear, "Office of the Solicitor General Participation Before the United States Supreme Court: Influences on the Decision-Making Process" (Ph.D. diss., Ohio State University, 2002), chap. 4.
118. Linda Greenhouse, "Affirmative Reaction: Can the Justices Buck What the Establishment Backs?" *New York Times,* March 30, 2003, sec. 4, p. 4. The cases were *Gratz v. Bollinger* (2003) and *Grutter v. Bollinger* (2003).
119. Seth P. Waxman, "Foreword: Does the Solicitor General Matter?" *Stanford Law Review* 53 (May 2001): 1115–26.
120. For contrasting arguments and evidence, see Segal, "Separation-of-Powers Games"; and Mario Bergara, Barak Richman, and Pablo T. Spiller, "Modeling Supreme Court Strategic Decision Making: The Congressional Constraint," *Legislative Studies Quarterly* 28 (May 2003): 247–280.

121. Mark A. Graber, "The Problematic Establishment of Judicial Review," in *The Supreme Court in American Politics: New Institutionalist Interpretations,* ed. Howard Gillman and Cornell Clayton (Lawrence: University Press of Kansas, 1999), 28–42.
122. Jan Crawford Greenburg, "Speculation Builds over Chief Justice Successor," *Chicago Tribune,* February 17, 2002, sec. 1, pp. 1, 10; Tony Mauro, "Kennedy on Campaign Trail?" *Legal Times,* April 1, 2002, 7.
123. See, for example, *Lawrence v. Texas* (2003).

Chapter 5

Policy Outputs

The last two chapters examined the processes that shape the Supreme Court's policies. In this chapter, I consider the substance of what the Court does. What kinds of issues does the Court address? How active is it as a policymaker? What is the ideological content of its policies? This chapter examines those questions by looking at the Court's policy outputs in the current era and in the past. It concludes by developing an explanation for historical patterns in the Court's outputs.

Areas of Activity: What the Court Addresses

During any given term, the Supreme Court resolves a broad range of issues in fields as varied as antitrust, environmental protection, and freedom of speech. In this sense the Court's agenda is highly diverse. But the Court generally devotes most of its efforts to a few policy fields. To a considerable degree, then, the Court is a specialist.

The Court's Current Activity

The content of the Court's agenda can be illustrated with the cases that it heard in the 2001 term. It is useful first to describe the issues in a fairly representative sample of cases decided during that term.

1. Whether a defendant facing a possible death sentence has the right to a jury instruction informing the jury that a life sentence would make the defendant ineligible for parole (*Kelly v. South Carolina*, 2002).

2. Whether the states' sovereign immunity from lawsuits prevents the Federal Maritime Commission from adjudicating a private party's complaint against a state (*Federal Maritime Commission v. South Carolina State Ports Authority*, 2002).

3. Whether a state supreme court rule that prohibits candidates for judgeships from announcing their views on disputed legal or political

issues violates freedom of speech under the First and Fourteenth Amendments (*Republican Party of Minnesota v. White*, 2002).

4. Whether the British Virgin Islands constitutes a foreign state, so that a corporation organized under its laws is subject to the diversity jurisdiction of the federal courts (*JPMorgan Chase Bank v. Traffic Stream Infrastructure Ltd.* (2002).

5. Whether an indigent defendant can be given a suspended prison sentence, which might be imposed in the future, if the defendant was not provided with an attorney in the case (*Alabama v. Shelton*, 2002).

6. Whether utility patents may be issued for newly developed plant breeds (*J. E. M. Ag Supply, Inc. v. Pioneer Hi-Bred International, Inc.*, 2001).

7. Whether the Internal Revenue Service can use the "aggregate estimation" method to determine the amount of tips that restaurant employees received (*United States v. Fior D'Italia, Inc.*, 2002).

8. Whether the prohibition of advertising and promotion for compounded drugs in the federal Food and Drug Administration Modernization Act of 1997 violates the guarantee of free speech in the First Amendment (*Thompson v. Western States Medical Center*, 2002).

9. When the federal government seeks forfeiture of cash belonging to a prisoner, whether sending a notice of the intended forfeiture by certified mail satisfies Fifth Amendment due process if there is no proof that the prisoner actually received the notice (*Dusenbery v. United States*, 2002).

10. Whether a complaint of employment discrimination in federal court must contain specific facts establishing a prima facie case of discrimination (*Swierkiewicz v. Sorema N. A.*, 2002).

Table 5-1 provides a more systematic picture of the Court's agenda in the 2001 term by summarizing the characteristics of the eighty decisions with full opinions in that term. The distribution of cases by category is similar to the distribution in other recent terms.

The Court's decisions were closely connected with the other branches of government. The federal government or one of its agencies was a party in nearly half the cases, and in many others a state or local government was a party. Moreover, most of the disputes between private parties were based directly on government policy, such as regulation of labor-management relations and protection against discrimination.

There were about equal numbers of constitutional and statutory cases. Observers of the Court tend to focus on its interpretations of the Constitution, which often involve fundamental issues about the structure and power of government. But the Court also acts as interpreter of federal statutes, adjudicating what are often important disputes about their meaning.

TABLE 5-1
Characteristics of Decisions by the Supreme Court with Full Opinions, 2001 Term

Characteristic	Number	Percentage
Number of decisions	80	—
Cases from lower federal courts	71	89
Cases from state courts	9	11
Original cases	0	0
Federal government party[a]	34	43
State or local government party[a]	28	35
No government party	18	23
Constitutional issue present[b]	41	51
No constitutional issue	39	49
Civil liberties issue present[b]	47	59
No civil liberties issue	33	41
Criminal cases[c]	20	25
Civil cases	60	75

Note: The data are based on listings of cases in *United States Supreme Court Reports, Lawyers' Edition*. Consolidated cases decided with one set of opinions were counted once.

a. Cases with both a federal government party and another government party were listed as federal government. Government as party includes agencies and individual government officials.

b. Cases were counted as having constitutional or civil liberties issues if the parties raised those issues, even if the Court decided them on the basis of other issues.

c. Includes actions brought by prisoners to challenge the legality of their convictions but excludes cases concerning rights of prisoners.

In the 2001 term, as has been true for three decades, the Court's primary area of activity was civil liberties. As in earlier discussions, the term *civil liberties* refers here to three general types of rights: procedural rights of people involved in government proceedings; the right of disadvantaged groups to equal treatment; and certain "substantive" rights, the most important of which are freedom of expression and freedom of religion. By that definition, more than half the Court's decisions fell in this area.

Related to the Court's civil liberties emphasis is its substantial work in criminal law and procedure. One quarter of the 2001 decisions resulted from criminal prosecutions, about average for recent terms. Some criminal cases involve statutory interpretation, but a large majority concern constitutional rights of due process.

The list of representative cases from the 2001 term illustrates two other areas in which the Court is active. Outside of civil liberties, the largest number of cases concern economic issues. While most civil liberties cases are based on constitutional questions, economic cases generally involve statutory interpretation. Most of these cases arise from government regulation of economic activity, such as labor-management relations, antitrust, and environmental protection. Issues related to tax law are also common.

Another major subject of Court activity is federalism, the division of power between federal and state governments. Federalism overlaps with other categories, and most federalism cases concern economic issues. This concern has been prominent in the past decade.

Taken together, civil liberties, economic policy, and federalism cover a substantial portion of the issues that arise in government. Still, the Court's emphasis on those issues constitutes something of a specialized focus. Most striking is its concentration on civil liberties. Although civil liberties cases are quite varied, the fact that half of the Court's decisions concern this single kind of issue is an indication of the Court's specialization.

Change in the Court's Agenda

The Court's agenda is far from static. Even over a few terms, the Court's attention to specific categories of cases sometimes increases or decreases substantially. The shape of its agenda as a whole changes more slowly, but over long periods it may undergo fundamental change.[1]

Changes in Specific Areas. Until 1980 the Supreme Court seldom dealt with issues concerning employee pension plans. Since then the Court has decided more than forty cases concerning these issues. The source of this change is simple: Congress enacted the Employee Retirement Income Security Act of 1974. This regulation of pension plans raised a variety of legal questions that the courts had to address, and the justices have seen a need to resolve many of these questions themselves. As a result, pensions have become a staple of the Court's work.

This kind of history is not unusual. When Congress adopts legislation that creates new legal questions and legal rights in a policy area, the Court's attention to that area often increases considerably. An especially striking example is employment discrimination. Until Congress legislated in this area, people who felt that they had suffered from discrimination had little basis for bringing cases to court. But Congress enacted a series of statutes in this field from 1963 on, creating a large number of legal questions to resolve. As a result, the Court has heard about 120 cases in this area over the past three decades.

The Court itself can open up new areas on its agenda with decisions that create legal rights or add to existing rights. When the Court held in

Roe v. Wade (1973) that the abortion laws of most states violated the constitutional right to privacy, it ensured that it would have to decide a stream of cases involving challenges to new abortion laws. The same was true of the Court's death penalty decisions in 1976, which established that capital punishment was constitutionally acceptable but also held that there were limits on its use.[2] Since then, the Court has addressed a wide range of issues involving the death penalty in more than eighty cases.

When Congress or the Court takes action that might open up a new area, the opening will actually occur only if litigants bring cases to the Court. Often, interest groups play an important role in this process. In *Reed v. Reed* (1971) the Court signaled that it was receptive to challenges of laws that treat women and men differently. The Women's Rights Project of the American Civil Liberties Union and other groups then acted to ensure that challenges to such laws would reach the Court.

Just as issues can rise on the Court's agenda, they can also recede. Often, a new statute or Court decision raises a series of issues that the Court resolves. Once they are resolved, the Court need not decide as many cases in this area. To a degree, this has been true of the Fourteenth Amendment's protection against sex discrimination. The justices may simply decide that they will devote less attention to a field of policy, a path they took in patent law. Congress can cut off an area by changing the law, as it did with cases involving the military draft when it ended the draft in 1973.

Changes in the Agenda as a Whole. Beyond such changes in specific areas, the overall pattern of the Court's agenda may change over a period of several decades. Indeed, comparison of the Court's 2001 agenda with those of the early 1930s indicates that there has been a fundamental change in the kinds of issues and cases the Court addresses. This change is documented by findings from Richard Pacelle's study of the Court's agenda for the 1933 through 1995 terms, summarized in Table 5-2. Pacelle has also illuminated the process by which this change occurred, and the discussion that follows is based primarily on his analysis.

The Court's agenda in the 1930s was similar to its agenda throughout the preceding half century.[3] Issues of procedural due process constituted a small proportion of the agenda, and other civil liberties issues were barely present. Far more numerous were cases that concerned economic issues, arising primarily from government economic policies. Also important but clearly secondary were cases about federalism.

By the 1960s civil liberties had replaced economics as the Court's primary concern, and this broad category has remained dominant ever since. Most categories of economic cases, including challenges to federal taxes and state regulatory policies, have declined precipitously in number.

TABLE 5-2
Percentages of Supreme Court Agenda Devoted to
Selected Issue Areas, in Selected Periods, 1933–1995 Terms

	Terms				
Issue area	1933– 1942	1948– 1957	1963– 1972	1978– 1987	1991– 1995
Civil liberties[a]	10.0	28.9	53.3	53.1	49.8
Racial equality[b]	0.5	1.8	6.3	4.6	2.6
Criminal procedure[b]	4.8	14.2	23.4	22.6	20.4
Federal taxation	16.8	7.4	4.0	2.8	3.0
Federalism	13.9	10.8	6.2	10.6	10.3

Sources: Richard L. Pacelle Jr., *The Transformation of the Supreme Court's Agenda from the New Deal to the Reagan Administration* (Boulder: Westview Press, 1991), 56–57, 147, 159. Data for 1991–1995 were provided by Richard Pacelle.

Note: Only cases with opinions of at least one page in length are included.

a. Includes due process, equality, and substantive rights such as freedom of expression and freedom of religion.

b. Included within civil liberties category.

Federal economic regulation has become a much smaller component of the agenda, although the number of cases arising in areas such as securities and environmental regulation has actually increased. Federalism cases are also less common than they were in the 1930s, but this category has had a resurgence since the 1970s and may continue to grow. Federalism aside, the major trend is clear: the Court has evolved from an institution concerned primarily with economic issues to one that gives attention primarily to individual liberties.

Many forces contributed to this change in the Court's agenda, ranging from public opinion to federal legislation. But actions by the Court itself had the most direct effect. Perhaps most important, the justices became more interested in protecting civil liberties and thus in hearing challenges to government policies that allegedly infringed on liberties. Because they had to make room on the agenda for civil liberties cases and because they were less interested in scrutinizing economic policies, the justices gave more limited attention to fields other than civil liberties.

But the shift in emphasis from economics to civil liberties was gradual rather than swift. The Court had to continue addressing important economic issues, particularly those that had caused conflicts between lower courts. Litigants also needed time to respond to the Court's growing support for civil liberties by bringing additional cases to the Court. And massive change in the agenda inevitably takes time; the Court could not have moved simultaneously into all the diverse areas of civil liberties that have occupied a place on its agenda since the 1960s. Inevitably, the shift was not total: the Court decides a great many cases that concern economic issues, even while its agenda emphasizes civil liberties.

A Broader View of the Agenda

If the Supreme Court's current agenda differs from the agendas of previous Courts, it also differs from those of other policymakers. In turn, those differences provide some perspective on the Court's role.

Comparison with Other Institutions. In some respects, the Supreme Court's agenda is similar to that of other appellate courts, especially state supreme courts and federal courts of appeals. To a considerable extent, all of these courts focus on government parties and government policy. Criminal cases are prominent on the agendas of virtually all appellate courts, and most give substantial attention to economic issues. Except for the rights of criminal defendants, however, civil liberties issues are relatively rare in lower appellate courts. The Supreme Court stands alone in the prominence of issues involving rights to equal treatment and freedom of expression.

Like the Court, the president is something of a specialist. But the president's agenda has its own emphases: foreign policy and maintenance of the nation's economic health. In contrast, the Court makes few decisions about foreign policy, and its decisions on economic policy barely touch the function of managing the economy.

In contrast, Congress is something of a generalist, spreading its activity across a large set of issues. One result is that the congressional agenda covers virtually all the types of policy that the Supreme Court deals with. But some of the issues that are central to the Court, especially in civil liberties, receive much less attention from Congress. And Congress gives a high priority to several fields, ranging from foreign policy to agriculture, that are less important to the Court.

The Court's Position. These comparisons of agendas underline the limited range of the Court's work. Its jurisdiction is very broad, but the bulk of its decisions are made in a few policy areas.

The Court's specialization affects its role in policymaking. By deciding as many civil liberties cases as it does, the Court can do much to shape law and policy in this area. In contrast, the Court's more limited activity in some major policy areas severely narrows its potential impact in those fields. It cannot have much effect on the law of contracts and personal injuries, to take two examples. Because of its agenda the Court today can

Iraq's ambassador to the United Nations speaks at a meeting of the Security Council in February 2003 about weapons inspections in Iraq; U.S. secretary of state Colin Powell listens. The Supreme Court plays only a minor role in shaping foreign policy, especially on issues of war and peace.

have little impact on government management of the economy and even less impact on foreign policy.[4] Many people consider these the two most important areas of government policy.

These realities should caution against the conclusion that the Supreme Court is the most important policymaker in the United States. The Court should not be regarded as preeminent when the range of its activities is so limited. It could not possibly be dominant as a policymaker except in federalism, civil liberties, and some limited areas of economic policy. For reasons that are discussed in the rest of this chapter and in Chapter 6, even here the Court's dominance is far from certain.

The Court's Activism

The Court's attention or inattention to various areas of policy helps determine where it is likely to play a significant role. But its impact also depends on how much it uses its decisions to make significant changes in government policy, engaging in what is labeled judicial activism.

Of the various forms of judicial activism, perhaps the most important is making decisions that conflict with policies of the other branches. This form of activism is often gauged by the Court's use of judicial review, its power to overturn acts of other policymakers on the ground that they violate the Constitution. The Court intervenes in government policy most directly and most clearly through its use of judicial review. And judicial review, unlike some other forms of activism, is easy to measure. For these reasons, it is a good focus for analysis of activism.

Overturning Acts of Congress

The most familiar use of judicial review comes in decisions holding that federal statutes are unconstitutional. Such rulings represent a striking assertion of power by the Court. When the Court overturns a federal law on constitutional grounds, it directly negates a decision by another branch of the federal government.

There is sometimes disagreement about whether the Court actually has struck down a statute. By one count, however, by the end of 2002 the Court had overturned 158 federal laws completely or in part.[5] This number in itself is noteworthy. On the one hand, it indicates that the Court has made fairly frequent use of its review power—on average, more than once every two years. On the other hand, the laws struck down by the Court constitute a minute fraction of the more than sixty thousand laws that Congress has adopted. A closer look at these decisions provides a better sense of their significance.[6]

One question is the importance of the statutes that the Court has overturned. The Court has struck down some statutes of major significance. Among these were the Missouri Compromise of 1820, concerning slavery in the territories, which the Court declared unconstitutional in the *Dred Scott* case in 1857; the laws prohibiting child labor that were struck down in 1918 and 1922; and the New Deal economic legislation that was overturned in 1935 and 1936.[7] In contrast, many of the Court's decisions declaring statutes unconstitutional have been unimportant to the policy goals of Congress and the president, either because the statutes were minor or because they were struck down only as they applied to particular circumstances.

A related question is the timing of judicial review. The Court's decisions striking down federal statutes fall into three groups of nearly equal size: those that came no more than four calendar years after a statute's enactment, those that came five to twelve years later, and those that occurred at least thirteen years later. Congress sometimes retains a strong commitment to a statute from an earlier period. But often few members care much if an older law is overturned: the statute becomes less relevant

TABLE 5-3
Number of Federal Statutes Held Unconstitutional by the Supreme Court, 1790–2002

Period	Number	Period	Number
1790–1799	0	1900–1909	9
1800–1809	1	1910–1919	6
1810–1819	0	1920–1929	15
1820–1829	0	1930–1939	13
1830–1839	0	1940–1949	2
1840–1849	0	1950–1959	5
1850–1859	1	1960–1969	16
1860–1869	4	1970–1979	20
1870–1879	7	1980–1989	16
1880–1889	4	1990–1999	23
1890–1899	5	2000–2002	11
		Total	158

Sources: Congressional Research Service, *The Constitution of the United States of America: Analysis and Interpretation* and *2000 Supplement* (Washington, D.C.: Government Printing Office, 1996, 2000); Kenneth Jost, *The Supreme Court Yearbook, 2000–2001* (Washington, D.C.: CQ Press, 2002); author's analysis of cases.

over time, or the collective point of view in Congress becomes less favorable to the provision in question.

For these reasons the Court's frequent use of its power to invalidate congressional acts is somewhat misleading. Any decision that strikes down a federal statute might seem likely to bring about a major conflict between the Court and Congress, but that is not necessarily the case. Conflict is most likely when the Court invalidates an important congressional policy within a few years of its enactment, but most decisions striking down statutes do not meet both those criteria.

Another way to gauge the significance of judicial review is in terms of the historical pattern of its use. As Table 5-3 shows, the Court has not overturned federal statutes at a consistent rate. Before 1865 it struck down only two statutes. The Court then began to exercise its judicial review power more actively, overturning thirty-five federal laws between 1865 and 1919. Two more increases, even more dramatic, followed: the Court struck down fifteen federal laws during the 1920s, and twelve from 1934 through 1936. Over the next quarter century, the Court used this power sparingly. But between 1960 and 2002, it overturned eighty-six statutes, far more than in any previous period of the same length and more than half of the total for the Court's entire history.

James Brady, at right, at the Supreme Court in 1997. In that
year the Court ruled that part of the "Brady bill," a gun control
law, violated states' rights under the Constitution.

The period of greatest conflict between the Court and Congress was
1918 to 1936, when the Court overturned twenty-nine federal laws. More
important, many of these laws were significant. Between 1918 and 1928,
the Court struck down two child labor laws and a minimum wage law,
along with several less important statutes. Then, between 1933 and 1936,
a majority of the Court engaged in a frontal attack on the New Deal program, an attack that ended with the Court's retreat in 1937.

Among all the statutes that the Court struck down between 1960 and
1994, a few were of major importance. *Buckley v. Valeo* (1976) and several
later decisions invalidated major provisions of the Federal Election Campaign Act on First Amendment grounds and thereby made comprehensive regulation of campaign finance impossible. In *Immigration and Naturalization Service v. Chadha* (1983), the Court struck down a relatively

minor provision of an immigration law. But its ruling indicated that the legislative veto, a widely used mechanism for congressional control of the executive branch, violated the constitutional separation of powers. These decisions were exceptions. In general, the laws overturned by the Court in the 1960–1994 period were not nearly as significant as the economic legislation that it struck down in the 1930s. Indeed, most of the Court's decisions striking down federal laws received little attention from the mass media or the general public.

Between 1995 and 2002, the Court invalidated thirty federal laws, a record number for an eight-year period. During this period, too, most of the laws involved were relatively minor. One exception was *Clinton v. City of New York* (1998), in which the Court ruled that Congress could not give presidents the power to veto individual items within budget bills and thereby ended a major innovation in policymaking.

The Court also handed down ten decisions that limited the power of Congress to regulate state governments. In these decisions the Court gave narrow interpretations to the Commerce Clause and the Fourteenth Amendment as bases for federal power while giving a broad interpretation to the Eleventh Amendment as a limit on lawsuits against states. In *Board of Trustees v. Garrett* (2001), for example, the Court ruled that Congress could not make it possible for disabled individuals to win monetary damages from states in lawsuits for discrimination. This set of decisions constitutes a substantial change in the federal-state balance. But it is not as consequential as the economic decisions of the 1920s and 1930s, because the current Congress is not inclined to assert federal power against the states in the areas where the Court has limited that power.

Overturning State and Local Laws

The Supreme Court's exercise of judicial review over state and local laws has less of an activist element than does its use of that power over federal laws. When the Court strikes down a state law, it does not put itself in conflict with the other branches of the federal government. Indeed, it may be supporting their powers over those of the states. Still, it is invalidating the action of another policymaker. For that reason, this form of judicial review is significant.

From 1790 to 2002, by one count, the Court overturned 1,261 state statutes and local ordinances. Most were struck down on the ground that they directly violated the Constitution, the others because they were superseded by federal law under the constitutional principle of federal supremacy. That is eight times the number of federal statutes struck down by the Court (see Table 5-3). The disparity is even greater than this figure suggests, because many of the Court's decisions overturning particular state and local laws also applied to similar laws in other states.

TABLE 5-4
Number of State Laws and Local Ordinances
Held Unconstitutional by the Supreme Court, 1790–2002

Period	Number	Period	Number
1790–1799	0	1900–1909	40
1800–1809	1	1910–1919	118
1810–1819	7	1920–1929	139
1820–1829	8	1930–1939	93
1830–1839	3	1940–1949	57
1840–1849	9	1950–1959	61
1850–1859	7	1960–1969	149
1860–1869	23	1970–1979	193
1870–1879	36	1980–1989	162
1880–1889	46	1990–1999	61
1890–1899	36	2000–2002	12
		Total	1,261

Sources: Congressional Research Service, *The Constitution of the United States of America: Analysis and Interpretation* and *2000 Supplement* (Washington, D.C.: Government Printing Office, 1996, 2000); Kenneth Jost, *The Supreme Court Yearbook, 2000–2001* (Washington, D.C.: CQ Press, 2002); author's analysis of cases.

As shown in Table 5-4, the rate at which the Court invalidates state and local laws has increased tremendously over time. One jump came in the 1860s, another early in the twentieth century. The highest rate of decisions striking down state and local laws occurred from the 1960s through the 1980s. In that period, the Court declared unconstitutional an average of seventeen such laws per year. The rate of invalidations has been much lower since 1990, returning to the level of the 1940s and 1950s. That decline probably reflects the same sympathy for the states that has led the Rehnquist Court to limit federal power over the states.

Although the Court struck down relatively few state laws before 1860, its decisions during that period were important because they limited state powers under the Constitution. For example, under John Marshall (1801–1835) the Court weakened the states with decisions such as *McCulloch v. Maryland* (1819), which denied the states power to tax federal agencies, and *Gibbons v. Ogden* (1824), which narrowed state power to regulate commerce.

The state and local laws the Court has overturned in more recent periods have been a mixture of the important and the minor. In the aggregate, the Court's decisions have given it a significant role in shaping state policy. During the late nineteenth century and the first third of the twentieth, the Court struck down a great deal of state economic legislation, including many laws regulating business practices and labor relations. The net effect was to turn back much of a major tide of public policy.

Some of the Court's decisions since the mid-1950s have also impinged on major elements of state policy. A series of rulings helped to break down the legal bases of racial segregation and discrimination in southern states. In 1973 the Court overturned the broad prohibitions of abortion that existed in most states, thereby requiring a general legalization of abortion, and it has struck down a number of new laws regulating abortion since then. And through a long series of decisions, the Court limited state power to regulate the economy in areas that Congress has preempted under its constitutional supremacy. In doing so, the Court shifted power further toward the federal government and away from the states. The current Court is reversing this shift to a degree, but it is not yet clear how far the reversal will extend.

Other Targets of Judicial Review

The Supreme Court can declare unconstitutional any government policy or practice, not just laws enacted by legislative bodies. The number of nonstatutory policies and practices that the Court has struck down is probably much larger than the 1,400 laws it has overturned. In 2001 and 2002, for example, the Court held that policies established by a local school board, a state attorney general, and a state supreme court were unconstitutional.[8]

The Court is especially active in overseeing criminal procedure under the Constitution, and it frequently holds that actions by police officers or trial judges violate the rights of defendants. One example is *Kyllo v. United States* (2001), in which the Court ruled that it was unconstitutional for law enforcement officers to use a "thermal imaging device" to detect illegal drugs in homes without a warrant. By playing this role, the Court has had a major impact on the criminal justice process.

Of particular interest is the Court's review of presidential orders and policies. Decisions of presidents or officials acting on their behalf can be challenged on the grounds that they are unauthorized by the Constitution or that they violate a constitutional rule. It is difficult to say how frequently the Court strikes down presidential actions as unconstitutional, because it is often unclear whether an action by the executive branch should be considered "presidential." But such decisions by the Court seem to be relatively rare.[9]

The Court has invalidated a few major actions by presidents, however. In *Ex parte Milligan* (1866), it held that President Abraham Lincoln had lacked the power to suspend the writ of habeas corpus for military prisoners during the Civil War. And in *Youngstown Sheet and Tube Co. v. Sawyer* (1952), it declared that President Harry Truman had acted illegally during the Korean War when he ordered the federal government to seize and operate major steel mills because their workers were preparing to go on strike. Decisions of another type, which limited presidents' power to withhold information from courts and their immunity from lawsuits, led to President Nixon's resignation and President Clinton's impeachment.[10]

Judicial Review: The General Picture

The Supreme Court's record of judicial review is complex. The Court has been more activist in some eras than others. On the whole, the level of activism has increased over time, in part because of growth in the volume of government activity that can be challenged. The Court has struck down far more state and local policies than federal policies, and it has done more to limit state and local action than federal action.

The Court's overall record is ambiguous. The justices have made considerable use of the power of judicial review, thereby making the Court a major participant in the policymaking process. Yet the justices also have been quite selective in using their power to strike down laws. Partly as a result, the great majority of public policies at all levels of government have continued without Court interference. Judicial review has given the Court a major role in policymaking, but it has not given the Court a dominant position in the national government.

Statutory Interpretation

Historically, only a minority of the Supreme Court's decisions have determined whether some government practice is unconstitutional. Instead, most have interpreted federal statutes. Statutory interpretation may seem routine, but it can involve activism in at least two senses.

First, the Court's statutory decisions often determine whether an administrative agency has interpreted a statute correctly in the process of implementing it. If the Court concludes that an agency has erred, it strikes down the agency's action as contrary to the statute. In 1996 the federal Food and Drug Administration decided that a statute giving the FDA power to regulate drugs and devices affecting the body extended to cigarettes and smokeless tobacco, and it issued a set of sweeping regulations as a means to reduce tobacco use by young people. Tobacco companies, manufacturers, and advertisers challenged the regulations. In *Food and Drug Administration v. Brown & Williamson Tobacco Corporation* (2000), the Court ruled that the statute did not give the FDA power to regulate tobacco products, thereby blocking a major anti-tobacco campaign.

More broadly, the Court often puts its own stamp on a statute through its interpretations of that statute over the years. It has done so with its decisions on antitrust, labor relations, and environmental protection. The

Court's decisions in these areas have shaped the coverage and operation of major statutes.

This process is exemplified by Title VII of the Civil Rights Act of 1964, the most important of the federal statutes that prohibit employment discrimination. As with many other statutes, Congress laid out the broad outlines of the law and left it to the other branches to fill in the gaps. Over the years the Court has resolved a number of major issues. For example, it has established and revised the guidelines that courts use to determine whether an employer has engaged in discrimination.[11] It ruled that a company's policies could violate Title VII on the basis of their impact, even if the employer did not intend to discriminate.[12] It held that sexual harassment may constitute sex discrimination under Title VII and set up rules to determine when an employer is legally responsible for harassment.[13] Through these and other rulings the Court has had a major impact on the use and impact of this statute.

The Content of Policy

In the preceding sections of this chapter I have examined the areas in which the Supreme Court concentrates its efforts and the extent of its activism. A third aspect of the Court's role as a policymaker is the substance or content of its policies. This content can best be understood in terms of its ideological direction and its beneficiaries.

The 1890s to the 1930s

Scrutinizing Economic Regulation. In 1915 the Supreme Court decided *South Covington & Cincinnati Street Railway Co. v. City of Covington.* The company, which ran streetcars between Covington, Kentucky, and Cincinnati, Ohio, challenged several provisions of a Covington ordinance regulating its operations. The Court struck down some provisions on the ground that they constituted a burden on interstate commerce between Ohio and Kentucky. The Court also declared invalid a regulation stipulating that the temperature in the cars never be permitted to go below fifty degrees Fahrenheit: "We therefore think . . . this feature of the ordinance is unreasonable and cannot be sustained"—apparently on the ground that the regulation violated the Fourteenth Amendment by depriving the company of its property without due process of law.

The *South Covington* case illustrates some important characteristics of the Court's decisions during the period from the 1890s to the late 1930s. In that period the Court dealt primarily with economic issues, especially government policies that affected private businesses. Most important, it ruled on challenges to growing government regulation of business practices.

The Court frequently ruled in favor of government in these cases, rejecting most challenges to federal and state policies and giving broad interpretations to some government powers.[14] But the Court also limited government regulatory powers under the Constitution, and over time its limits on regulation became tighter. This development is reflected in the number of laws involving economic policy that the Court struck down each decade: 44 from 1900 to 1909, 112 from 1910 to 1919, and 133 from 1920 to 1929.[15] The Court's attacks on government regulation were strongest in the mid-1930s, when it declared unconstitutional most of the major statutes in President Franklin Roosevelt's New Deal program to deal with the Great Depression.

The theme of limiting government regulatory powers was reflected in the Court's constitutional doctrines. At the national level, the Court gave narrow interpretations to congressional powers over taxation and interstate commerce. In contrast, the Court read the general limitation on federal power in the Tenth Amendment broadly as a bar to certain federal action on the ground that it interfered with state prerogatives. At the state level, the Court ruled in 1886 that corporations were "persons" with rights protected by the Fourteenth Amendment.[16] Further, it interpreted the Fourteenth Amendment requirement that state governments provide "due process of law" in making decisions as an absolute prohibition of regulations that interfered unduly with the liberty and property rights of businesses. The Court's ruling against the streetcar temperature regulation was one of many such decisions.

The Court's Beneficiaries. The business community benefited from the Court's policies during this period, and major corporations benefited the most. Much of the regulatory legislation the Court overturned or limited was aimed at the activities of large businesses, because legislators believed that these businesses abused their great economic power. The railroads were the most prominent example. Although the Court allowed a good deal of government control over railroads, it also struck down a large body of railroad regulation.[17] In the decade from 1910 to 1919, the Court overturned forty-one state laws in cases brought by railroad companies. Major corporations such as railroads might be considered the clientele of the Court from the 1890s to the 1930s.

Large corporations did not simply benefit from the Court's policies; they helped to bring them about.[18] Beginning in the late nineteenth century, the corporate community employed much of the best legal talent in the United States to challenge the validity of regulatory statutes, and the effective advocacy of these attorneys laid some of the groundwork for the Court's policies favoring business.

Corporate interests came to the judiciary because of their defeats elsewhere in government. On the whole, Congress and the state legislatures were friendly to business interests, but they did enact a good many regulations of private enterprise. In scrutinizing these regulations closely, the Court served as a court of last resort for corporations in a political sense as well as the legal sense.

Civil Liberties: A Limited Concern. Civil liberties, as I have defined them, were a minor concern of the Court between 1890 and the mid-1930s. Only occasionally did it hear cases dealing with issues such as the procedural rights of criminal defendants and discrimination against disadvantaged groups.

The Court issued a number of specific decisions that favored civil liberties in this period.[19] But the justices gave much less protection to individual liberties than to the economic rights of businesses. The Court's limited support for racial equality was exemplified by *Plessy v. Ferguson* (1896), in which it promoted racial segregation by ruling that state governments could mandate "separate but equal" facilities for different racial groups. In 1908 the Court held that only a limited set of the procedural rights for criminal defendants in the Bill of Rights were "incorporated" into the Due Process Clause of the Fourteenth Amendment and thus applicable to proceedings in state courts.[20] Late in that era, the Court ruled that the Due Process Clause protected freedom of speech and freedom of the press from state violations. But in a series of decisions it held that the federal government could prosecute people whose expressions allegedly endangered military recruitment and other national security interests.[21]

Overview. In ideological terms, the Court of this period was predominately conservative. Most of its activism was on behalf of advantaged interests such as business corporations. It did little to protect disadvantaged groups such as racial minorities.

This conservatism was not new; the dominant themes of the Court's work in earlier periods were also conservative. The Court provided considerable support for the rights of property holders and much less support for values such as civil liberties.

Because of this history, observers of the Supreme Court in the New Deal period might well have concluded that the Court was a fundamentally conservative institution. Indeed, this was the position of two distinguished observers in the early 1940s. Henry Steele Commager argued in 1943 that, with one possible exception, the Court had never intervened on behalf of the underprivileged; in fact, it frequently had blocked efforts by Congress to protect the underprivileged.[22] Two years earlier, Attorney General Robert Jackson, a future Supreme Court justice, reached this stark conclusion: "Never in its entire history can the Supreme Court be said to have for a single hour been representative of anything except the relatively conservative forces of its day." [23] Jackson may have exaggerated for effect, but he captured an important theme in the Court's history.

1937 to 1969

Even before Commager and Jackson described this record of conservatism, the Court began a shift in its direction that one historian has called "the Constitutional Revolution of 1937." That revolution, he said,

altered fundamentally the character of the Court's business, the nature of its decisions, and the alignment of its friends and foes. From the Marshall Court to the Hughes Court, the judiciary had been largely concerned with questions of property rights. After 1937, the most significant matters on the docket were civil liberties and other personal rights. . . . While from 1800 to 1937 the principal critics of the Supreme Court were social reformers and the main supporters people of means who were the principal beneficiaries of the Court's decisions, after 1937 roles were reversed, with liberals commending and conservatives censuring the Court.[24]

Acceptance of Government Economic Policy. In the first stage of the revolution, the Court abandoned its opposition to government intervention in economic matters. That step came quickly. In a series of decisions beginning in 1937, majorities accepted the constitutional power of government—particularly the federal government—to regulate and to manage the economy. This shift culminated in *Wickard v. Filburn* (1942), in which the Court held that federal power to regulate interstate commerce extended so far that it applied to a farmer growing wheat for his own livestock.

This collective change of heart proved to be of long duration. The Court consistently upheld major economic legislation against constitutional challenge, striking down only one minor provision of federal law regulating business in the period from the 1940s through the 1960s.[25] Supporting federal supremacy in economic matters, the Court struck down many state laws on the ground that they impinged on the constitutional powers of the federal government or that they were preempted by federal statutes. But in other respects it gave state governments as well more freedom to make economic policy.

The Court continued to address economic issues involving interpretations of federal statutes. In some instances it overrode decisions of regulatory agencies such as the Interstate Commerce Commission and the National Labor Relations Board, holding that those decisions misinterpreted statutes. Some of these interventions were significant, but the Court did not challenge the basic economic programs of the federal government.

Support for Civil Liberties. In a 1938 decision, *United States v. Carolene Products Co.,* the Court signaled that there might be a second stage of the revolution. The case was one of many in which the Court upheld federal economic policies. But in what would become known as "footnote 4," Justice Harlan Stone's opinion for the Court argued that the Court was justified in taking a tolerant view of government economic policies while it gave "more exacting judicial scrutiny" to policies that infringed on civil liberties.

This second stage took a long time to develop. In the 1940s and 1950s, the Court gave more support to civil liberties than it had in earlier eras, but it did not make a strong and consistent commitment to the expansion of individual liberties. This stage of the revolution finally came to full fruition in the 1960s. Civil liberties issues dominated the Court's agenda for the first time, and the Court's decisions expanded liberties in many fields, from civil rights of racial minority groups to procedural rights of criminal defendants to freedom of expression.

As in the preceding era, the Court's policy position was reflected in the constitutional doctrines it adopted. Departing from its earlier view, the Court of the 1960s ruled that nearly all the rights of criminal defendants in the Bill of Rights were incorporated in the Fourteenth Amendment and therefore applied to state proceedings. In interpreting the Equal Protection Clause of the Fourteenth Amendment, the Court held that some government policies challenged as discriminatory would be given "strict scrutiny," if the groups that the law disfavored were especially vulnerable or if the rights involved were especially important.

The Court's sympathies for civil liberties were symbolized by *Griswold v. Connecticut* (1965), which established a new constitutional right to privacy. A majority of the justices discovered this right in provisions of the Bill of Rights nearly two centuries after those provisions were written.

The Court's direction after 1937 is illustrated by the pattern of decisions declaring laws unconstitutional. Figure 5-1 shows the number of economic statutes and statutes limiting civil liberties that the Court overturned in each decade of the twentieth century. The number of economic laws the Court struck down declined precipitously between the 1920s and the 1940s and remained relatively low in the 1950s and 1960s. In contrast, the number of statutes struck down on civil liberties grounds became significant in the 1940s and 1950s and rose sharply in the 1960s, reflecting the Court's growing liberalism. The reversal of these trends in the 1980s is also noteworthy; I discuss its implications later in this section.

The Court's Beneficiaries. The groups that the Court's policies benefited most were those that gained from expansions of legal protections for civil

FIGURE 5-1

Number of Economic and Civil Liberties Laws (Federal, State, and Local)
Overturned by the Supreme Court by Decade, 1900s–1990s

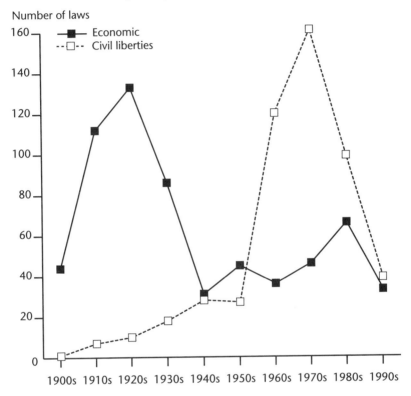

Sources: Congressional Research Service, T*he Constitution of the United States of America: Analysis and Interpretation* and *1998 Supplement* (Washington, D.C.: Government Printing Office, 1996, 1999); Kenneth Jost, *The Supreme Court Yearbook, 1998–1999* (Washington, D.C.: CQ Press, 2000); coded by the author.

Note: Civil liberties category does not include laws supportive of civil liberties.

liberties. Among them were socially and economically disadvantaged groups, criminal defendants, and people who took unpopular political stands. In 1967, during the Court's most liberal period, an unsympathetic editorial cartoonist depicted the Court as a Santa Claus whose list of gift recipients included communists, pornographers, extremists, drug push-ers, criminals, and perverts.[26] Whatever one may think of this characteri-zation, it underlines the change in the Court.

The segment of the population that the Court supported most strongly was black citizens, particularly in the fields of education and voting rights. The Court also made great efforts to protect the civil rights movement when southern states attacked the movement in the late 1950s and 1960s. Like the Court's policies favoring corporations in an earlier era, this support reflected effective litigation efforts, chiefly those of the NAACP Legal Defense Fund.

The Court was generally more favorable to liberties than the other branches of government. Congress did not adopt a strong civil rights bill attacking racial discrimination until 1964, ten years after *Brown v. Board of Education*. The Court's support for some other liberties diverged even more from the positions of the other branches. The procedural rights of criminal defendants had few advocates in the executive and legislative branches. Congress did much to attack leftist political groups such as the Communist Party. As it had done when it favored business interests, the Court provided relief for groups that fared less well elsewhere in government.

The Burger and Rehnquist Courts

In the period since 1969, the Supreme Court's policies have become considerably more conservative. The strength of this trend is difficult to gauge, and the Court frequently surprises observers who think they understand its direction. Reacting to the Court's decisions at the end of the 2002 term, for instance, one commentator said they "represent a shockingly progressive set of decisions from a supposedly conservative court." [27] As is often the case, it is more difficult to characterize the Court in the current era than in prior eras.

Uneven Support for Civil Liberties. On the whole, especially under Chief Justice Rehnquist, the Court has narrowed legal protections for individual liberties. The Court's shift is reflected in the declining rate of success for parties bringing civil liberties claims, shown in Table 4-4 (page 134). As Figure 5-1 shows, the number of laws struck down on the ground that they violated constitutional protections of civil liberties increased in the 1970s but declined dramatically after that.

The reduction in support for civil liberties came most quickly and has gone the furthest on defendants' rights. Since the early 1970s, for example, the Court has narrowed the *Miranda* rules for police questioning of suspects and the *Mapp* rule disallowing the use of evidence obtained through illegal searches, although it reaffirmed *Miranda v. Arizona* itself in *Dickerson v. United States* (2000). Even today the Court frequently supports defendants' rights in individual cases, but its general tendency is to interpret those rights narrowly. One illustration is its decision in *Atwater v.*

City of Lago Vista (2001), in which it upheld the arrest and temporary jailing of an automobile driver who was charged with a misdemeanor for which the maximum penalty was a $50 fine.

On issues of equality, the Court moved in a conservative direction more slowly and unevenly. The Burger Court was the first to strike down laws under the Equal Protection Clause on the ground that they discriminated against women. It also held that northern-style school segregation, in which schools were not explicitly segregated by law, could be unconstitutional. It generally gave broad interpretations to federal laws against discrimination but limited constitutional challenges to discrimination by private institutions that are connected to government. The Rehnquist Court has interpreted antidiscrimination laws more narrowly than its predecessor across a wide range of issues. It has approved the termination of court orders that maintained racial integration of public schools and limited the power of the federal government to enforce antidiscrimination laws against states. On the whole, however, the Court has continued to strengthen legal protections against sex discrimination.

Freedom of expression is the only field in which the Court has directly overruled major Warren Court decisions favoring civil liberties—specifically, on standards determining obscenity.[28] The Court has narrowed some other First Amendment protections as well. But this is the field in which the Rehnquist Court gives the greatest support to civil liberties. Most noteworthy are its protections for commercial speech such as advertising and its limits on government power to regulate spending in political campaigns.

More Limits on Economic Regulation. In interpreting federal statutes that regulate economic practices, the Burger and Rehnquist Courts have taken more conservative positions than the Warren Court. For example, in antitrust law the Court has moved away from Warren Court rulings that had made certain business practices automatically illegal.[29] In labor law the Court has given more support to employers, and for the most part it has interpreted environmental laws narrowly.

The Burger Court maintained the Court's broad interpretation of government powers under the Constitution to regulate economic activity. In contrast, the Rehnquist Court has taken some steps to limit those powers. It has expanded the right of property owners to monetary compensation when government regulates the use of their property. As in civil liberties, the Rehnquist Court has limited federal power over state governments in the economic arena.

The Court's Beneficiaries. To a considerable degree, state governments have benefited from policies of the Burger and Rehnquist Courts. The

Court has limited federal power over state governments, and the Rehnquist Court has struck down relatively few state laws. Yet the Court has been less favorable to states when they seek to regulate economic practices in areas where Congress has enacted legislation.

The Court's chief beneficiary has been the business community. The Court's policies generally have favored business interests across a wide range of fields, from labor law to freedom of speech. This support for business is symbolized by a series of decisions that allow a business to require that employees and consumers take legal grievances to an arbitration system specified by the business rather than to court.

The Court has not been uniformly favorable to business interests, however. As in any other era, the Court's current policies defy easy generalization. Still, both the Court's major beneficiaries and its dominant ideological direction differ from those of the late 1930s to the late 1960s.

Explaining the Court's Policies

In the preceding sections, I described changes over time in the Supreme Court's agenda, the extent of its activism, and the content of its policies. All these changes are summarized in Table 5-5.

The magnitude of these changes underlines the need for explanation: What forces can account for the various elements of the Court's policies? I have discussed these forces at several points earlier in the book, but in this section I pull them together and apply them to the broad patterns described in this chapter.

The Court's Environment

Freedom from External Pressures. The life terms of Supreme Court justices give them considerable freedom from the rest of government and from the general public. This freedom is reinforced by the reluctance of Congress and the president to use their powers over the Court as an institution. The Court's relative freedom from external pressures distinguishes it from the other branches of government.

The Court's freedom is reflected in some of the positions that it takes in individual decisions. Political realities would not allow Congress or a state legislature to support the right to burn the American flag as a form of political protest, nor could they prohibit student-led prayers at public schools' football games. But the Court could and did make such decisions.

More important, the Court has adopted some broad lines of policy that run counter to the majority view in the general public and elsewhere in government. To a considerable degree, it resisted the widespread support

TABLE 5-5
Summary of the Supreme Court's Policies During Three Historical Periods

Period	Predominant Area on Agenda	Extent of Activism	Content of Policy
1890s to 1930s	Economic regulation	Variable, becoming more inclined to strike down legislation	Mixed, primarily conservative
1937 to 1969	Economic regulation, then civil liberties	Initially low, becoming higher and then very high in 1960s	Generally liberal, very liberal in 1960s
Burger and Rehnquist Courts	Civil liberties	High, declining somewhat since 1990s	Moderate in 1970s, then increasingly conservative

Note: Characterizations of each period are approximate and subject to disagreement. Extent of activism is gauged primarily by striking down of government policies.

for regulation of business in the early twentieth century. Even more striking was the Court's expansion of the procedural rights of criminal defendants in the 1960s. No elected body, even a court, could have adopted so many rules that favored so unpopular a segment of society.

Influence from the Other Branches

The Court is not entirely free from external pressure. Congress and the president do hold substantial powers over the Court. Although these powers are seldom used, their use is often threatened. The other branches can legislate to raise the justices' salaries or leave them as they are, allow the Court's interpretations of statutes to stand or override them, and control its jurisdiction. They also can shape the implementation of the Court's decisions. Because such threats and criticisms are unpleasant in themselves, and because they might affect the Court's public standing, the justices have an incentive to minimize direct conflicts with Congress.

It is difficult to ascertain the impact of this incentive on the Court's policies. There are, however, specific instances when the justices seemed to avoid or minimize conflict with the other branches; the Court's retreat from some of its expansions of civil liberties in the late 1950s and its refusal to decide whether American participation in the Vietnam War was unconstitutional are two examples. More broadly, the Court has limited its use of judicial review to strike down significant national policies. It is noteworthy that the Court has struck down far more state laws than federal laws. The activism of the Warren Court in civil liberties was directed primarily at the states, and on the whole that Court was sympathetic to the federal government.[30] The Rehnquist Court's limitations on federal power have provoked little conflict with the other branches because members of Congress have been largely sympathetic toward those limitations.[31]

Societal Influence. The justices are also influenced by developments in society as a whole. Those developments can affect the justices' attitudes toward issues such as women's rights and illegal drugs. They can exert an influence on their own as well.

One form of influence concerns what might be called a requirement of minimum support: the justices are unlikely to take a sustained policy position that lacks significant support outside the Court, especially from the segments of society whose judgment is most important to them. Avoiding such positions helps to maintain support for the Court and respect for its members. Another form of influence derives from the litigation process. The Court acts on the cases that come to it: the Court cannot reshape its agenda without action by litigants and, more generally, without interest groups that support litigation and the broad social movements from which groups develop.

These influences are reflected in the two most distinctive patterns in the Court's policies during the twentieth century. The Court's resistance to government regulation of the economy before 1937 may have had only minority support in society, but most of the business community and much of the legal community strongly approved that position. Corporations and their representatives engaged in a concerted litigation campaign, bringing to the Court a steady flow of litigation and strong legal arguments against government economic policies.

The Court's expansions of civil liberties from the 1940s to the 1970s also benefited from social support. If these expansions were not always popular, they were favored by significant portions of society as a whole, including political elites and the legal community.[32] The development of organizations such as the NAACP and the ACLU and other social changes allowed civil liberties to take a more prominent place on the Court's agenda and for the Court to broaden its interpretations of constitutional rights.[33]

To a degree, the Court's increased conservatism since the 1970s reflects changing attitudes in the general public and a growth in litigation by conservative groups. By the same token, there is probably too little support for the Court to reverse fully its earlier expansions of government regulatory power and of protections for civil liberties. The Court has considerable freedom from societal opinion and social trends, but its freedom is not total.[34]

Policy Preferences and the Appointment Power

The freedom the justices do have generally allows them to make their own judgments about the issues they face. Those judgments are based in part on their assessments of cases in legal terms. But because the questions before the Court seldom have clear legal answers, justices' policy preferences are the chief basis for the positions they take.

The importance of policy preferences suggests that a great deal about the Court's policies can be explained simply and directly: during any given period in the Court's history, its policies have reflected the collective preferences of its members. Most of the justices who served from the 1890s to the 1930s were political conservatives who generally accepted government restrictions on civil liberties but questioned government regulation of business enterprises. In contrast, the justices who came to the Court from the late 1930s to the late 1960s were predominately liberals who supported government management of the economy and, in most instances, broader protections of civil liberties.

This explanation is not entirely satisfying because it does not show why certain preferences predominated on the Court during particular periods. One reason is that some national values were dominant during the periods in which justices were developing their attitudes. Another is that the justices came from backgrounds that instilled particular values in them. Most important, the higher-status backgrounds that predominated during most of the Court's history fostered sympathy for the views and interests of higher-status segments of society. Further, the prevailing ideology in elite segments of the legal profession shapes the views of its members, including future Supreme Court justices. The most direct source of the Court's collective preferences, however, is the decisions that presidents make in appointing justices.

Indeed, the predominant pattern of Supreme Court policy at any given time tends to reflect patterns of presidential appointments. If a series of appointees is politically conservative, the Court is likely to become a conservative body. And because vacancies occur on the Court with some frequency—on the average, once every two years—most presidents can have a significant impact on the Court's direction.

Robert Dahl argued that for this reason, "The policy views dominant on the Court are never for long out of line with the policy views dominant among the lawmaking majorities of the United States." [35] In Dahl's judgment, the president's power to make appointments has limited the frequency with which the Court overturns major federal statutes: justices generally take the same view of policy as members of Congress and the president, so they seldom upset the policies of these branches. I think there is much to Dahl's argument. But because of several complicating factors, the appointment power produces only imperfect control by "lawmaking majorities."

One factor is time lag. Most justices serve for many years, so the Court usually reflects the views of past presidents and Senates more than those of the current president and Senate. That is why Fred Rodell suggested that the aphorism, "the Supreme Court follows the election returns" be amended to refer to the returns "of ten or twelve years before." [36]

The lag varies chiefly because presidents have differing opportunities to make appointments. Richard Nixon could select four justices during his first term in office, while Franklin Roosevelt and Jimmy Carter made none in the four years after they took office. Had Roosevelt been able to replace two conservative justices early in his first term, the Court probably would not have blocked much of his New Deal program. Carter's luck was even worse; the absence of vacancies during his term, combined with his failed reelection bid in 1980, made him the first president to serve at least four years without appointing any justices. Bill Clinton chose two justices in his first two years in office, but the absence of vacancies in the next six years limited his impact on the Court's direction. A president's influence on the Court depends on its ideological configuration and on which members leave it as well as the simple number of appointments.

Another complicating factor is the deviation of justices from presidential expectations. Presidents usually get most of what they want from their appointees, but this is not a certainty. The unprecedented liberalism of the Court in the 1960s resulted largely from Dwight Eisenhower's miscalculations in nominating Earl Warren and William Brennan. The current Court would be more conservative if Sandra Day O'Connor, Anthony Kennedy, and especially David Souter had not diverged from the expectations of the Republican presidents who chose them.

The role of chance in shaping the Court's general direction also deserves emphasis. Chance plays a part in the timing of Court vacancies and in the performance of justices relative to their appointers' expectations. For that matter, the identity of the president who fills vacancies on the Court sometimes reflects chance. The close electoral victories of John Kennedy in 1960 and Richard Nixon in 1968 were hardly inevitable. The election of George W. Bush in 2000 was even narrower than Kennedy's or Nixon's. These presidents had a major impact on the Court's policies with their appointments, and Bush may achieve a similar impact.

The policy orientations of the Supreme Court between the 1890s and the 1960s reflected the existence of strong lawmaking majorities during two periods: the conservative Republican governments that dominated much of the period from the Civil War to the Great Depression, and the twelve-year tenure of Franklin Roosevelt accompanied by heavily Democratic Senates. These orientations also reflected patterns of resignations and deaths, unexpected behavior on the part of justices, and other factors that were a good deal less systematic. By the same token, if these factors had operated differently since 1969, the current Court might be less conservative—or even more so—than the one that actually exists. The forces that shape the Court's policy positions, like so much about the Court, are highly complex.

Conclusion

In this chapter I have examined a wide range of subjects concerning the Supreme Court's policy outputs. A few conclusions merit emphasis.

First, in some periods the Court's policymaking has had fairly obvious themes. During the first part of the twentieth century, the dominant theme was review of government economic policies. Later, the primary theme was review of practices that infringed on individual civil liberties. In each instance, the theme was evident in both the Court's agenda and the content of its decisions.

Second, these themes and the Court's work as a whole reflect both the justices' policy preferences and the influence of the Court's environment. In large part the Court's policies are what its members would like them to be. But the Court is subject to environmental influences that limit the divergence between Supreme Court decisions and the policies adopted by the other branches of government. In a different way, the president's appointment power establishes a direct link between the justices' policy preferences and their political environment.

Finally, the Court's role as a policymaker—though clearly significant—is a limited one. The Court gives considerable attention to some areas of policy but scarcely touches others. Some critical matters, such as foreign policy, are left almost entirely to the other two branches. Even in the areas that the Court gives the most attention, it seldom disturbs the basic features of national policy.

The significance of the Supreme Court as a policymaker ultimately depends on the impact of its decisions, the subject of Chapter 6. After examining the effect of the Court's decisions, I make a broader assessment of the Supreme Court's role in the policymaking process.

NOTES

1. This discussion of agenda change is drawn in part from Richard L. Pacelle Jr., *The Transformation of the Supreme Court's Agenda from the New Deal to the Reagan Administration* (Boulder: Westview Press, 1991); and Pacelle, "The Dynamics and Determinants of Agenda Change in the Rehnquist Court," in *Contemplating Courts,* ed. Lee Epstein (Washington, D.C.: CQ Press, 1995), 251–274. Numbers of cases involving particular issues or statutes were calculated from data in the U.S. Supreme Court Judicial Database created by Harold Spaeth, updated by the author.
2. The primary case was *Gregg v. Georgia* (1976).
3. Sandra L. Wood, Linda Camp Keith, Drew Noble Lanier, and Ayo Ogundele, "The Supreme Court, 1888–1940: An Empirical Overview," *Social Science History* 22 (summer 1998): 212–213.
4. On the Court and foreign policy, see Thomas M. Franck, *Political Questions/Judicial Answers: Does the Rule of Law Apply to Foreign Affairs?* (Princeton: Princeton University Press, 1992).
5. Because of ambiguities, different observers have obtained different numbers of laws overturned. The numbers of federal and state laws struck down by the Court that are presented in this chapter are based on data in Congressional Research Service, *The Constitution of the United States of America: Analysis and Interpretation* and *2000 Supplement* (Washington, D.C.: Government Printing Office, 1996, 2002); Kenneth Jost, *The Supreme Court Yearbook, 2000–2001* (Washington, D.C.: CQ Press, 2002); and my calculations for the 2001 term. The Congressional Research Service count has two unusual features. First, although the count is of statutes, when the Court overturned different sections of the same statute in different decisions, the service counts these as two different statutes. The second unusual feature concerns decisions that nullify state laws on the ground that they are preempted by

federal laws: apparently most, but not all, of these decisions are treated as declarations that the state law is unconstitutional.

6. The distinctions made in the paragraphs that follow are drawn chiefly from Robert A. Dahl, "Decision-Making in a Democracy: The Supreme Court as a National Policy-Maker," *Journal of Public Law* 6 (fall 1957): 279–295.

7. *Scott v. Sandford* (1857); *Hammer v. Dagenhart* (1918); *Bailey v. Drexel Furniture Co.* (1922). Decisions overturning New Deal economic legislation include *United States v. Butler* (1936) and *Schechter Poultry Corp. v. United States* (1935).

8. The decisions were, respectively, *Good News Club v. Milford Central School* (2001); *Lorillard Tobacco Company v. Reilly* (2001); and *Republican Party of Minnesota v. White* (2002).

9. Robert Scigliano, "The Presidency and the Judiciary," in *The Presidency and the Political System*, 3d ed., ed. Michael Nelson (Washington, D.C.: CQ Press, 1990), 471–499. See David A. Yalof, "The Presidency and the Judiciary," in *The Presidency and the Political System*, 7th ed., ed. Michael Nelson (Washington, D.C.: CQ Press, 2003), 501–503.

10. The decisions were *United States v. Nixon* (1974) and *Clinton v. Jones* (1997).

11. See, for example, *Desert Palace, Inc. v. Costa* (2003).

12. *Griggs v. Duke Power Co.* (1971).

13. *Meritor Savings Bank v. Vinson* (1986); *Burlington Industries v. Ellerth* (1998).

14. Wood et al., "The Supreme Court, 1888–1940," 215–216; William G. Ross, *A Muted Fury: Populists, Progressives, and Labor Unions Confront the Courts, 1890–1937* (Princeton: Princeton University Press, 1994).

15. To obtain these figures and others to be presented later in the chapter, I categorized decisions that struck down laws according to whether they pertained to economics, civil liberties, or other subjects. The criteria that I used were necessarily arbitrary; other criteria would have resulted in slightly different totals.

16. *Santa Clara County v. Southern Pacific Railroad Co.* (1886).

17. James W. Ely Jr., *Railroads and American Law* (Lawrence: University Press of Kansas, 2001); Richard C. Cortner, *The Iron Horse and the Constitution: The Railroads and the Transformation of the Fourteenth Amendment* (Westport, Conn.: Greenwood Press, 1993).

18. Benjamin Twiss, *Lawyers and the Constitution* (Princeton: Princeton University Press, 1942).

19. John Braeman, *Before the Civil Rights Revolution: The Old Court and Individual Rights* (Westport, Conn.: Greenwood Press, 1988).

20. *Twining v. New Jersey* (1908).

21. See, for example, *Schenck v. United States* (1917). See also David Rabban, *Free Speech in Its Forgotten Years* (New York: Cambridge University Press, 1997).

22. Henry Steele Commager, "Judicial Review and Democracy," *Virginia Quarterly Review* 19 (summer 1943): 428. The possible exception was *Wing v. United States* (1896).

23. Robert H. Jackson, *The Struggle for Judicial Supremacy* (New York: Knopf, 1941), 187.

24. William E. Leuchtenburg, *The Supreme Court Reborn: The Constitutional Revolution in the Age of Roosevelt* (New York: Oxford University Press, 1995), 235.

25. *United States v. Cardiff* (1952).

26. Ken Alexander, *San Francisco Examiner*, December 14, 1967, 42.

27. Dahlia Lithwick, "The Breakfast Table," *Slate*, at *slate.msn.com*, June 23, 2003.

On the Court's position since 1969, see Frederick P. Lewis, *The Context of Judicial Activism: The Endurance of the Warren Court Legacy in a Conservative Age* (Lanham, Md.: Rowman & Littlefield, 1999); Earl M. Maltz, *The Chief Justiceship of Warren Burger, 1969–1986* (Columbia: University of South Carolina Press, 2000); and Martin H. Belsky, ed., *The Rehnquist Court: A Retrospective* (New York: Oxford University Press, 2002).

28. *Miller v. California* (1973).
29. Lino A. Graglia, "Economic Rights," in *The Burger Court: Counter-Revolution or Confirmation?* ed. Bernard Schwartz (New York: Oxford University Press, 1998), 154–165.
30. Lucas A. Powe Jr., *The Warren Court and American Politics* (Cambridge, Mass.: Harvard University Press, 2000).
31. See Keith E. Whittington, "Taking What They Give Us: Explaining the Court's Federalism Offensive," *Duke Law Journal* 51 (2001): 477–520.
32. See Powe, *Warren Court and American Politics*, 485–501.
33. Charles R. Epp, *The Rights Revolution: Lawyers, Activists, and Supreme Courts in Comparative Perspective* (Chicago: University of Chicago Press, 1998), chaps. 3 and 4.
34. See John R. Howard, *The Shifting Wind: The Supreme Court and Civil Rights from Reconstruction to Brown* (Albany: State University of New York Press, 1999).
35. Dahl, "Decision-Making in a Democracy," 285.
36. Fred Rodell, *Nine Men* (New York: Random House, 1955), 9. The original aphorism was coined by author Finley Peter Dunne and put in the mouth of his character Mr. Dooley in 1901. See Finley Peter Dunne, *Mr. Dooley on Ivrything and Ivrybody,* selected by Robert Hutchinson (New York: Dover Publications, 1963), 160.

Chapter 6

The Court's Impact

The last two weeks of June 2002 followed the usual pattern for the end of the Supreme Court's term: the Court handed down decisions in several cases with important and controversial issues. These decisions received considerable attention in the news media, and commentators spoke once again of the Court's power to resolve so many major issues of law and policy.

A closer look at the Court's decisions makes clear how much the Court did *not* resolve.

The Court ruled in *Zelman v. Simmons-Harris* that states could include religious schools in voucher programs that provide parents with money to pay for school tuition. Because only three states had voucher programs that included private schools, proponents of such programs in other states would have to persuade their state legislatures to adopt them. Thirty-seven states have provisions in their constitutions that forbid government funding of religious schools, so the ability of those states to extend voucher programs to religious schools depends on how courts interpret those provisions and how they respond to arguments that such provisions conflict with the U.S. Constitution.[1]

In *Board of Education v. Earls,* the Court upheld a school district policy requiring students who participate in extracurricular activities to take drug tests but left uncertain whether a drug-testing requirement could be extended to all students, a question that courts might have to address in later cases. And school districts with the power to require drug testing might not use that power. Among other considerations, the expense of a testing program could work against its adoption in cash-strapped districts.

The Court's decision in *Atkins v. Virginia* prohibited the execution of criminal defendants who are mentally retarded, executions that were allowed in twenty states. Inevitably, large numbers of defendants who had been sentenced to death or who faced possible death sentences would cite the Court's decision. But the Court did not set criteria or procedures to determine whether a defendant was retarded. Lower courts will have to address those issues, and their answers will help to determine how much impact the Court has.

The Court is the highest interpreter of federal law, and people often think of it as the final arbiter of the issues it addresses. Occasionally, the Court *is* the final arbiter: its decision in *Bush v. Gore* resolved the presidential election of 2000. But that is unusual. Most of the time the Court is one of many institutions that shape law and policy on an issue.

Often the Court decides only one aspect of an issue or offers general guidelines that other policymakers have to fill in. Even when the Court rules decisively on an issue, other institutions may limit the impact of that ruling or negate it altogether. Congress and the president can write a new statute to override the Court's interpretation of an old one. Congress and the states can amend the Constitution to overcome a constitutional decision. Judges and administrators can carry out a Supreme Court policy as they see fit. And the Court's ultimate impact on society depends on the actions of other institutions in and out of government. The Court influences the strength of the labor movement and the status of women, but so do many other forces—including some that are likely to have far greater impact than the Court.

This chapter explores the impact of Supreme Court decisions. I begin by looking at what happens to the litigants themselves. The remainder of the chapter examines the broader effects of the Court's policies: their implementation, responses to them by legislatures and chief executives, and their effects on society as a whole.

Outcomes for the Parties

Whatever else it does, a Supreme Court decision affects the parties in the case. But the Court's ruling does not always determine the final outcome for the two sides. Indeed, a great deal can happen to the parties after the Court rules in their case.

If the Court affirms a lower court decision, that decision usually becomes final. If the Court reverses, modifies, or vacates a decision, it almost always remands (sends back) the case to the lower court for "further proceedings consistent with this opinion," or the like. When it remands a case, the Court sometimes gives the lower court little leeway about what to do. More often, the lower court has wide discretion about how to apply the Court's ruling, and the party who wins in the Court may end up the ultimate loser.

Cases in which the Court overturns a criminal conviction on procedural grounds are good examples. The defendant is often retried, and the retrial may produce a second conviction. That was the result for Charles Dickerson, in whose 2000 case the Court reaffirmed the *Miranda* rules for police questioning.[2] Wilbert Rideau, whose murder conviction was overturned by the Court in 1963, was tried and convicted twice more, had each conviction overturned by appellate courts, and in 2003 was awaiting a fourth trial.[3]

Most such outcomes are quite consistent with the Supreme Court rulings that preceded them. But lower court judges occasionally respond to remands in questionable ways, using the leeway that the Supreme Court provides to reach a result that conflicts with the Court's intent. A litigant who feels that a lower court has failed to follow the Supreme Court's directions after a remand can bring the case back to the Court for a second ruling. After a 1997 remand to the federal Fifth Circuit Court of Appeals, that court reinstated its original judgment in the case. A commentator said that the court was "thumbing its nose at the Supreme Court."[4] The losing party came back to the Supreme Court, the Court accepted the case, and in 1999 it reversed the court of appeals and remanded the case a second time. Justice Souter's opinion for the Court gently chided the Fifth Circuit for its failure to apply the Court's ruling properly.[5]

The ultimate outcome for the parties is often determined outside of court. Sometimes the parties settle the case, with the Court's decision providing leverage for the party that it favored. But some winning parties are in too weak a position to achieve a favorable outcome. This was the case with the freelance authors who won a 2001 case against the *New York Times* over compensation for inclusion of their articles in electronic databases. The winning authors expected the *Times* to negotiate with them over compensation. But the newspaper responded by announcing that it would not work with those authors in the future.[6]

Other branches of government may become involved after the Supreme Court rules in a case. In New York, state legislators intervened after the Court's decision in *Board of Education v. Grumet* (1994). In *Grumet* the Court struck down a New York statute that had created a school district for a religious enclave, allowing children from the enclave to receive publicly funded special education services while remaining separate from students outside the group. In response the governor and legislature enacted three successive statutes, each designed to meet the Court's objections to the original statute while maintaining the same separate district. New York's highest court ruled that the first two of these statutes were also unconstitutional. A lower court upheld the third statute in 2001, and its opponents decided not to appeal, so the religious enclave ultimately won.[7]

The lives of Supreme Court litigants can undergo all kinds of twists after their cases conclude. In *Runyon v. McCrary* (1976), the parents of three-year-old Michael McCrary challenged the whites-only admissions policy of a Virginia private school. The Court ruled in their favor, holding that this policy violated federal law. Justice Byron White, nicknamed "Whizzer" White when he was a football star, wrote a strong dissent arguing that the Court should have ruled against the McCrarys. Michael McCrary grew up to become a football player himself, and he ultimately played for the Baltimore Ravens of the National Football League. In 2001 he was honored by the NFL Players Association for his good works off the field. The honor he received was the Byron "Whizzer" White Award.[8]

Implementation of Supreme Court Policies

More important than the outcome of a case for the litigants are the broader effects of the legal rules that the Court lays down in its opinions. Like statutes or presidential orders, these rules have to be implemented—put into effect—by administrators and judges. Judges are obliged to apply the Court's interpretations of law whenever they are relevant to a case. Administrators, ranging from cabinet officers to police officers, are expected to follow Court-created rules that are relevant to their work.

The responses of judges and administrators to the Court's rules of law can be examined in terms of their compliance and noncompliance with these rules. But the Court's decisions may evoke responses ranging from complete rejection to enthusiastic acceptance and extension, and the concept of compliance does not capture all the possible variations.

The Effectiveness of Implementation

Implementation is an imperfect process. People sometimes assume that when Congress enacts a statute, other policymakers automatically do what is required to make the statute effective. In reality, implementation of statutes is far from automatic. Indeed, congressional policies frequently fail to achieve their objectives because they are implemented poorly. The same is true of Supreme Court decisions: judges and administrators may not carry them out fully, thereby creating a gap between the Court's goals and the actual results.

This does not mean that implementation always works badly; any policymaker, including the Supreme Court, is likely to have a mixed record in getting its policies put into effect. Some of the Court's decisions are carried out more effectively than others, and specific decisions are implemented better in some places or situations than in others.

On the whole, the Court achieves considerable success in getting its policies carried out by lower courts, especially appellate courts. When the Court issues a decision with a new rule of law, judges generally do their best to follow its lead, even on issues as controversial as abortion. And when a series of decisions in a field of law indicates a broader change in the Court's position in that field, lower courts tend to follow the new trend.[9]

It is rare for judges explicitly to say they will not follow the Court's doctrines. More common is what might be called implicit noncompliance, in which a court purports to follow the Supreme Court's lead but actually evades the implications of the Court's ruling. A Supreme Court ruling on sentencing practices was "rendered a dead letter" in Illinois through a 2003 decision by the state supreme court, according to a justice who dissented from the Illinois decision.[10]

The Court enjoys considerable success in gaining compliance from administrative bodies, especially at the federal level.[11] Yet implementation problems seem more common among administrators than among judges. For example, some evidence exists that the Immigration and Naturalization Service has evaded the Court's 2001 decision limiting the time that noncitizens can be imprisoned pending deportation.[12]

State trial courts resemble administrative agencies in some respects, and some of the Court's decisions about trial procedures have been implemented poorly. One example is the Court's decision in *Tate v. Short* (1971), holding that an indigent person cannot be sentenced to jail because of inability to pay a fine. Judges in some courts ignore that ruling, and in 2002 the city of Wichita, Kansas, paid $2.7 million to compensate people who were jailed for their failure to pay fines.[13]

Two Case Studies of Implementation

School desegregation and police investigations illustrate the implementation of the Court's decisions. Both examples highlight the difficulties of implementation and variation in its success.

School Desegregation. Before the Supreme Court's 1954 decision in *Brown v. Board of Education,* separate schools for black and white students existed throughout the Deep South and in most districts of border states such as Oklahoma and Maryland. The Court's decision required that these dual school systems be eliminated. Full desegregation in the border states took time, but considerable compliance with the Court's ruling came within a few years. In contrast, policies in the Deep South changed very slowly. As late as 1964–1965, there was no Deep South state in which even 10 percent of the black students went to school with any white students—a minimal definition of desegregation.[14] This resistance requires a closer look.

Judges and school officials in the Deep South responded to the *Brown* decision in an atmosphere hostile to desegregation. Visible opinion among white citizens was strongly opposed to desegregation; the opinion of black citizens was far less important because a large proportion of them were prevented from voting. Throughout the South, public officials encouraged resistance to the Supreme Court. Governor Orval Faubus of Arkansas, for example, intervened to block desegregation in Little Rock in 1957.

In this atmosphere, school officials generally sought to maintain the status quo. Most administrators personally favored segregation and did everything possible to preserve it. Those administrators who wanted to comply with the Court's ruling were deterred from doing so by pressure from state officials and local citizens.

In places where the schools did not comply on their own, parents could file suits in the federal district courts to challenge the continuation of segregated systems. In many districts no suits ever were brought; one reason was fear of retaliation.

Even where suits were brought, their success was hardly guaranteed. In its second decision in *Brown* in 1955, the Supreme Court gave federal district judges substantial freedom to determine the appropriate schedule for desegregation in a school district. Many judges themselves disagreed with the *Brown* decision, and all felt local pressure to proceed slowly, if at all. As a result, few demanded speedy desegregation of the schools, and many supported school officials in resisting change. Some judges did support the Court wholeheartedly, but they found it difficult to overcome delaying tactics by school administrators and elected officials.

After a long period of resistance, officials in the southern states began to comply. In the second decade after *Brown,* most dual school systems in the South were finally dismantled. Although school segregation was not eliminated altogether, the proportion of black students attending school with whites increased tremendously, as shown in Table 6-1.

The major impetus for this change came from Congress. The Civil Rights Act of 1964 allowed federal funds to be withheld from institutions that practiced racial discrimination. In carrying out that provision, the Department of Health, Education, and Welfare required that schools make a "good-faith start" toward desegregation to receive federal aid. Faced with a threat to important financial interests, school officials felt some compulsion to go along. The 1964 act also allowed the Justice Department to bring desegregation suits where local residents were unable to do so, and this provision greatly increased the potential for litigation against school districts that refused to change their policies. The Court re-

TABLE 6-1
Percentage of Black Elementary and Secondary Students Going to School with Any Whites, in Eleven Southern States, 1954–1973

School year	Percentage	School year	Percentage
1954–1955	0.001	1964–1965	2.25
1956–1957	0.14	1966–1967	15.9
1958–1959	0.13	1968–1969	32.0
1960–1961	0.16	1970–1971	85.6
1962–1963	0.45	1972–1973	91.3

Sources: Southern Education Reporting Service, *A Statistical Summary, State by State, of School Segregation-Desegregation in the Southern and Border Area from 1954 to the Present* (Nashville: Southern Education Reporting Service, 1967) (for 1954–1967); U.S. Bureau of the Census, *Statistical Abstract of the United States* (Washington, D.C.: Government Printing Office, 1971 and 1975) (for 1968–1973).

Note: The states are Alabama, Arkansas, Florida, Georgia, Louisiana, Mississippi, North Carolina, South Carolina, Tennessee, Texas, and Virginia.

inforced the congressional action with decisions in 1968 and 1969 that demanded effective desegregation without further delay.[15]

In the 1970s, the Court turned its attention to the North. In many northern cities, a combination of housing patterns and school board policies had created a situation in which white and nonwhite students generally went to different schools. In a Denver case, *Keyes v. School District No. 1* (1973), the Court held that segregation caused by government in such cities violated the Fourteenth Amendment and required a remedy. In a line of decisions over the next decade, the Court spelled out rules by which to identify segregation that violated the Constitution and to devise remedies for such segregation.

On the whole, federal district judges in the North supported the Court more than had their southern counterparts. Many were willing to order sweeping remedies for segregation in the face of strong local opposition to those remedies, especially busing. One judge ordered the imposition of higher property taxes to pay for school improvements that might facilitate desegregation in Kansas City. Another held a city in New York State and some of its council members in contempt for failing to approve new public housing for a similar purpose.[16] Ironically, the Court found some of these remedies *too* sweeping.

Few northern school districts took significant steps to eliminate segregation until they were faced with a court order or pressure from federal administrators. For the most part, however, northern districts complied with desegregation orders rather than resisting them. Compliance was increased by the willingness of some district judges to supervise school desegregation directly and closely. Congress and some presidents took steps to limit northern desegregation, but their actions were mostly symbolic and had little impact.

Once desegregation plans were put in place, the question arose as to whether and when such plans could be terminated. In a pair of decisions in 1991 and 1992, the Court indicated that these plans need not remain permanent even if ending them would produce high levels of racial segregation in a school district.[17] With support for desegregation declining, many administrators have accepted this invitation and returned to systems in which students are assigned to schools based on where they reside. That development has contributed to growing segregation of schools in the past decade. Not surprisingly, school officials have been most willing to follow the Court's lead when the Court's rulings are consistent with what they want to do.

Police Investigation. The Warren Court imposed substantial procedural requirements on the police in two areas of criminal investigation, issuing a landmark decision in each. In search and seizure, *Mapp v. Ohio* (1961) extended to the states the "exclusionary rule," under which evidence illegally seized by the police cannot be used against a defendant in court. The *Mapp* decision provided an incentive for police to follow rules for legal searches that the Court established in other decisions. In the area of interrogation, *Miranda v. Arizona* (1966) required that suspects be given a series of warnings before police questioned them if their statements were to be used as evidence. How have judges and police officers responded to those rules?

Lower court responses to *Mapp* and *Miranda* have been mixed. Some state supreme courts criticized the decisions and interpreted them narrowly. At the trial level, many judges who sympathize with the police are reluctant to exclude evidence from trials on the basis of Supreme Court rules. But some lower court judges have applied the Court's rulings vigorously.

Although the basic rules of *Mapp* and *Miranda* remain standing, the Burger and Rehnquist Courts have narrowed their protections of suspects. Many lower courts have followed this new direction enthusiastically. But some state supreme courts that support the rulings of the 1960s have found a legitimate means to establish broader protections of procedural rights by declaring that rights denied by the Court under the U.S. Constitution are protected independently by state constitutions. The most important example concerns the Court's ruling in *United States v. Leon* (1984). In *Leon* the Court held that evidence seized on the basis of a search warrant that was improperly issued could be used in court if the officers engaging in the search had a "good faith" belief that the warrant was justified. At least fourteen state supreme courts have held that there is no good faith exception to the search rules in their own constitutions.[18]

Inevitably, *Mapp* and *Miranda* have been unpopular in the law enforcement community. Most police officers want maximum freedom for their investigative activities and resent court decisions that impose constraints on them. But they also want their evidence to stand up in court. The result has been a complex pattern of police behavior.

In the case of police questioning, it appears that reading the *Miranda* warnings to suspects gradually has become standard practice in most places.[19] One reason is that providing these warnings has had less impact than expected on the ability of police officers to obtain confessions and incriminating information from suspects.[20] The great majority of suspects waive their *Miranda* rights and answer questions, in part because officers structure the situation to encourage waivers. One common approach is exemplified by this statement from a detective to a suspect:

In order for me to talk to you specifically about the injury with [the victim], I need to advise you of your rights. It's a formality. I'm sure you've watched television with the cop shows right and you hear them say their rights and so you can probably recite this better than I can, but it's something I need to do and we can get this out of the way before we talk about what's happened.[21]

Even if suspects invoke their right to remain silent or to wait for a lawyer, officers sometimes can get them to change their minds. Some of the means that officers use to do so are of questionable legality. In some California police departments, for example, officers have told suspects who invoke their *Miranda* rights that they want to ask questions off the record, since nothing the suspect says can be used in court.[22] What most suspects do not know is that under *Harris v. New York* (1971), statements obtained by officers who do not comply with *Miranda* can be used to impeach a defendant's testimony in court.

To a considerable degree, then, police officers have learned to live with *Miranda,* complying partially with its requirements and continuing to get the information they seek from most suspects. Indeed, *Miranda* serves them well in one important respect: when suspects sign a form in which they waive their rights, it is difficult for them to contest the use of their statements in court. Yet most officers still perceive *Miranda* as a constraint on their ability to obtain evidence. That perception is reflected in the amicus briefs from law enforcement organizations that argued for abandoning *Miranda* when the Court considered (but ultimately rejected) that step in 2000.[23]

Before the *Mapp* decision, as one scholar put it, state and local law enforcement officers "*systematically* ignored the requirements of the Fourth Amendment because there was no reason to pay attention to it." [24] *Mapp* was intended to achieve greater compliance with search rules by providing a reason for compliance—potential exclusion of evidence from cases in court. To a degree, it has achieved this goal.[25] Faced with potential loss of evidence, many police departments changed their practices substantially. Most important, some made much greater use of search warrants.[26]

But the available evidence indicates that compliance is far from perfect. One example is a study based on a sample of searches by a metropolitan police department in the early 1990s. The authors of the study concluded that at least 30 percent of the searches violated constitutional rules.[27]

Some noncompliance is inadvertent, reflecting the complexity and ambiguity of the body of rules that police are asked to follow in searches and seizures. According to one judge, "The law is so muddy that the police can't find out what they are allowed to do even if they wanted to." [28] Other noncompliance is intentional, resulting most fundamentally from the conflict that police officers often perceive: if they follow the applicable legal rules, they cannot obtain evidence they see as critical. Because violations of the rules for searches often do not result in the exclusion of evidence, officers may resolve this conflict by violating those rules. Indeed, one scholar concluded that "for many police officers," the exclusionary rule "is not a significant influence when contemplating a search or seizure." [29]

Explaining the Implementation Process

It should be clear by now that the effectiveness with which Supreme Court policies are implemented varies a great deal. That effectiveness depends on several conditions: communication of policies to relevant officials, the motivations of those officials to follow or resist the Court's policies, the Court's authority, and the sanctions it can use to deter noncompliance.

Communication. Judges and administrators can carry out Supreme Court decisions well only if they know what the Court wants them to do. The communication process begins with the Court's opinions. Ideally, an opinion would state the Court's legal rules with sufficient precision and specificity that an official who reads the opinion would know how to apply those rules to any other case or situation. Frequently, however, opinions fall far short of that ideal: there is considerable ambiguity in the Court's messages.

Much of this ambiguity is unavoidable. The Court's opinions proclaim general legal principles in the context of specific cases. As the example of police searches indicates, the application of those principles to other cases or situations often is uncertain. In Florida, members of the state supreme court differed on whether the state's death penalty law was consistent with the Supreme Court's 2002 decision on the role of juries in determining death sentences.[30]

Officials who are uncertain about what the Court wants may not carry out the Court's intent properly even if they would like to do so. When officials do *not* want to carry out the Court's intent, ambiguity gives them leeway to interpret decisions as they see fit. For example, the Court's vague timetable for school desegregation gave southern judges and school administrators an excuse to delay desegregation.

Whether the Court's position on an issue is clear or ambiguous, its decisions must be transmitted to relevant judges and administrators. This process is not automatic. Even judges seldom monitor the Supreme Court's output systematically to identify relevant decisions. Instead, decisions come to the attention of officials through other channels.

One channel is the mass media. A few Supreme Court decisions are sufficiently interesting that they receive heavy publicity in newspapers and on television. But most decisions garner much less attention from the mass media. Americans collectively get more news from television than from any other source, but only a minority of decisions get any coverage on the network news programs. And that coverage is typically quite limited and sometimes misleading.[31]

Attorneys communicate decisions to some officials. Through their arguments in court proceedings and administrative hearings, lawyers bring favorable precedents to the attention of judges and administrators. Staff lawyers in administrative agencies often inform agency personnel of relevant decisions. But administrators such as teachers and public welfare workers lack that source of information.

Another channel of information is professional hierarchies. State trial judges often become aware of the Court's decisions when they are cited by state appellate courts. Police officers learn of decisions from departmental superiors. Here, too, there is considerable potential for misinformation, especially when the communicator disagrees with a decision. Many state supreme courts and most police officials conveyed negative views of liberal criminal justice decisions by the Warren Court when they informed their subordinates of those decisions.

Effective communication of decisions depends on the receivers as well as the channels of transmission. Legally trained officials are the most capable of understanding decisions and their implications. Police officers and other nonlawyers who work regularly with the law also have some advantage in interpreting decisions. On the whole, administrators who work outside the legal system have the greatest difficulty in interpreting what they learn about Supreme Court rulings.

Where transmission problems exist, they have an obvious and significant impact. Policymakers who do not know of a decision cannot implement it. By the same token, those who misunderstand the Court's requirements will not follow them as intended. Police officers who do not fully understand the complex body of rules for searches cannot fully comply with those rules. In sum, effective transmission of the Court's policies, like clarity in the policies themselves, is needed for their effective implementation.

Motivations for Resistance. If policymakers know of a Supreme Court policy that is relevant to a choice they face, they must decide what to do with that policy. As one would expect, officials are likely to carry out a policy faithfully if they think it is a good policy and that they will benefit from doing so. But if that policy conflicts with their policy preferences or their self-interest, they may resist the Court's lead.

When appellate judges fail to implement Supreme Court decisions fully, the most common reason is a conflict between those decisions and their policy preferences. After the Court adopts a new policy, lower court judges may conclude that it has made a serious mistake. Those judges sometimes rebel against the Court's policy, though their rebellion is usually quiet.

Disagreement about judicial policy tends to follow ideological lines. That tendency is illustrated by conflict between the Supreme Court and the Ninth Circuit Court of Appeals on the West Coast.[32] For many years the Ninth Circuit has been the most liberal court of appeals, distinctly more liberal than the Supreme Court. It is relatively common for three-judge panels of the Ninth Circuit to take positions that diverge from those of the Supreme Court. This divergence is reflected in the frequency with which the Supreme Court reverses the Ninth Circuit. Indeed, in each of its first three decisions in the 2002 term, the Court overturned Ninth Circuit decisions unanimously and summarily, without holding oral argument.[33]

Trial judges and administrators may also disagree with Supreme Court decisions. Beginning with a pair of decisions in 1962 and 1963, the Court prohibited organized religious observances such as classroom prayer and Bible reading exercises in public schools.[34] A great many teachers and school administrators disapprove of those decisions, and some disapprove strongly. As a result, many schools have maintained the prohibited practices or modified them only marginally. For example, some southern schools have continued student-led prayers at football games despite a 2000 decision to the contrary.[35]

Supreme Court policies may conflict with officials' self-interest if they threaten existing practices that serve important purposes. In 1972 the Court ruled that mayors could not serve as judges in traffic court if their towns receive a substantial portion of their revenue from traffic fines. But precisely because they *do* benefit enormously from that revenue, some Ohio towns have ignored the Court's decision.[36]

Elected officials sometimes have good reason not to carry out highly unpopular decisions. Conservative groups have enjoyed some success in campaigning against elected judges who give broad interpretations to the rights of criminal defendants. For that reason, judges may avoid following Supreme Court policies that require such broad interpretations. For the same reason, school board members in conservative areas are unlikely to take strong stands against school prayers.

Because their positions are secure, federal judges might seem to be immune from these political concerns. But they too may wish to avoid incurring public wrath. Full adherence to *Brown v. Board of Education* would have made the lives of district judges less pleasant because of the reactions of their friends and neighbors. J. Skelly Wright of Louisiana, who did adhere to *Brown,* found that his life was greatly affected. "You never know whether people really want to talk with you and I don't see a lot of people anymore." [37] Wright also had to endure public attacks, including a demonstration in which white parents and children from integrated New Orleans schools brought an effigy of Wright in a coffin into the state capitol, to the applause of legislators.[38]

Wright and a few other judges were willing to accept the costs of supporting the Supreme Court, and several northern federal judges ordered school desegregation despite the prospect of severe public criticism. But they are exceptions. If officials expect to suffer serious consequences for carrying out a decision fully, few will do so.

Differences in the implementation of Supreme Court policies result chiefly from differences in the policy preferences and self-interest of implementers. Police departments tend to resist decisions that limit their powers but follow with alacrity those that expand them. The Deep South and the border states responded differently to the *Brown* decision because attitudes toward race and segregation were not the same in the two regions.

The Court's Authority. In 2003 the Supreme Court upheld California's "three-strikes" law, which required long sentences for people convicted of a felony after two prior convictions for serious or violent felonies. Two months later the federal court of appeals for the Ninth Circuit reviewed a long sentence under the law. In a concurring opinion, Judge Stephen Reinhardt protested that this sentence was "unconscionable and unconstitutional," but he voted to uphold it "under compulsion of the Supreme Court's decision." [39]

Judge Reinhardt's action was hardly unique. In 1995, for example, another court of appeals judge criticized a Supreme Court decision as "unsound when decided" and "inconsistent with later decisions" of the Court, but he felt compelled to follow that decision.[40] These two judges were accepting both the Supreme Court's authority to make conclusive judgments about the law and their own obligation to comply with the Court's decisions. This acceptance has considerable effect on the implementation of those decisions, motivating officials to carry out policies that they view negatively.

The Court's authority is strongest for judges, who have been socialized to accept the leadership of higher courts and who also benefit from acceptance of judicial authority. This strong authority is reflected in the general willingness of judges to follow the Court's lead. But judges may give narrow interpretations to Court decisions with which they strongly disagree, thereby limiting the impact of those decisions while acknowledging the Court's authority. The Court ruled in 2002 that a worker who was in the United States illegally could not be awarded back pay for an employer's violation of federal labor law, and the logic of its decision seemed to limit the rights of these workers more broadly. A few months later, however, a federal district judge in California held that the Court intended only to rule out back pay for such workers and that they *could* sue and receive other monetary damages for labor law violations. In all likelihood, that decision reflected disagreement with the spirit of the Court's decision.[41]

The Court's authority extends to administrators. Some school officials eliminate religious observances that they would prefer to maintain because they accept their duty to follow Supreme Court rulings.[42] On the whole, however, the Court's authority is weaker for administrators than it is for judges. Administrative agencies are somewhat removed from the judicial system and its norm of obedience to higher courts, and relatively few administrators have had the law school training that supports this norm. As a result, administrative officials find it somewhat easier to justify deviation from Supreme Court policies than judges do.

The Court's authority tends to decline as organizational distance from the Court increases. Officials at the grassroots level may not feel obliged to adjust their policies to the Court's decisions. State trial judges typically orient themselves more closely to appellate courts in their state than to the Supreme Court, several steps away from them in the judicial hierarchy.

The Court's authority is an important reason for acceptance of its policies. Especially within the judiciary, the authority attached to Supreme Court decisions increases compliance with those decisions. But the

Court's authority has limits: it does not always outweigh the motivations that move some officials toward noncompliance. In the same case in which Judge Reinhardt reluctantly followed the Supreme Court's three-strikes ruling, his colleague Harry Pregerson dissented despite that ruling: "In good conscience, I cannot go along with the sentence imposed" in the case.[43]

Sanctions for Disobedience. In 1906 the Supreme Court ordered a stay of execution for a Tennessee prisoner. The local sheriff responded by allowing the prisoner to be lynched. In response, the Court held the sheriff in contempt of court and ordered him to jail.[44]

This episode was the only time the Court has held an official in contempt for failure to comply with its decisions, but it illustrates the Court's power to punish noncompliance through sanctions. Such sanctions can give judges and administrators an incentive to follow the Court's lead, an incentive more concrete than the Court's authority.

For judges, the most common sanction is reversal. If a judge does not follow an applicable Supreme Court policy, the losing litigant may appeal the case and secure a reversal of the judge's decision. This sanction is significant, chiefly because it suggests that a judge erred. Indeed, lawyers and judges sometimes evaluate judicial performance by the frequency of reversals. The Court can give an extra sting to its reversals by rebuking the lower court. In *Kirk v. Louisiana* (2002), for example, the Court's *per curiam* opinion said that the reasoning of the Louisiana Court of Appeal "plainly violates our holding in *Payton v. New York.*"[45]

The threat of reversal helps the Supreme Court to draw lower courts toward its policies. When she was inducted into the National Cowgirl Hall of Fame in 2002, Justice O'Connor spoke of her childhood ambition to become a cattle rancher. "And I now find myself riding herd on lower court judges."[46]

But reversal has its limits as a sanction. Judges who feel strongly about an issue may be willing to accept reversals on that issue as the price of following their personal convictions. As noted earlier, the relative liberalism of the federal court of appeals for the Ninth Circuit has led the Court to reverse an unusually large number of its decisions in recent years. These reversals have had only a limited effect on the Ninth Circuit's liberals.

For that matter, failure to follow the Supreme Court's lead does not always lead to reversal. The losing litigant may not appeal. Moreover, the great majority of judges are reviewed by a court other than the Supreme Court, and the reviewing court may share their opposition to the Court's policies.

For administrators, the most common sanction is a court order that directs compliance with a decision. If a public welfare agency fails to follow an applicable Supreme Court policy, someone who is injured by its failure may bring a lawsuit to compel compliance with the Court's decision. Any suit hurts the agency because of the trouble and expense it entails. A successful suit is even worse, because an order to comply with a Supreme Court rule puts an agency under judicial scrutiny and may embarrass agency officials. The agency may also be required to pay monetary damages to the person who brought the lawsuit.

But this sanction has weaknesses. Most important, it can occur only if people bring lawsuits against agencies, and they do not always do so. To take one example, public school religious observances that violate the Supreme Court's rulings have gone unchallenged in many communities. If a lawsuit is threatened or actually brought, agencies can usually change their practices in time to avoid serious costs.

In situations in which compliance is difficult to ascertain, sanctions lose some of their efficacy. *Batson v. Kentucky* (1986) prohibits prosecutors from removing prospective jurors because of their race, but this practice has not been eliminated, even though it is frequently challenged. Prosecutors offer nonracial reasons for their removal of nonwhite jurors, and judges may not be confident that those reasons are just pretexts.[47]

Still, to follow a policy that conflicts with a Supreme Court ruling carries risks that officials usually prefer to avoid. This attitude helps to account for the frequency with which administrative organizations on their own initiative eliminate practices prohibited by the Court. Administrators whose actions require court enforcement, such as officials in some regulatory agencies, have even more reason to avoid noncompliance that may cost them judicial support.

Police practices in searches and seizures illustrate both the strength and limitations of this sanction. Under *Mapp*, noncompliance with rules for searches prevents the use of evidence in court. As a result, officers frequently comply with rules that they would prefer to ignore. Officers, however, seldom receive any personal sanctions for noncompliant practices that cause evidence to be thrown out. Moreover, illegal searches may not prevent convictions. Most defendants plead guilty, and by doing so they generally waive their right to challenge the legality of searches. Trial judges often give the benefit of the doubt to police officers on borderline evidentiary questions. And evidence that is ruled illegal may not be needed for a conviction. Thus, police officers have an incentive to avoid illegal searches, but not so strong an incentive that they always try to follow the applicable rules.

This discussion suggests two conditions that affect the implementation process. First, interest groups can play an important part in enforcement of Supreme Court decisions. The American Civil Liberties Union frequently challenges religious observances in public schools, and by doing so it has enhanced compliance with the Court's rules. Second, the Court's decisions are easiest to enforce when the affected policymakers are few in number and highly visible. It is relatively simple for the Court to oversee the fifty state governments that must carry out its decisions on the drawing of legislative districts. It is far more difficult for the Court to oversee the day-to-day activities of all the police officers who investigate crimes.

In general, the sanctions available to the Court are fairly weak, so help from Congress and the president can make a great deal of difference when the Court faces widespread noncompliance. In enforcing school desegregation, that help was a necessity.

Summary. The Supreme Court's policies are implemented more effectively in some settings than in others. Judges generally carry out the Court's policies more fully than administrators because communication of decisions to judges is relatively good; most judges accord the Court considerable authority; and their self-interest is less likely to conflict with the implementation of decisions. For similar reasons, federal judges and administrators are probably better implementers of decisions than are their state counterparts. The Court's decisions are communicated to them more effectively, and its authority and sanctions affect them more directly.

On the whole, the Court's policies are implemented fairly well. But the gap between the rules of law that the Court establishes and the actions taken by judges and administrators is often considerable. To a degree, this gap reflects the Court's limited power: it can exert little control over the implementation process. Most important, the sanctions that the Court can apply to disobedient officials are relatively weak compared with those available to Congress and the president. But more striking than this difference is the similarity in the basic positions of Court, Congress, and president: each proclaims policies that have uncertain and often unhappy fates in the implementation process.

Responses by Legislatures and Chief Executives

After the Supreme Court hands down its decisions, Congress, the president, and their state counterparts can respond in various ways that affect the Court's decisions and the Court itself.

Congress

Congress has considerable ability to modify or override the Court's decisions. It also shapes the implementation of decisions, and it may use its powers to attack justices or the Court as a whole.

Enron executive Sherron Watkins prepares to testify at a 2002 congressional hearing. Watkins's revelations and other evidence of corporate misdeeds led Congress to overturn a 1991 Supreme Court decision that had limited lawsuits for securities fraud.

Statutory Interpretation. In *Lampf v. Gilbertson* (1991), the Supreme Court interpreted federal statutes to mean that in most lawsuits for securities fraud, investors must file the suits within three years of the time the fraud was committed and within one year after the fraud was discovered. A decade later the Enron Corporation collapsed amid charges of massive frauds against investors, and corporate fraud became a major issue. Congress responded in 2002 by enacting a statute aimed at protecting investors against corporate misdeeds. One section of the statute overturned *Lampf* by extending the time limits for securities fraud suits to five years after the fraud was committed and two years after it was discovered.

This congressional action was completely legitimate because Congress is supreme in statutory law: it can override the Supreme Court's interpretation of a statute simply by adopting a new statute with different language that supersedes the Court's reading of the old law. Congress can also ratify or extend the Court's interpretation of a statute, but overrides of statutory decisions are especially significant.

A substantial proportion of statutory decisions receive some congressional scrutiny, and proposals to override decisions are common. Most of these proposals fail, for the same reasons that most bills of any type fail: legislation must navigate successfully through several decision points at which it can be killed, and there is usually a presumption in favor of the status quo. Still, overrides are far from rare. Over the past three decades, on average, more than ten statutory decisions have been overturned in each two-year Congress. Of the statutory decisions in the Court's 1978–1989 terms, Congress had overridden more than 5 percent by 1996.[48] Some overrides follow quickly after a decision. In 2002, for example, Congress overturned a decision on corporate taxes that was only a year old.[49] Others come considerably later. One 1998 statute removed part of the exemption of major league baseball from the antitrust laws, an exemption that the Court first established in a 1922 decision.[50]

In most respects, the politics of congressional response to the Court's statutory decisions resembles congressional politics generally.[51] The initiative for bills to overturn decisions often comes from interest groups. Just as groups that fail to achieve their goals in Congress frequently turn to the courts for relief, groups whose interests suffer in the Supreme Court frequently turn to Congress.

The success of efforts to overturn statutory decisions depends on the same broad array of factors that influence the fates of other bills in Congress. The political strength of the groups that favor or oppose overrides is important. Not surprisingly, the federal executive branch enjoys considerable success in getting Congress to overturn unfavorable decisions, while nearly all decisions that work to the detriment of criminal defendants are left standing.[52] When a significant group favors action and organized opposition does not exist, Congress may override a decision quickly and easily. Many successful overrides are enacted not as separate bills but as provisions of broader bills such as appropriations, and members of Congress who vote for those bills sometimes are unaware that they are overriding a Supreme Court decision.

Congress does not always have the last word when it overrides a statute, because the new statute is subject to judicial interpretation. In *Westfall v. Erwin* (1988), the Court held that federal officials could be sued for personal injuries under some circumstances. A few months later Congress overrode *Westfall* by allowing the attorney general to certify that an employee who had been sued was acting as a federal official and thereby substituting the federal government for the employee as a defendant. But in *Gutierrez de Martinez v. Lamagno* (1995), the Court weakened the override by holding that the attorney general's certification could be challenged in court.

Constitutional Interpretation. When the Court interprets the Constitution, the most direct and decisive way to overturn its decision is through

a constitutional amendment. But that route is very difficult: the amending process is arduous, and there is a widespread reluctance to tamper
with the Constitution. It is far easier to adopt a new statute, but a constitutional decision cannot be overturned directly by a statute. Under some
circumstances, however, a statute can negate or limit the effects of a constitutional decision.

If the Court has nullified or limited a statute on constitutional
grounds, Congress can enact a second statute to try to meet the Court's
objections. Congress frequently takes such action.[53] One example is the
response to *Reno v. American Civil Liberties Union* (1997), in which the
Court struck down on First Amendment grounds a 1996 statute aimed at
limiting children's exposure to sexually oriented material on the Internet.
A year later Congress enacted the Child Online Protection Act, aimed at
achieving the same goal without running into the First Amendment problems that the Court had cited in *Reno*. In 2002 the Court rejected a challenge to this second statute. But after the Court remanded the case to the
federal court of appeals for the Third Circuit, that court struck down the
statute on other grounds.[54]

When the Court holds that a right is not protected by the Constitution,
Congress often can protect that right by enacting a statute. One effort to
do so has gone back and forth between Congress and the courts.[55] In *Employment Division v. Smith* (1990), the Court made it easier under the First
and Fourteenth Amendments for governments to justify rules that treat
religion neutrally but that put a burden on a particular religious practice.
Congress enacted the Religious Freedom Restoration Act (RFRA) in 1993
to restore the broader pre-*Smith* standard of protection for religion. But
in *City of Boerne v. Flores* (1997), the Court held that RFRA was unconstitutional as applied to state and local governments because it went beyond
congressional power to enforce the Fourteenth Amendment. Congress
then responded with the Religious Land Use and Institutionalized Persons Act of 2000, which re-established some of the rights protected by
RFRA on the basis of congressional power to regulate interstate commerce and the use of federal funds. A federal district judge upheld the
new law in 2002.[56]

In situations where constitutional decisions cannot be negated by
statute, members of Congress may introduce resolutions to overturn them
with constitutional amendments. In recent years, resolutions have been
submitted on a variety of issues. The range of these issues is suggested by
a sampling of resolutions introduced in 2003, shown in Table 6-2.

Not surprisingly, few of the efforts to propose amendments achieve
the necessary two-thirds votes in both houses. Only five times has Congress proposed an amendment that was aimed directly at Supreme Court
decisions. One of these, proposed in 1924 to give Congress the power to

TABLE 6-2
Selected Resolutions Introduced in Congress for Constitutional Amendments to Overturn Supreme Court Decisions, 1999–2003

Purpose	Decisions that would be overturned
Limiting the number of consecutive terms that members of Congress can serve	*U.S. Term Limits v. Thornton* (1995)
Giving Congress power to limit campaign spending	*Buckley v. Valeo* (1976), later decisions
Allowing organized prayer in public schools	*Engel v. Vitale* (1962)
Giving federal and state governments power to prohibit flag desecration	*Texas v. Johnson* (1989), *United States v. Eichman* (1990)
Prohibiting abortion under most circumstances	*Roe v. Wade* (1973), *Planned Parenthood v. Casey* (1992), other decisions

regulate child labor, was not ratified by the states. (A few amendments have indirectly negated Supreme Court decisions.) Since the child labor proposal, the only amendment that Congress has proposed in order to overturn a decision was the Twenty-sixth Amendment, adopted in 1971. In *Oregon v. Mitchell* (1970), the Court had ruled that Congress could not regulate the voting age in elections to state office; Congress acted quickly to propose an amendment overturning the decision, and the states quickly ratified it.

In contrast with the Twenty-sixth Amendment, the most prominent failed campaigns for amendments in recent years were aimed at decisions that increased legal protections for civil liberties. Even highly unpopular decisions, such as prohibitions of school prayer, stood up against efforts to overturn them. In these instances, the general reluctance to amend the Constitution was compounded by a special reluctance to limit the protections of rights in the Bill of Rights.

That reluctance is illustrated by the effort to propose an anti–flag-desecration amendment. In *Texas v. Johnson* (1989), the Supreme Court struck down a state statute prohibiting flag burning on the ground that it punished people for political expression. Four months later Congress enacted a federal statute against flag burning, written in an effort to meet the Court's objections to the Texas statute. But in *United States v. Eichman* (1990), the Court held that the new statute was also unconstitutional.

Members of Congress then sought a constitutional amendment to allow prohibition of flag desecration. Its passage seemed inevitable, because most members of Congress share an abhorrence of flag burning and because a member's vote against the amendment might provide an election opponent with a powerful issue. But both houses defeated a flag-desecration amendment in 1990. Similar amendments won approval in the House every two years from 1995 through 2001, but each time they failed in the Senate. These repeated failures underline the difficulty of amending the Constitution, especially in ways that might limit civil liberties. (In 2003 the House approved yet another flag-burning amendment; its prospects in the Senate were uncertain.)

Affecting the Implementation of Decisions. By passing legislation, Congress can influence the implementation of Supreme Court decisions by other institutions. Its most important tool is money. Congress can provide or fail to provide funds to carry out a decision. It can also affect responses to decisions by state and local governments through its control over federal grants to them. Congressional use of this latter power was critical in achieving school desegregation in the Deep South.

In a 2001 education statute, Congress employed the same power in two different ways. The first was related to *Boy Scouts of America v. Dale* (2000), in which the Court held that the First Amendment allows the Boy Scouts to prohibit membership to gay men and boys. In response, some schools ended their ties with the Scouts. One provision of the 2001 law required that no federal funds be provided to schools that "deny equal access" or "discriminate against" the Scouts. Another provision required that schools receiving federal money allow "constitutionally protected prayer." By enacting this provision, Congress gave school districts an incentive to interpret the Court's limitations on school religious observances narrowly.[57]

Occasionally, a Supreme Court decision requires implementation by Congress itself. In these situations Congress generally has accepted its obligation with little resistance. The legislative veto is an exception. In *Immigration and Naturalization Service v. Chadha* (1983), the Court indicated that any statutes allowing Congress as a whole, one house, or a committee to "veto" proposed executive branch actions are invalid. After the decision, Congress eliminated legislative veto provisions from several statutes. But it maintained others and, by 1999, had adopted more than four hundred new legislative veto provisions—most requiring that specific congressional committees approve action by administrative agencies. To maintain good relations with congressional committees and to avoid even more stringent congressional controls, agency officials are willing to accept these provisions rather than challenge their legality.

Thus, political realities have allowed noncompliance with *Chadha* to continue.[58]

Attacks on the Court and Its Members. When members of Congress dislike the Supreme Court's policies, they may attack the Court or the justices directly. The easiest way to do so is verbally, and members of Congress sometimes denounce the Court publicly. More concretely, Congress can take formal legislative action of several types.

One type of action concerns jurisdiction. The Constitution allows Congress to alter the Court's appellate jurisdiction through legislation, although it is uncertain whether Congress can narrow the Court's jurisdiction to prevent it from protecting constitutional rights. Congress used this power in 1869, withdrawing the Court's right to hear appeals in habeas corpus actions to prevent it from deciding a pending challenge to the post–Civil War Reconstruction legislation. In *Ex parte McCardle* (1869), the Court ruled that Congress had acted properly.

Since then, Congress has not directly limited the Court's jurisdiction to prevent it from ruling in a field of policy. In the past half century Congress has considered many bills that would have limited the Court's jurisdiction in areas of civil liberties activism, on issues such as abortion and school busing. Only two—on legislative districting in 1964 and school prayer in 1979—have passed either house, and none has been enacted.

The most extreme action that Congress can take against individual justices is to remove them through impeachment. Members of Congress sometimes talk of impeachment when they dislike a justice's policy positions. In 1997, for example, House Majority Whip Tom DeLay of Texas reportedly used the Court's 1979 decision upholding affirmative action by employers as an example of judicial activism that would justify impeachment.[59] But impeachment based only on disagreement over policy is extremely unlikely.

Congress controls the Court budget, limited only by the constitutional prohibition against reducing the justices' salaries. Dissatisfaction with the Court's policies sometimes makes Congress unwilling to increase the justices' salaries or approve the Court's budget requests. The clearest example occurred during the 1960s, a time when many members were displeased with the Court's civil liberties policies. In 1964 Congress singled out the justices by increasing their salaries by $3000 less than those of other federal judges. A year later the House defeated a proposal to restore the $3000, after a debate in which several members attacked the Court and Robert Dole of Kansas suggested that this pay increase be contingent on the Court's reversing a legislative districting decision that he disliked.[60]

Despite such moves, it is striking how little use Congress has made of its enormous powers over the Court over the past century. Of the many actions that members of Congress threatened against the conservative Court in the early part of the twentieth century, culminating in Franklin Roosevelt's Court-packing plan, none was carried out.[61] All the attacks on the liberal Court in the second half of the century resulted in nothing more serious than the salary "punishment" of 1964 and 1965. Why has Congress been so hesitant to use its powers, even at times when most members are unhappy about the Court's direction?

Several factors help to explain this hesitancy. First, there are always some members of Congress who agree with the Court's policies and lead its defense. Second, serious forms of attack against the Court, such as impeachment and reducing its jurisdiction, seem illegitimate to many people. Finally, when threatened with serious attack, the Court sometimes retreats to reduce the impetus for congressional action. For these reasons, the congressional bark at the Supreme Court has been a good deal worse than its bite.

The President

Presidents can influence how Congress uses its power over the Court, and they may also act on their own to shape the outcomes of decisions.

Influencing Congressional Response. The president can influence congressional responses to the Supreme Court by taking a position on proposals for action. Sometimes it is the president who first proposes anti-Court action. The most dramatic example in the last century was Franklin Roosevelt's Court-packing plan.

Since the 1960s, conservative presidents have encouraged efforts in Congress to limit or overturn some of the Court's liberal rulings on civil liberties. For example, George Bush led the effort to overturn the Court's flag-burning decisions in 1989 and 1990. George W. Bush's administration supported legislation to reestablish prohibitions of "virtual" child pornography after a 2002 decision striking down a federal statute in that field; the legislation passed the House but received no Senate action. For his part, Bill Clinton supported legislation in response to conservative decisions on regulation of tobacco and prohibition of guns in and around schools.

Using Executive Power. As chief executive, the president has a number of means to shape the implementation of Supreme Court decisions. For one thing, presidents can decide whether to support the Court with the power of the federal government when its decisions encounter open resistance from officials with the responsibility to carry them out.

The most coercive form of federal power is deployment of the military. In 1957, when a combination of state interference and mob action prevented court-ordered desegregation of the schools in Little Rock,

Arkansas, Dwight Eisenhower abandoned his earlier position against the use of federal troops to enforce *Brown v. Board of Education*. In 1962 President John Kennedy used federal troops to enforce desegregation at the University of Mississippi.

Presidents can also use litigation and their control over federal funds, and the Johnson administration used both mechanisms vigorously to break down segregated school systems in the Deep South. More recently, federal funds have been the subject of a battle that began with *Communications Workers of America v. Beck* (1988). This decision held that nonunion members are not required to pay the portion of union dues that is used for purposes (such as political activities) other than collective bargaining. In 1992 President George Bush ordered companies with federal contracts to notify their nonunion workers of the right to obtain refunds for part of their dues. President Clinton rescinded the order shortly after taking office in 1993. Shortly after *he* took office in 2001, President George W. Bush issued a new order similar to his father's. Two years later a federal court of appeals upheld his authority to do so.[62]

When Supreme Court decisions affirm federal power, presidents and members of their administrations can decide how much use to make of their power. A 2001 decision ruled that state laws allowing the medical use of marijuana violated a federal drug law, and the Bush administration vigorously attacked California programs to provide medical marijuana.[63] The next year, when the Court broadly interpreted a federal law under which public housing tenants could be evicted when guests or members of their households violated drug laws, the secretary of Housing and Urban Development asked local housing authorities to treat such evictions as a last resort.[64]

Presidential Compliance.   Occasionally, a Supreme Court decision requires compliance by the president, either as a party in the case or—more often—as head of the executive branch. Some presidents and commentators have argued that the president need not obey an order of the Supreme Court, which is a coequal body rather than a legal superior. In any case, presidents would seem sufficiently powerful to disobey the Court with impunity.

In reality their position is not that strong. The president's political power is based largely on the ability to obtain support from other policymakers. This ability, in turn, depends in part on perceptions of the president's legitimacy. Because disobedience of the Court would threaten this legitimacy, Samuel Krislov argued, presidents "cannot afford to defy the Court."[65]

That conclusion is supported by presidential responses to two highly visible Court orders. In *Youngstown Sheet and Tube Co. v. Sawyer* (1952), the

Court ruled that President Harry Truman had acted illegally during the Korean War when he seized steel mills to keep them operating if a threatened strike took place. The Court ordered an end to the seizure, and Truman immediately complied.

Even more striking is *United States v. Nixon* (1974). During the investigation of the Watergate scandal, President Richard Nixon withheld recordings of certain conversations in his offices that were sought by special prosecutor Leon Jaworski. In July 1974 the Supreme Court ruled unanimously that Nixon must yield the tapes.

In oral argument before the Court, the president's lawyer had indicated that Nixon might not comply with an adverse decision. But he did comply. At the least, this compliance speeded Nixon's departure from office. He released transcripts of some of the tapes; the content provided strong evidence of presidential misdeeds; and opposition to impeachment evaporated. Fifteen days after the Court's ruling, Nixon announced his resignation.

In light of that result, why did Nixon comply with the Court order? He apparently did not realize how damaging the evidence in the tapes actually was. Perhaps more important, noncompliance would have damaged his remaining legitimacy fatally. For many members of Congress, noncompliance in itself would have constituted an impeachable offense, one on which there would be no dispute about the evidence. Under the circumstances, compliance may have been the better of two unattractive choices.

State Legislatures and Governors

State governments have no direct power over the Supreme Court as an institution. But state legislatures and governors, like Congress and the president, can influence the impact of the Court's decisions in a variety of ways.

Any legislature can rewrite a statute to try to meet the Court's constitutional objections to it. After the Court struck down existing death penalty laws in *Furman v. Georgia* (1972), thirty-five state legislatures soon wrote new laws that were designed to avoid arbitrary use of capital punishment and thus meet the objections raised by the pivotal justices in *Furman*. In a series of decisions since 1976, the Court has upheld some of the new statutes and overturned others. States whose laws were rejected by the Court have then adopted the forms that the Court had found acceptable. For example, in *Ring v. Arizona* (2002), the Court struck down an Arizona law that allowed judges rather than juries to find the "aggravating circumstance" that is necessary to impose the death penalty. Idaho had a similar law, and in 2003 the state legislature maintained the death penalty by adopting a new law that gave juries the power to determine aggravat-

Richard Nixon (far right) leaves the White House after resigning from the presidency in 1974. A Supreme Court decision two weeks earlier made it impossible for Nixon to finish his term in office.

ing circumstances. Through such adjustments, the states have nearly nullified the impact of *Furman.*

In the case of term limits, voters rather than legislators have sought to limit the Court's impact. After a 1995 decision that the states could not impose term limits on members of Congress, voters in ten states adopted initiatives that would punish any member of Congress who did not support a constitutional amendment establishing term limits by putting on the ballot next to that member's name, "disregarded voters' instruction on term limits." In *Cook v. Gralike* (2001), the Court ruled that these laws were unconstitutional as well.

More frequently than Congress, state legislatures have adopted statutes that seem clearly to violate the Court's decisions. In the decade after *Brown v. Board of Education,* southern states passed a large number of statutes to prevent school desegregation. Some states have enacted laws to restore public school religious observances that the Court invalidated. Most noncomplying statutes are overturned quickly by the federal courts. One example was a 1999 Louisiana law that required schools to allow "students and teachers desiring to do so to observe a brief time in prayer or meditation" each day.[66] These and similar statutes win enactment because they allow legislators to gain personal satisfaction and political credit by expressing opposition to the Court's rulings.

Occasionally, state legislatures act to protect rights that the Supreme Court has held to be unprotected by the Constitution. As discussed earlier, the Court ruled in *City of Boerne v. Flores* (1997) that Congress lacked the power to expand protection for religious practices against state regulation. Since then, several legislatures have enacted similar laws to provide expanded protection in their own states.

Like presidents, governors can influence both legislative responses to the Court's decisions and their implementation. Southern governors helped to block school desegregation in the 1950s and 1960s through their efforts to stir up resistance. Some governors have played a similar role in opposition to the Court's limitations on religious observances in public schools. In 2002 Texas governor Rick Perry appeared at a required public school assembly in which a minister led students in a prayer, contrary to the Court's long-standing rules.[67]

Legislatures, governors, and their local counterparts must act to put some Supreme Court decisions into effect. *Gideon v. Wainwright* (1963) and later decisions required that indigent criminal defendants be provided with legal counsel. The Court's decisions spurred state and local governments to increase their commitment to defense for the indigent. That commitment has been reflected in substantially higher levels of funding, and low-income defendants are in a far better position than they were prior to 1963.

But funding of counsel has never been adequate throughout the country, and it has become less so with growth in the number of criminal cases and declining support for assistance to criminal defendants. As a report on Texas concluded, the quality of indigent defense varies enormously even within individual states.[68] Although the Court has achieved considerable change in state and local practices, they still fall short of what many people saw as the promise of the *Gideon* decision.

State legislatures and governors engage in direct defiance of the Court's decisions more often than do Congress and the president. This difference may result chiefly from the sheer number of states rather than from differences in the behavior of state and federal officials. Still, it suggests that the Court may face special difficulties when it seeks to bring about fundamental changes in state policies. Yet resistance to the Court by state governments should not be exaggerated. Undoubtedly, their most frequent response to the Court's decisions is compliance. And much of what governors and legislatures do to limit the Court's impact, such as their reinstatement of the death penalty, is an effort to maintain the policies they want within the constraints of the Court's rulings.

Two Policy Areas

Patterns of response to the Court's decisions by the other two branches of government can be examined more closely with a look at two areas in which the Court and other policymakers often interact.

Civil Rights Statutes. Beginning in 1957, Congress adopted a series of statutes that prohibited discrimination along racial and other lines. The Supreme Court has issued a number of major decisions and many minor ones interpreting these provisions.

Democrats controlled the House throughout the period from 1957 through 1994, and they enjoyed a Senate majority for all but six of those years.[69] Through the mid-1980s, the Court generally gave broad interpretations to the civil rights laws, a stance that was consistent with the majority view in Congress. But Congress did override some decisions that narrowed the reach of the laws. The Pregnancy Discrimination Act of 1978 overturned a 1976 decision that exclusion of pregnancy from programs providing pay to disabled workers did not violate the Civil Rights Act of 1964.[70] Congress in 1988 reversed *Grove City College v. Bell* (1984), which had limited the reach of several statutes prohibiting discrimination by recipients of federal funds. And even with Republicans in control of the Senate, Congress amended the Voting Rights Act in 1982 to reverse a 1980 decision that established a heavy burden of proof for people trying to prove racial discrimination in election rules.[71]

In comparison with its predecessors, the Rehnquist Court has given narrower interpretations to civil rights laws. This stance aroused opposition from Congress in the early 1990s. The Civil Rights Act of 1991 overrode eight different Rehnquist Court decisions, most of them on employment discrimination. But since 1995, with Republican majorities in both houses most of the time, Congress has had little to complain about in the Court's decisions on civil rights laws. The Court has limited some civil rights laws on the ground that they went beyond congressional power under the Constitution, and those decisions might seem likely to spur a major confrontation. But with a conservative Congress, there have been no serious attacks on the Court or its decisions.

The Republican administrations of the 1980s and early 1990s were less favorable than Congress to broad interpretation of the civil rights laws, and this stance shaped legislative response to the Court's decisions. The reversal of *Grove City* was delayed by President Reagan's opposition, and ultimately it was enacted by an override of his veto. The Civil Rights Act of 1991 became law only after President Bush had vetoed an earlier version. Congress would have done even more to reverse conservative decisions under a Democratic president. But presidents can do much more to block action than to bring it about, and, even with a Democratic president in the late 1990s, the Court's narrow readings of civil rights laws were secure.

Abortion. In the three decades since the Supreme Court struck down state prohibitions of abortion in *Roe v. Wade,* states have enacted a wide range of statutes to regulate abortion in ways intended to making abortions more difficult to obtain. These restrictive laws are regularly challenged by abortion providers and groups that support *Roe.*

The Court has ruled on a number of these challenges. For the most part, it has struck down laws that substantially limit access to abortion, although it has been somewhat more willing to accept restrictive laws since 1989. The Court did uphold federal and state restrictions on the funding of abortion in the Medicaid program for people with low incomes. For the most part, lower courts have also given close scrutiny to restrictive laws, following the Court's lead.

State legislators who seek greater limitations on abortion have looked for ways to regulate abortion as much as the Court will allow—and sometimes more. When the Court's 1989 decision on a Missouri law suggested that the justices might reverse *Roe* in a future case, Utah, Louisiana, and Guam enacted statutes that would prohibit abortion under most circumstances—statutes that lower courts struck down after the Court largely reaffirmed *Roe* in 1992.[72]

During the 1990s, a majority of states enacted a new type of regulation, one prohibiting an abortion method that opponents label "partial-birth abortion." The Court struck down these laws in *Stenberg v. Carhart* (2000). Following a well-established pattern in this field, legislators immediately began to draft new laws that might meet the Court's objections to the existing ones. Meanwhile, state legislators continue to look for other ways to restrict abortion, such as heavy regulation of medical facilities that perform abortions.

At the federal level, the Reagan and George Bush administrations established restrictions on the availability of abortion in some areas of federal activity, such as the military. In the early 1990s, Congress took steps to overturn some of the restrictions, but President Bush used the veto power to block these initiatives. One example involved the "gag rule," a set of regulations by the Department of Health and Human Services that broadly prohibited family planning clinics funded by the federal government from engaging in activities that encouraged or facilitated abortion. The Court upheld these regulations in *Rust v. Sullivan* (1991). Later that year Congress passed a bill intended to overturn the regulations, but President Bush vetoed it; he vetoed similar legislation in 1992.

Two days after he became president, Bill Clinton eliminated the regulations of family planning clinics along with several other restrictions on abortion. When the Court ruled in 1993 that abortion clinics could not use a civil rights law to sue people who engaged in protests that obstructed access to the clinics, the Clinton administration encouraged Congress to pass a statute aimed at curbing those protests.[73] Congress did so in 1994, allowing criminal prosecutions and civil lawsuits against those engaged in activities such as blockading abortion clinics. After Congress came under Republican control in 1995, Clinton used veto threats and actual vetoes to limit anti-abortion legislation. The election of George W. Bush in 2000 eliminated that barrier, but as of 2003, Congress and President Bush had taken only limited steps to restrict abortion.

The abortion issue illustrates the importance of legislative responses to the Court's decisions. Even a seemingly definitive ruling in *Roe v. Wade* did not prevent Congress and state legislatures from enacting laws limiting access to abortion, and legislatures have done a great deal to shape the law of abortion within the constraints of the Court's decisions. The issue also underlines the role of chief executives. Governors in some states have encouraged restrictions on abortion, while other governors have prevented their enactment. The difference in the actions of the George Bush and Clinton administrations underscores the president's importance in influencing federal responses to the Court's abortion decisions.

Impact on Society

Talking with his chief of staff in 1971, President Nixon said, "What this Court has done is ruined this country." [74] Although few people would ascribe so much power to the Supreme Court, commentators often conclude that the Court's decisions have considerable impact on American society. For more than a century, to take one example, the Court has been blamed for increases in crime.[75] More friendly observers speak of the Court as a powerful force for good. The belief that the Court shapes society is reflected in the attention that interest groups, the mass media, and political leaders give to the Court. But just how strong is the Court's impact? This is an important question, perhaps the most important one that one can ask about the Court.

A General View

Any government policy can have a wide range of effects on society, including some that are indirect and quite unexpected. Certainly, this is true of Supreme Court decisions. Often, however, it is difficult to distinguish between the Court's impact and that of other forces contributing to the same result. For this reason, it is seldom possible to make firm judgments about the effects of the Supreme Court on society.

Still, there is reason to be skeptical about assertions that the Court has sweeping effects on American society. In reality, the effects of Supreme Court policies on society are constrained a great deal by the context in which those policies operate.

Much of that context is governmental. The Supreme Court seldom issues directives to people or institutions outside government. Rather, its decisions establish legal rules to govern decisions within government. This means that the Court's impact on society is mediated by other public policymakers.

One reason, discussed earlier, is that the impact of decisions can be narrowed by other policymakers. A popular comic strip concluded in 1999 that "senseless violence" was the result of taking "God, the Bible, and prayer out of public schools." [76] The cartoonist seemed to assume that public schools actually ended prayer and Bible-reading exercises after the Court prohibited these practices. In reality, these practices remained widespread.

More broadly, the Court is seldom the only government agency that deals with a particular set of issues. Rather, in most areas the Court is one policymaker among many that render decisions and undertake initiatives. In environmental policy, for example, Congress sets the basic legal rules, administrative agencies elaborate on these rules and apply them to specific cases, and lower courts resolve most disagreements over agency decisions. The Court's participation is limited to resolving a few of the legal questions that arise in the lower courts. The Court can still have considerable impact, but it can hardly determine the character of environmental policy by itself.

The Court's policies also operate within a context of nongovernmental action. The direct impact of most decisions depends largely on the responses of people outside government. Especially important are the actions of institutions and people to whom the Court gives greater freedom. These beneficiaries of the Court's policies may not take full advantage of the freedom that the Court provides them. One reason is that they may not be aware of favorable decisions. But even those who know about such decisions do not always act on them. For example, welfare recipients may not insist on their procedural rights because they do not want to alienate officials who hold power over them.

Forces outside of government also limit the broad impact of Supreme Court decisions on society. The crime rate and the quality of education are affected by family socialization, the mass media, and the economy. Those forces are likely to exert a much stronger impact on the propensity to commit crimes or the performance of students than does a Supreme

Court policy. This limitation is common to all public policies, no matter which branch issues them. But the Supreme Court is in an especially weak position, because it has little control over the behavior of the private sector and because it seldom makes comprehensive policy in a particular area.

Despite all these limitations, Supreme Court decisions can and do have significant effects on society. Frequently, they exert an impact by shaping government policies on major issues. In this way, to take two examples, the Court helps to determine whether businesses merge and whether people are compensated for acts of discrimination.

One illustration of the Court's impact is a 1938 decision allowing companies to hire new employees as permanent replacements for workers who were on strike.[77] For several decades, companies made little use of the Court's ruling. But in the 1980s, President Reagan fired air traffic controllers who had gone on strike. By doing so he encouraged private employers to take similar action, and they thereby accelerated a decline in the power of organized labor.

The Court can exert a major impact in more subtle ways. In the 1960s, it required the states to eradicate the overrepresentation of rural areas in their legislatures. As a result, the urban and suburban areas that gained equal representation receive billions of dollars more in state spending than they would have without the Court's rulings.[78]

Some Areas of Court Activity

We can gain a better sense of the Court's impact on society and the forces that determine that impact by looking at a few areas of the Court's activity. These examples demonstrate that the Court's impact is complex, highly variable, and sometimes quite difficult to measure.

Abortion. Prior to the Court's 1973 decisions in *Roe v. Wade* and *Doe v. Bolton,* two-thirds of the states allowed abortion only under quite limited circumstances, and there were only four states in which abortion was generally legal. With its decisions the Court disallowed nearly all significant legal restrictions on abortion. In every year since 1976, more than 1 million legal abortions have been performed. In light of the sequence of events, it seems reasonable to conclude that the Court is responsible for the large numbers of legal abortions. But the reality is more complicated, and it is impossible to assess the Court's impact with any precision.[79]

As Figure 6-1 shows, the number of legal abortions increased by about 150 percent between 1972 and 1979. This massive change suggests that the Court made a great deal of difference. But the rate of increase was actually greater between 1969 and 1972. That increase reflected changes in state laws before and during that period, as some states relaxed their general prohibitions of abortion and a few eliminated most restrictions. If the Court had never handed down *Roe v. Wade,* the number of legal abortions probably would have continued to rise because of continuing change in state laws and because the numbers were already increasing in the states that allowed abortion. But it is impossible to know how state laws would have evolved and how the abortion rate would have changed if the Court had not intervened.

After the Court decided *Roe v. Wade,* other government policies shaped its impact. Decisions by the federal government and most states to fund abortions through Medicaid only under limited circumstances have affected the rate of abortion among low-income women. Decisions not to perform abortions in government-run medical facilities have also affected the abortion rate. The number of legal abortions is influenced by an array of other policies, from rules for medical clinics that receive federal money to state-mandated waiting periods before abortions can be performed. The Court influences these policies through its rulings on what kinds of restrictions on abortion are allowable, but that influence falls far short of full control.

The abortion rate is affected by conditions other than government policy, conditions that the Court affects very little.[80] First, the number of abortions largely depends on the number of unintended pregnancies and on women's choices to seek abortions. A second condition is the ability of women who want abortions to obtain them. Only a small minority of privately owned hospitals perform abortions. Urban areas generally have clinics that perform abortions, but many rural areas lack such clinics. The number of facilities that perform abortions has declined substantially in the past two decades. These patterns reflect personal beliefs about abortion on the part of medical personnel as well as restrictive laws and pressures against providing abortions, ranging from disapproval in the local community to threatened and actual violence. This decline helps to explain the lower numbers of abortions in recent years.

Roe v. Wade had an unexpected political impact. The decision greatly strengthened the movement against legalized abortion by creating a perceived need for action and a target to attack. By the same token, the groups that had sought legalization of abortion found it difficult to maintain their strength after their major goal had been accomplished. As a result, opponents of legalized abortion had an advantage for several years in influencing elections and legislation. This advantage helped to bring about the array of federal and state restrictions on abortion that followed *Roe.* More broadly, the Court helped to make abortion a major issue in national politics, one that affects government action on a variety of other issues.

FIGURE 6-1

Estimated Numbers of Legal Abortions and Related Government Policy Actions, 1966–2000

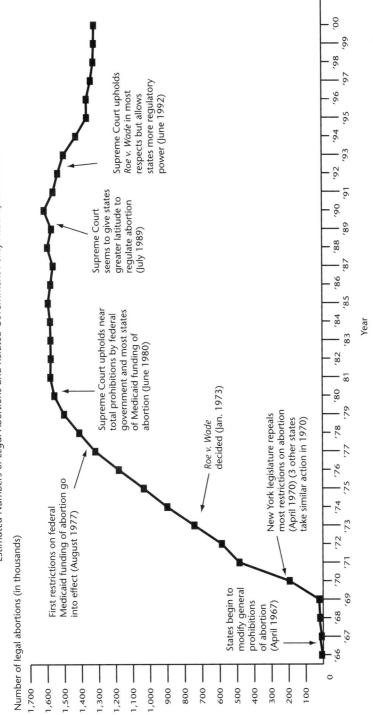

Sources: Estimated numbers of abortions taken from Gerald N. Rosenberg, *The Hollow Hope: Can Courts Bring About Social Change?* (Chicago: University of Chicago Press, 1991), 180 (for 1968–1985); and Lawrence B. Finer and Stanley K. Henshaw, "Abortion Incidence and Services in the United States in 2000," *Perspectives on Sexual and Reproductive Health* 35 (January–February 2003): 8 (for 1986–2000).

Political Dissent. In its First Amendment cases, the Supreme Court often reviews government policies aimed at people who take unpopular political positions. The Court has a mixed record in these cases, but over the last four decades it has made a number of decisions limiting censorship and punishment of political dissenters. In the 1960s it struck down government policies that penalized people for association with groups on the far left. During the Vietnam War it issued decisions shielding opponents of official U.S. policy from punishment for their activities. In an era without such direct confrontations between government and political dissenters, the Rehnquist Court established some additional protections. For example, it struck down criminal penalties for burning the flag as a political statement and limited economic retaliation against public employees and business owners who criticize government policy.

The impact of these decisions is difficult to measure, but in all likelihood they have limited government action against dissent and thereby encouraged dissenters. For example, the Court's protection of opponents of the war in Vietnam probably encouraged the open expression of opposition.

Yet the Court has not brought about a massive increase in the level of political dissent in the United States. One reason is that the Court's support for political dissent has not gone as far as it could have. Another is that government officials do not always comply with the letter of the Court's decisions, and noncompliance with their spirit is quite common. But perhaps most important are conditions in the private sector. For one thing, most people simply do not hold the highly unpopular views about political matters that the Court has sought to protect.

Further, people realize that the Court cannot prevent all the negative consequences of political dissent. Companies can threaten employees with firing even for discussing their salaries.[81] Homeowners' associations can punish people for putting political signs on their property.[82] People may refrain from saying what they think because they fear that neighbors will ostracize them or people in the community will attack them. Threats and violence have been directed against environmentalists who oppose economic activities that are important in their area. Some opponents of government-sponsored religious activities experience property damage, harassment, and death threats.[83] When one father opposed mandatory student drug tests in a rural Texas school, he received threats and faced what a reporter called "life as a pariah."[84]

Incentives to avoid unpopular speech become especially strong in times of perceived dangers to national security. Since September 2001 critics of government anti-terrorist policies have felt formal and informal pressures, some quite heavy, against expressing their dissent. These pressures were symbolized by the admonition of presidential press secretary

Ari Fleischer that "people have to watch what they say." [85] The war in Iraq in 2003 created its own pressures against dissent.

It is not surprising that people often choose to remain silent rather than express controversial views. This result underlines the limits on the Court's ability to change basic social realities.

Racial Equality

In debates over the Supreme Court's impact, no issue is given as much attention as racial equality. The Warren Court of the 1950s and 1960s did a great deal to combat racial discrimination. It ruled against discrimination in education and voting, it upheld federal laws prohibiting discrimination, and it sought to protect the civil rights movement from legal attacks. To a degree, that line of policy extended back to the Court of the 1940s and forward to the Court of the 1970s. Implicitly, the Court was making a commitment to improve the status of black Americans. To what extent have the Court's policies achieved that goal?

Change in Status. The first question to ask is how much the status of black Americans has changed. This is the subject of considerable disagreement, in part because progress has varied so much among different areas of life.

Politically, racial barriers to black voting in the South were overcome. This change contributed to growth in the number of black elected officials in the country, from about three hundred in 1965 to nine thousand in 2000.[86] And white officials, especially in the South, have become considerably more willing to respond to black concerns.

Socially, the segregation of American life has broken down unevenly. Segregation of hotels and restaurants went from a standard practice to an anomaly. Legally segregated school systems have disappeared from the Deep South and the border states, but the level of actual segregation among schools remains high and has increased somewhat since the 1980s.[87] This school segregation reflects the high level of housing segregation, which has declined little since 1970.[88]

Economically, discrimination in employment has not disappeared, but it has declined considerably. This decline and substantial growth in education levels have helped to bring about a major improvement in economic status, but the disparity between the races remains wide. Indeed, the ratio between the average incomes of blacks and whites has not changed much since 1970, remaining at about 60 percent both for individuals and for families. Black children are more than twice as likely to live in poverty as white children.[89]

The Court's Impact. To the extent that progress toward racial equality has occurred, how much can be ascribed to the Supreme Court? Certainly, there are other important sources of change, including the other branches of government, the mass media, and the civil rights movement itself. In some respects these sources are considerably more powerful than the Court.

The Court's relative weakness is clear in education and voting, the areas in which it was most active. The Court's rulings against dual school systems and devices to limit black voting in the South had only limited effects in themselves. It was the enactment of the Civil Rights Act of 1964 and the Voting Rights Act of 1965 and their vigorous enforcement by the Johnson administration that broke down official school segregation and made the right to vote effective.

Because constitutional protections against discrimination do not apply directly to the private sector, the initiative in attacking housing and employment discrimination had to come from the other branches. Congress enacted statutes in the 1960s that mandated equal treatment in these areas, and the executive branch is responsible for enforcing them. In the 1970s and early 1980s, the Court generally gave broad interpretations to the laws against employment discrimination, interpretations that strengthened them. Some evidence indicates that these laws have had a significant impact on the economic status of black citizens, and the Court's decisions might be given a small degree of responsibility for that impact.

Perhaps the Court had important indirect effects in that its early civil rights decisions helped to spur passage of federal legislation and strengthened the civil rights movement. The development of a mass civil rights movement in the South was probably inevitable, and the Supreme Court was hardly the major force contributing to its development. But the Court may have speeded the movement's growth. Its decisions in education and other areas created hope for change and established rights to be vindicated by political action. This is especially true of the *Brown* decision, which had considerable symbolic importance for some people.[90] The Court's protection of the civil rights movement itself did not eliminate the harassment of civil rights groups in the South or the violence against their members, but the Court helped the movement to withstand the pressures placed on it.

The series of civil rights laws adopted from 1957 on also may owe something to the Court. In education and voting, the Court initiated government action against discrimination and helped to create expectations that Congress and the executive branch were pressed to fulfill. It is true that congressional action was most directly responsible for bringing about school desegregation in the Deep South. But if the Court had not issued the *Brown* decision, Congress might have had less impetus to act against segregation at all.

An Assessment. The issue of racial equality illustrates both the strengths and limitations of government in achieving societal change. Public policy has helped to bring about significant reductions in the disadvantages of black Americans. But these disadvantages have hardly disappeared, and even a stronger government commitment to equality could not have eliminated them altogether.

For the Supreme Court specifically, the assessment is also mixed. The Court has had little direct impact on discrimination in the private sector. Even in the public sector, it has been weak in the enforcement of rights. But it has helped to initiate and support processes of change, and its members probably can take some credit for progress toward racial equality. If the Court's effects have been more limited than many people had hoped, the Court *has* contributed to significant social change.

Conclusion: The Court, Public Policy, and Society

It is now possible to reach some general conclusions about the role of the Supreme Court as a public policymaker. As this chapter and chapter 5 suggest, that role is fundamentally limited in some respects but still quite important.

The most obvious limitation on the Court's role is that it decides relatively few issues. One effect is to ensure that the Court is only a minor participant in fields such as foreign policy, in which it does not address most major issues. Even in its areas of specialization, the Court intervenes only in limited ways. It makes decisions on a small sample of the issues that affect the rights of criminal defendants or freedom of expression. And the Court has been cautious about substituting its judgment for that of Congress and the president.

When the Court does intervene, its impact is often reduced by the actions of other institutions and individuals. A ruling that public schools must eliminate organized prayers does not guarantee that those observances will disappear. Efforts to broaden freedom of expression may be stymied by conditions in society that the Court cannot influence.

These limitations must be balanced against the Court's strengths. Certainly, a great many Supreme Court decisions have significant direct effects. School desegregation decisions determine the schools that students attend. Interpretations of the Voting Rights Act shape the course of local politics. The Court's decisions can determine whether development projects are blocked to protect the environment.[91] The effects of capital punishment decisions are literally matters of life and death for some people.

The Court also helps to shape political and social change. Its partial opposition to government regulation of private business was ultimately overcome, but the Court slowed a fundamental change in the role of government. If *Roe v. Wade* was not as consequential as most people think, it *has* been the focus of a major national debate and struggle for more than a quarter century. The Court's decisions have not brought about racial equality, even in conjunction with other forces, but they have helped to spur changes in race relations.

As the examples of abortion and civil rights suggest, the Court is perhaps most important in creating conditions for action by others. Its decisions help to put issues on the national agenda so that other policymakers and the general public consider them.[92] The Court is not highly effective in enforcing rights, but it often legitimates efforts to achieve rights and thereby provides the impetus for people to take legal and political action. Its decisions affect the positions of interest groups and social movements, strengthening some and weakening others.

The Supreme Court, then, is neither all-powerful nor inconsequential. Rather, it is one of many institutions that shape American society in significant ways. That is a more limited role than some have claimed for the Court. But the role that the Court does play is an extraordinary one for a single small body that possesses little tangible power. In this sense, perhaps more than any other, the Supreme Court is a remarkable institution.

NOTES

1. Tresa Baldas, "School Voucher Suits Hitting States," *National Law Journal,* January 13, 2003, A1, A8.
2. *Dickerson v. United States* (2000); *United States v. Dickerson* (4th Cir. 2001).
3. *Rideau v. Louisiana* (1963); *Rideau v. Whitley* (5th Cir. 2000); Michael Perlstein, "Rideau's Attorneys File for Change of Venue," *New Orleans Times-Picayune,* May 31, 2003, 3.
4. Rex Bossert, "Asbestos Case Deepens Rift in 5th Circuit," *National Law Journal,* February 16, 1998, A6.
5. *Ortiz v. Fibreboard Corp.,* 527 U.S. 815, 831 (1999).
6. Felicity Barringer, "Some Writers Accuse Times of Hiring Ban," *New York Times,* September 25, 2001, C8. The decision was *New York Times Co. v. Tasini* (2001).
7. *Grumet v. Pataki* (N.Y. Ct. App. 1999); Tamar Lewin, "Controversy Over, Enclave Joins School Board Group," *New York Times,* April 20, 2002, B4. See Michael A. Bamberger, *Reckless Legislation: How Lawmakers Ignore the Constitution* (New Brunswick, N.J.: Rutgers University Press, 2000), 113–124.
8. "Sharper Remains a Raven with New $22 Million Deal," *Washington Post,* April 24, 2001, D3; post from Michael R. Masinter on the "CONLAWPROF" listserv, May 22, 2001.
9. See, for instance, Donald R. Songer, Jeffrey A. Segal, and Charles M. Cameron, "The Hierarchy of Justice: Testing a Principal-Agent Model of Supreme Court–Circuit Court Interactions," *American Journal of Political Science* 38 (August 1994): 673–696.

10. *People v. Crespo*, 788 N.E.2d 1117, 1125 (Ill. Sup. Ct. 2001, as modified 2003), referring to *People v. Thurow* (Ill. Sup. Ct. 2003). The Supreme Court decision was *Apprendi v. New Jersey* (2000).

11. James F. Spriggs II, "Explaining Federal Bureaucratic Compliance with Supreme Court Opinions," *Political Research Quarterly* 50 (September 1997): 577–578.

12. Elizabeth Amon, "INS Flouts Court on Prisoners, Critics Say," *National Law Journal*, August 12, 2002, A1, A12; *Seretse-Khama v. Ashcroft* (D.D.C. 2002). The decision was *Zadvydas v. Davis* (2001).

13. Roy Sylvester and Jean Hays, "City Pays Millions to Settle Lawsuit," *Wichita Eagle*, May 8, 2002.

14. Harrell R. Rodgers Jr. and Charles S. Bullock III, *Law and Social Change: Civil Rights Laws and Their Consequences* (New York: McGraw-Hill, 1972), 75.

15. *Green v. School Board* (1968); *Alexander v. Holmes County Board of Education* (1969).

16. *Missouri v. Jenkins* (1990); *Spallone v. United States* (1989). On *Spallone*, see Lisa Belkin, *Show Me a Hero: A Tale of Murder, Suicide, Race, and Redemption* (Boston: Little, Brown, 1999).

17. *Board of Education v. Dowell* (1991); *Freeman v. Pitts* (1992).

18. Christopher Paul Fischer, "'I Hear You Knocking, But You Can't Come In': The North Dakota Supreme Court Again Declines to Decide Whether the State Constitution Precludes a Good Faith Exception to the Exclusionary Rule," *North Dakota Law Review* 76 (2000): 145.

19. Richard A. Leo, "The Impact of *Miranda* Revisited," *Journal of Criminal Law and Criminology* 86 (spring 1996): 652–653; Paul G. Cassell and Bret S. Hayman, "Police Interrogation in the 1990s: An Empirical Study of the Effects of *Miranda*, *UCLA Law Review* 43 (February 1996): 887–892.

20. This discussion is based in part on Welsh S. White, *Miranda's Waning Protections: Police Interrogation Practices after Dickerson* (Ann Arbor: University of Michigan Press, 2001); and George C. Thomas III and Richard A. Leo, "The Effects of Miranda v. Arizona: 'Embedded' in Our National Culture?" *Crime and Justice* (2002): 203–271.

21. Leo, "Impact of *Miranda* Revisited," 663. See Stephen J. Schulhofer, "*Miranda's* Practical Effect: Substantial Benefits and Vanishingly Small Social Costs," *Northwestern University Law Review* 90 (winter 1996): 507–510; and David Simon, *Homicide: Life on the Killing Streets* (Boston: Houghton Mifflin, 1991), 193–207.

22. Charles D. Weisselberg, "Deterring Police from Deliberately Violating Miranda: In the Stationhouse After Dickerson," *Michigan Law Review* 99 (March 2001): 1121–67.

23. The case was *Dickerson v. United States* (2000).

24. Jerome H. Skolnick, *Justice Without Trial: Law Enforcement in Democratic Society*, 3d ed. (New York: Macmillan, 1994), 277 (emphasis in original).

25. Evidence on the impact of *Mapp* is discussed in L. Timothy Perrin, H. Mitchell Caldwell, Carol A. Chase, and Ronald W. Fagan, "If It's Broken, Fix It: Moving Beyond the Exclusionary Rule," *Iowa Law Review* 83 (May 1998): 678–711.

26. Bradley C. Canon, "Is the Exclusionary Rule in Failing Health? Some New Data and a Plea against a Precipitous Conclusion," *Kentucky Law Journal* 62 (1974): 702–725; Myron W. Orfield Jr., "The Exclusionary Rule and

Deterrence: An Empirical Study of Chicago Narcotics Officers," *University of Chicago Law Review* 54 (summer 1987): 1024–49; and Craig D. Uchida and Timothy S. Bynum, "Search Warrants, Motions to Suppress and 'Lost Cases': The Effects of the Exclusionary Rule in Seven Jurisdictions," *Journal of Criminal Law and Criminology* 81 (winter 1991): 1034–66.

27. Jon B. Gould and Stephen D. Mastrofski, "Suspect Searches: Assessing Police Behavior Under the Constitution," unpublished paper, 2003.

28. Harold J. Rothwax, *Guilty: The Collapse of Criminal Justice* (New York: Random House, 1996), 41. See Perrin et al., "If It's Broken, Fix It," 727–732.

29. Christopher Slobogin, "Why Liberals Should Chuck the Exclusionary Rule," *University of Illinois Law Review* (1999): 369.

30. *Bottoson v. Moore* (Fla. Sup. Ct. 2002). The Supreme Court's decision was *Ring v. Arizona* (2002).

31. Elliot E. Slotnick and Jennifer A. Segal, *Television News and the Supreme Court: All the News That's Fit to Air?* (New York: Cambridge University Press, 1998).

32. Kevin Matthew Scott, "Double Agents: An Exploration of the Motivations of Court of Appeals Judges" (Ph.D. diss., Ohio State University, 2002), chap. 5.

33. *Early v. Packer* (2002); *Immigration and Naturalization Service v. Ventura* (2002); *Woodford v. Visciotti* (2002).

34. *Engel v. Vitale* (1962); *Abington School District v. Schempp* (1963).

35. Diana Jean Schemo, "Revival of School Prayer Has Limited Success," *New York Times*, October 23, 2001, A16. The decision was *Santa Fe Independent School District v. Doe* (2000).

36. Michael J. Berens, "Holding the Purse Strings," *Columbus Dispatch*, November 19, 1996, 1A, 2A.

37. J. W. Peltason, *Fifty-Eight Lonely Men: Southern Federal Judges and School Desegregation* (Urbana: University of Illinois Press, 1971), 9.

38. "Parents Stage Demonstration," *New Orleans Times Picayune*, November 24, 1960, quoted in Robert Coles, *Children of Crisis: A Study of Courage and Fear* (Boston: Little, Brown, 1967), 385 n. 2.

39. *Wallace v. Castro*, 2003 65 Fed. Appx. 618, 619 (9th Cir. 2003). The Supreme Court decision was *Lockyer v. Andrade* (2003).

40. *Khan v. State Oil Co.*, 93 F.3d 1358, 1363 (7th Cir. 1996).

41. *Singh v. Jutla* (N.D. Calif. 2002). The Supreme Court's decision was *Hoffman Plastic Compounds v. National Labor Relations Board* (2002).

42. William K. Muir Jr., *Prayer in the Public Schools: Law and Attitude Change* (Chicago: University of Chicago Press, 1967); Richard Johnson, *The Dynamics of Compliance* (Evanston, Ill.: Northwestern University Press, 1967).

43. *Wallace v. Castro*, at 619.

44. *United States v. Shipp* (1909). See Mark Curriden and Leroy Phillips Jr., *Contempt of Court* (New York: Faber and Faber, 1999).

45. *Kirk v. Louisiana*, 536 U.S. 635, 635–636 (2002).

46. Gracie Bonds Staples, "A Roundup of Cowgirl Memories," *Atlanta Journal and Constitution*, July 21, 2002, 1K.

47. *Shelling v. State of Texas* (Texas Ct. App. 2001); "Fear of a Black Jury," *Harper's Magazine*, July 2000, 26–29; Sheri Lynn Johnson, "Batson Ethics for Prosecutors and Trial Court Judges," *Chicago-Kent Law Review* 73 (1998): 475–507.

48. William N. Eskridge Jr., "Overriding Supreme Court Statutory Interpretation Decisions," *Yale Law Journal* 101 (November 1991): 338; updating through 1996 is from Lori Hausegger and Lawrence Baum, "Behind the Scenes: The Supreme Court and Congress in Statutory Interpretation," in *Great Theatre: The American Congress in Action*, ed. Herbert F. Weisberg and Samuel C. Patterson (New York: Cambridge University Press, 1998), 224–247.
49. The decision was *Gitlitz v. Commissioner* (2001).
50. *Federal Baseball Club, Inc. v. National League of Professional Baseball Clubs* (1922).
51. Michael E. Solimine and James L. Walker, "The Next Word: Congressional Response to Supreme Court Statutory Decisions," *Temple Law Review* 65 (1992): 425–458; R. Shep Melnick, *Between the Lines: Interpreting Welfare Rights* (Washington, D.C.: Brookings Institution, 1994), 261–264.
52. Eskridge, "Overriding Statutory Decisions," 348, 351, 359–367.
53. J. Mitchell Pickerill, "Judicial Review and the Lawmaking Process: The Role of the Supreme Court in the Legislative Process" (Paper presented at the annual meeting of the Midwest Political Science Association, Chicago, April 1998).
54. The decisions were *Ashcroft v. American Civil Liberties Union* (2002) and *American Civil Liberties Union v. Ashcroft* (3d Cir. 2003).
55. See Carolyn N. Long, *Religious Freedom and Indian Rights: The Case of Oregon v. Smith* (Lawrence: University Press of Kansas, 2000), 227–276.
56. *Freedom Baptist Church v. Township of Middletown* (E.D. Pa. 2002).
57. The provision on school religion is 20 U.S.C. 7904; the provision on the Boy Scouts is 20 U.S.C. 7905.
58. Louis Fisher and Neal Devins, *Political Dynamics of Constitutional Law*, 3d ed. (St. Paul: West Publishing Co., 2001), 116–123. For a different interpretation, see Jessica Korn, *The Power of Separation: American Constitutionalism and the Myth of the Legislative Veto* (Princeton: Princeton University Press, 1996), 39–40.
59. Bruce Fein, "Judge Not," *New York Times*, May 8, 1997, A23. The decision was *United Steelworkers v. Weber* (1979).
60. U.S. Congress, House, *Congressional Record*, 89th Cong., 1st sess., 1965, 111, pt. 4, 5275. See John R. Schmidhauser and Larry L. Berg, *The Supreme Court and Congress: Conflict and Interaction, 1945–1968* (New York: Free Press, 1972), 8–12.
61. William G. Ross, *A Muted Fury: Populists, Progressives, and Labor Unions Confront the Courts, 1890–1937* (Princeton: Princeton University Press, 1994).
62. *UAW-Labor Employment and Training Corporation v. Chao* (D.C. Cir. 2003).
63. Greg Winter, "U.S. Cracks Down on Medical Marijuana in California," *New York Times*, October 31, 2001, A12. The decision was *United States v. Oakland Cannabis Buyers' Cooperative* (2001).
64. "HUD Chief Cautions on '1-Strike' Eviction Law," *Los Angeles Times*, April 17, 2002, A10. The decision was *Department of Housing and Urban Development v. Rucker* (2002).
65. Samuel Krislov, *The Supreme Court in the Political Process* (New York: Macmillan, 1965), 140.
66. *Doe v. School Board of Ouachita Parish* (5th Cir. 2001).

67. Jay Root, "Falwell Backs Perry Prayer Push," *Fort Worth Star-Telegram*, November 1, 2001, 5B.
68. Allan K. Butcher and Michael K. Moore, "Muting Gideon's Trumpet: The Crisis in Indigent Criminal Defense in Texas" (Report to the state bar of Texas from the Committee on Legal Services to the Poor in Criminal Matters, September 2000).
69. On Congress-Court interaction in civil rights, see William N. Eskridge Jr., "Reneging on History? Playing the Court/Congress/President Civil Rights Game," *California Law Review* 79 (May 1991): 613–684.
70. *General Electric Co. v. Gilbert* (1976).
71. *City of Mobile v. Bolden* (1980).
72. The decisions were *Webster v. Reproductive Health Services* (1989) and *Planned Parenthood v. Casey* (1992).
73. The decision was *Bray v. Alexandria Women's Health Clinic* (1993).
74. John W. Dean, *The Rehnquist Choice* (New York: Free Press, 2001), 98.
75. Hank Harvey, "A Hanging Judge from Ohio," *Toledo Blade,* October 12, 1997, F3; Paul G. Cassell and Richard Fowles, "Handcuffing the Cops? A Thirty-Year Perspective on *Miranda*'s Harmful Effects on Law Enforcement," *Stanford Law Review* 50 (April 1998): 1132.
76. "B.C.," *Columbus Dispatch,* August 11, 1999, 9E.
77. *National Labor Relations Board v. Mackay Radio & Telegraph Company* (1938).
78. Stephen Ansolabehere, Alan Gerber, and James Snyder, "Equal Votes, Equal Money: Court-Ordered Redistricting and Public Expenditures in the American States," *American Political Science Review* 96 (December 2002): 767–777. Perhaps the pivotal decision was *Reynolds v. Sims* (1964).
79. This discussion of abortion is based in part on Gerald N. Rosenberg, *The Hollow Hope: Can Courts Bring About Social Change?* (Chicago: University of Chicago Press, 1991), 175–201; and Matthew E. Wetstein, "The Abortion Rate Paradox: The Impact of National Policy Change on Abortion Rates," *Social Science Quarterly* 76 (September 1995): 607–618.
80. This paragraph draws from Lawrence B. Finer and Stanley K. Henshaw, "Abortion Incidence and Services in the United States in 2000," *Perspectives on Sexual and Reproductive Health* 35 (January/February 2003): 6–15; and Stanley K. Henshaw and Lawrence B. Finer, "The Accessibility of Abortion Services in the United States, 2001," *Perspectives on Sexual and Reproductive Health* 35 (January/February 2003): 16–24.
81. Mary Williams Walsh, "The Biggest Company Secret," *New York Times,* July 28, 2000, C1, C19.
82. Laura Mansnerus, "Battling Homeowner Associations' Restrictions," *New York Times,* August 13, 2002, A18; Carol Lloyd, "The Myth of 'Privatopia,'" *San Francisco Chronicle,* December 17, 2002.
83. Frank S. Ravitch, *School Prayer and Discrimination: The Civil Rights of Religious Minorities and Dissenters* (Boston: Northeastern University Press, 1999).
84. Jim Yardley, "Family in Texas Challenges Mandatory School Drug Test," *New York Times,* April 17, 2000, A1, A16.
85. Bill Carter and Felicity Barringer, "In Patriotic Time, Dissent is Muted," *New York Times,* September 28, 2001, B8.
86. Gerald David Jaynes and Robin M. Williams Jr., *A Common Destiny: Blacks and American Society* (Washington, D.C.: National Academy Press, 1989), 238; Joint Center for Political and Economic Studies, "Number of Black

Elected Officials in the United States, by State and Office, January 2000," accessed at *www.jointcenter.org/DB/detail/BEO.htm* on February 28, 2003.

87. Erica Frankenberg, Chungmei Lee, and Gary Orfield, "A Multiracial Society with Segregated Schools: Are We Losing the Dream?" (Civil Rights Project, Harvard University, 2003), accessed at *www.civilrightsproject.harvard.edu* on January 21, 2003.

88. See Lance Freeman, "Minority Housing Segregation: A Test of Three Perspectives," *Journal of Urban Affairs* 22 (2000): 15–35; and Margery Austin Turner and Felicity Skidmore, eds., *Mortgage Housing Discrimination: A Review of Existing Evidence* (Washington, D.C.: Urban Institute, 1999).

89. U.S. Census Bureau, "Housing and Household Economic Statistics" (August 2002); U.S. Bureau of Labor Statistics and Bureau of the Census, "Annual Demographic Survey: March Supplement" (March 2002).

90. Bradley C. Canon, "The Supreme Court as a Cheerleader in Politico-Moral Disputes," *Journal of Politics* 54 (August 1992): 637–653.

91. See Traci Watson, "Developers Rush to Build in Wetlands After Ruling," *USA Today,* December 6, 2002, A15.

92. Roy B. Flemming, John Bohte, and B. Dan Wood, "One Voice Among Many: The Supreme Court's Influence on Attentiveness to Issues in the United States, 1947–1992," *American Journal of Political Science* 41 (October 1997): 1223–50.

Glossary of Legal Terms

Affirm. In an appellate court, to reach a decision that agrees with the result reached in the case by the lower court.

Amicus curiae. "Friend of the court." A person, private group or institution, or government agency, not a party to a case, that participates in the case (usually through submission of a brief) at the invitation of the court or on its own initiative.

Appeal. In general, a case brought to a higher court for review. In the Supreme Court, a small number of cases are designated as appeals under federal law; formally, these must be heard by the Court.

Appellant. The party that appeals a lower court decision to a higher court.

Appellee. A party to an appeal who wishes to have the lower court decision upheld and who responds when the case is appealed.

Brief. A document submitted by counsel to a court, setting out the facts of the case and the legal arguments in support of the party represented by the counsel.

Certiorari, Writ of. A writ issued by the Supreme Court, at its discretion, to order a lower court to send a case to the Supreme Court for review. Most cases come to the Court as petitions for writs of certiorari.

Civil cases. All legal cases other than criminal cases.

Class action. A lawsuit brought by one person or group on behalf of all persons in similar situations.

Concurring opinion. An opinion by a member of a court that agrees with the result reached by the court in the case but offers its own rationale for the decision.

Dicta. *See Obiter dictum.*

Discretionary jurisdiction. Jurisdiction that a court may accept or reject in particular cases. The Supreme Court has discretionary jurisdiction over most cases that come to it.

Dissenting opinion. An opinion by a member of a court that disagrees with the result reached by the court in the case.

Habeas corpus. "You have the body." A writ issued by a court to inquire whether a person is lawfully imprisoned or detained. The writ demands that the persons holding the prisoner justify the detention or release the prisoner.

Holding. In a majority opinion, the rule of law necessary to decide the case. That rule is binding in future cases.

In forma pauperis. "In the manner of a pauper." In the Supreme Court, cases brought in forma pauperis by indigent persons are exempt from the Court's usual fees and from some formal requirements.

Judicial review. Review of legislation or other government action to determine its consistency with the federal or state constitution; includes the power to strike down policies that are inconsistent with a constitutional provision. The Supreme Court reviews government action only under the federal Constitution, not state constitutions.

Jurisdiction. The power of a court to hear a case in question.

Litigants. The parties to a court case.

Majority opinion. An opinion in a case that is subscribed to by a majority of the judges who participated in the decision. Also known as the opinion of the court.

Mandamus. "We command." An order issued by a court that directs a lower court or other authority to perform a particular act.

Mandatory jurisdiction. Jurisdiction that a court must accept. Cases falling under a court's mandatory jurisdiction must be decided officially on their merits, though a court may avoid giving them full consideration.

Modify. In an appellate court, to reach a decision that disagrees in part with the result reached in the case by the lower court.

Moot. A moot case is one that has become hypothetical, so that a court need not decide it.

Obiter dictum. (Also called *dictum* [sing.] or *dicta* [pl.].) A statement in a court opinion that is not necessary to resolve the case before the court. Dicta are not binding in future cases.

Original jurisdiction. Jurisdiction as a trial court.

Per curiam. "By the court." An unsigned opinion of the court, often quite brief.

Petitioner. One who files a petition with a court seeking action or relief, such as a writ of certiorari.

Remand. To send back. When a case is remanded, it is sent back by a higher court to the court from which it came, for further action.

Respondent. The party in opposition to a petitioner or appellant, who answers the claims of that party.

Reverse. In an appellate court, to reach a decision that disagrees with the result reached in the case by the lower court.

Standing. A requirement that the party who files a lawsuit have a legal stake in the outcome.

Stare decisis. "Let the decision stand." The doctrine that principles of law established in earlier judicial decisions should be accepted as authoritative in similar subsequent cases.

Statute. A written law enacted by a legislature.

Stay. To halt or suspend further judicial proceedings. The Supreme Court sometimes issues a stay to suspend action in a lower court while the Supreme Court considers the case.

Vacate. To make void or annul. The Supreme Court sometimes vacates a lower court decision, requiring the lower court to reconsider the case.

Writ. A written court order commanding the designated recipient to perform or not perform acts specified in the order.

Selected Bibliography

Chapter 1 and General

Epstein, Lee, Jeffrey A. Segal, Harold J. Spaeth, and Thomas G. Walker. *The Supreme Court Compendium: Data, Decisions and Developments,* 3d ed. Washington, D.C.: CQ Press, 2003.

Gillman, Howard, and Cornell Clayton, eds. *The Supreme Court in American Politics: New Institutionalist Interpretations.* Lawrence: University Press of Kansas, 1999.

Perry, Barbara A. *The Priestly Tribe: The Supreme Court's Image in the American Mind.* Westport, Conn.: Praeger, 1999.

Rehnquist, William H. *The Supreme Court,* new ed. New York: Knopf, 2001.

Slotnick, Elliot E., and Jennifer A. Segal. *Television News and the Supreme Court: All the News That's Fit to Air?* New York: Cambridge University Press, 1998.

Stephenson, Donald Grier Jr. *Campaigns and the Court: The U.S. Supreme Court in Presidential Elections.* New York: Columbia University Press, 1999.

Chapter 2

Abraham, Henry J. *Justices, Presidents, and Senators: A History of the U.S. Supreme Court Appointments from Washington to Clinton,* rev. ed. Lanham, Md.: Rowman & Littlefield, 1999.

Atkinson, David N. *Leaving the Bench: Supreme Court Justices at the End.* Lawrence: University Press of Kansas, 1999.

Dean, John W. *The Rehnquist Choice.* New York: Free Press, 2001.

Maltese, John Anthony. *The Selling of Supreme Court Nominees.* Baltimore: Johns Hopkins University Press, 1995.

Ward, Artemus. *Deciding to Leave: The Politics of Retirement from the United States Supreme Court.* Albany: State University of New York Press, 2003.

Watson, George L., and John A. Stookey. *Shaping America: The Politics of Supreme Court Appointments.* New York: HarperCollins, 1995.

Yalof, David Alistair. *Pursuit of Justices: Presidential Politics and the Selection of Supreme Court Justices.* Chicago: University of Chicago Press, 1999.

Chapter 3

Kluger, Richard. *Simple Justice: The History of Brown v. Board of Education and Black America's Search for Equality.* New York: Knopf, 1976.

Lawrence, Susan E. *The Poor in Court: The Legal Services Program and Supreme Court Decision Making.* Princeton, N.J.: Princeton University Press, 1990.

McGuire, Kevin T. *The Supreme Court Bar: Legal Elites in the Washington Community.* Charlottesville: University Press of Virginia, 1993.

Pacelle, Richard L., Jr. *Between Law and Politics: The Solicitor General and the Structuring of Civil Rights, Gender, and Reproductive Rights Litigation.* College Station: Texas A & M Press, 2003.

Perry, H. W., Jr. *Deciding to Decide: Agenda Setting in the United States Supreme Court.* Cambridge, Mass.: Harvard University Press, 1991.

Sorauf, Frank J. *The Wall of Separation: The Constitutional Politics of Church and State.* Princeton, N.J.: Princeton University Press, 1976.

Walker, Samuel. *In Defense of American Liberties: A History of the ACLU,* 2d ed. Carbondale: Southern Illinois University Press, 1999.

Wasby, Stephen L. *Race Relations Litigation in an Age of Complexity.* Charlottesville: University Press of Virginia, 1995.

Chapter 4

Brenner, Saul, and Harold J. Spaeth. *Stare Indecisis: The Alteration of Precedent on the Supreme Court, 1946–1992.* New York: Cambridge University Press, 1995.

Clayton, Cornell W., and Howard Gillman, eds. *Supreme Court Decision-Making: New Institutionalist Approaches.* Chicago: University of Chicago Press, 1999.

Epstein, Lee, and Jack Knight. *The Choices Justices Make.* Washington, D.C.: CQ Press, 1998.

Epstein, Lee, and Joseph F. Kobylka. *The Supreme Court and Legal Change: Abortion and the Death Penalty.* Chapel Hill: University of North Carolina Press, 1992.

Maltzman, Forrest, James F. Spriggs II, and Paul J. Wahlbeck. *Crafting Law on the Supreme Court: The Collegial Game.* New York: Cambridge University Press, 2000.

Murphy, Walter F. *Elements of Judicial Strategy.* Chicago: University of Chicago Press, 1964.

Segal, Jeffrey A., and Harold J. Spaeth. *The Supreme Court and the Attitudinal Model Revisited.* New York: Cambridge University Press, 2002.

Spaeth, Harold J., and Jeffrey A. Segal. *Majority Rule or Minority Will: Adherence to Precedent on the U.S. Supreme Court.* New York: Cambridge University Press, 1999.

Chapter 5

Belsky, Martin H., ed. *The Rehnquist Court: A Retrospective.* New York: Oxford University Press, 2002.

Epp, Charles R. *The Rights Revolution: Lawyers, Activists, and Supreme Courts in Comparative Perspective.* Chicago: University of Chicago Press, 1998.

Leuchtenburg, William E. *The Supreme Court Reborn: The Constitutional Revolution in the Age of Roosevelt.* New York: Oxford University Press, 1995.

McCloskey, Robert G., rev. by Sanford Levinson. *The American Supreme Court,* 3d ed. Chicago: University of Chicago Press, 2000.

Pacelle, Richard L., Jr. *The Transformation of the Supreme Court's Agenda From the New Deal to the Reagan Administration.* Boulder, Colo.: Westview Press, 1991.

Rabban, David. *Free Speech in Its Forgotten Years.* New York: Cambridge University Press, 1997.

Schwartz, Bernard, ed. *The Burger Court: Counter-Revolution or Confirmation?* New York: Oxford University Press, 1998.

Wolfe, Christopher. *Judicial Activism: Bulwark of Freedom or Precarious Security?* rev. ed. Lanham, Md.: Rowman & Littlefield, 1997.

Chapter 6

Canon, Bradley C., and Charles A. Johnson. *Judicial Policies: Implementation and Impact,* 2d ed. Washington, D.C.: CQ Press, 1999.

Goldstein, Robert Justin. *Burning the Flag: The Great 1989–1990 American Flag Desecration Controversy.* Kent, Ohio: Kent State University Press, 1996.

Keynes, Edward, with Randall K. Miller. *The Court vs. Congress: Prayer, Busing, and Abortion.* Durham, N.C.: Duke University Press, 1989.

Leo, Richard A., and George C. Thomas III, eds. *The Miranda Debate: Law, Justice, and Policing.* Boston: Northeastern University Press, 1998.

Peltason, J. W. *Fifty-Eight Lonely Men: Southern Federal Judges and School Desegregation,* 2d ed. Urbana: University of Illinois Press, 1971.

Ravitch, Frank S. *School Prayer and Discrimination: The Civil Rights of Religious Minorities and Dissenters.* Boston: Northeastern University Press, 1999.

Rosenberg, Gerald N. *The Hollow Hope: Can Courts Bring About Social Change?* Chicago: University of Chicago Press, 1991.

White, Welsh S. *Miranda's Waning Protections: Police Interrogation Practices After Dickerson.* Ann Arbor: University of Michigan Press, 2001.

Sources on the Web

There are many sources on the Supreme Court on the World Wide Web. Some of the most useful sources are listed here; several of these websites have links to other useful sites. Access to each of these websites is available without charge.

Many colleges and universities subscribe to the LexisNexis Academic database, which provides access to all published court decisions as well as articles in newspapers, law reviews, and legal newspapers. The database includes the text of briefs submitted to the Supreme Court in cases with oral arguments.

As is true of websites in general, the content of these sites can change over time, and websites sometimes disappear altogether. Each of the sites listed below has been maintained for several years.

Supreme Court of the United States (*www.supremecourtus.gov/*). This is the Court's official website. The site includes the Court's rules and the calendar for oral arguments in the current term. The website includes the docket sheets in each case that comes to the Court, sheets that list all the briefs filed and the actions taken by the Court. The site also provides transcripts of oral arguments, which are available a few weeks after the arguments.

FindLaw (*www.findlaw.com/casecode/supreme.html/*). This website includes a database of Supreme Court decisions since 1893. Under "Supreme Court resources" it has links to a wide range of other sites, including several media organizations. Some of the links provide biographical information on the justices.

Legal Information Institute (*supct.law.cornell.edu/supct/*). The law school at Cornell University provides this website, which includes collections of Supreme Court decisions and other kinds of information about the Court. Connected with the website is a free e-mail subscription service that sends copies of the syllabi that summarize the Court's decisions on the same day they are handed down. Those syllabi are linked to the text of the opinions in each case.

On the Docket (*www.medill.nwu.edu/docket/*). This site is maintained by the Medill School of Journalism at Northwestern University. It provides summaries and links to information sources for each case that is scheduled for oral argument during the current term.

The Oyez Project (*www.oyez.org/oyez/frontpage*). Jerry Goldman of Northwestern University has created this site. The most important feature is an extensive collection of audiotapes of oral arguments in the Court. The site also provides a "virtual tour" of the Supreme Court building.

Office of the Solicitor General (*www.usdoj.gov/osg/*). This website provides several types of information on the solicitor general's office and on the Court. The site includes a file of briefs filed by the solicitor general's office in the Supreme Court. The site also provides considerable information on the solicitor general's office itself, including an extensive (although now a bit outdated) bibliography. Another feature is the "help/glossary" file, which defines terms related to the Court and also provides information on the Court's procedures.

The Constitution of the United States of America: Analysis and Interpretation (*www.access.gpo.gov/congress/senate/constitution/toc.html*). For many years the Congressional Research Service of the Library of Congress has published a massive volume summarizing the Supreme Court's interpretations of each provision of the Constitution, along with citations of the relevant cases. Also included are lists of all federal, state, and local statutes that the Court has declared unconstitutional and all Supreme Court decisions overruled by subsequent decisions. The most recent edition of this volume and the most recent supplement are available at this site.

Case Index

Index